South Essex College
Further & Higher Education, Thurrock Campus
Woodview Grays Essex RM16 2YR
Tel: 01375 391199 Fax: 01375 373356
Minicom: 01375 362740

D0293966

South Essex College

Further & Higher Education, Thurrock Campus
Woodview Grays Essex RM16 2YR
Tel: 01375 391199 Fax: 01375 373356
Minicom: 01375 362740

Thurrock and Basildon College
Learning Resource Centre

Constructing Childhood

Theory, Policy and Social Practice

Allison James and Adrian L. James

© Allison James, Adrian L. James 2004

All rights reserved. No reproduction, copy or transmission of this
publication may be made without written permission.

No paragraph of this publication may be reproduced, copied or transmitted
save with written permission or in accordance with the provisions of the
Copyright, Designs and Patents Act 1988, or under the terms of any licence
permitting limited copying issued by the Copyright Licensing Agency,
90 Tottenham Court Road, London W1T 4LP.

Any person who does any unauthorised act in relation to this publication
may be liable to criminal prosecution and civil claims for damages.

The authors have asserted their rights to be identified
as the authors of this work in accordance with the Copyright,
Designs and Patents Act 1988.

First published 2004 by
PALGRAVE MACMILLAN
Houndmills, Basingstoke, Hampshire RG21 6XS and
175 Fifth Avenue, New York, N.Y. 10010
Companies and representatives throughout the world

PALGRAVE MACMILLAN is the global academic imprint of the Palgrave
Macmillan division of St. Martin's Press, LLC and of Palgrave Macmillan Ltd.
Macmillan® is a registered trademark in the United States, United Kingdom
and other countries. Palgrave is a registered trademark in the European Union
and other countries.

ISBN 0–333–94890–4 hardback
ISBN 0–333–94891–2 paperback

This book is printed on paper suitable for recycling and made from fully
managed and sustained forest sources.

A catalogue record for this book is available from the British Library.

Library of Congress Cataloging-in-Publication Data
James, Allison.
    Constructing childhood : theory, policy, and social practice / Allison James
and Adrian L. James.
        p. cm.
    Includes bibliographical references and index.
    ISBN 0–333–94890–4 (cloth) — ISBN 0–333–94891–2 (pbk.)
    1. Children—Great Britain.   2. Socialization—Great Britain.
    3. Children and adults—Great Britain.   4. Children—Government
    policy—Great Britain.   I. James, Adrian L.   II. Title.

    HQ792.G7J35 2004
    305.23'0941—dc22

                                                    2003070290

10   9   8   7   6   5   4   3   2   1
13 12 11 10 09 08 07 06 05 04

Printed in China

Thurrock and Basildon College
Learning Resources Centre

Barcode 01004994
          W

S/LOAN
305.23 JAM
18.11.04

To our parents,
To our children
And to Le Petit Prince
Who helped us understand so much

We should once again address social scientists, and
aspire to contribute a comparative dimension to the
enlightenment project of a science of human variation
in time and space. Our object must be to confront the
models current in the social sciences with the
experiences and models of our subjects, while insisting
that this should be a two way process.

(Adam Kuper (1994) 'Culture, identity and the project of a
cosmopolitan anthropology', *Man CN. S.*, 29: 551.)

Contents

Acknowledgements

At the time of completing this book we are based in an office at the Norwegian University of Science and Technology, Trondheim, and the view from the window is of the fjords and wooded mountain sides – all of which, for the Norwegians, symbolises 'the good childhood'. Our many thanks go to our Norwegian friends and colleagues at NOSEB, the centre for childhood research, who invited us here and with whom we have been able to develop and refine the ideas in this book. Particular thanks go to Anne-Trine Kjørholt, Jens Qvortrup and Randi Dyblie Nilsen who organised the workshops within which different aspects of the politics of childhood were so fruitfully explored, discussions which have contributed so much to the final version of this text.

Special thanks go to Sally McNamee with whom some of the initial thinking for this project were teased out in our conversations over the last 2 years and to colleagues at the Danish University of Education, Copenhagen who also provided early inspiration. To those unnamed others who have heard and, then questioned, earlier incarnations of portions of this text also we give our thanks. Only through such processes of refinement have we been able to reach the conclusions we present here.

Allison James
Adrian L. James
July 2003

PART I

Towards a Cultural Politics of Childhood

Introduction

'Do as you're told!'

This phrase, uttered by many if not *all* parents at some time in the process of bringing up their children, encapsulates the key issues that we set out to address in this book under the more general rubric of a 'cultural politics of childhood'. It encapsulates the authority of parents over their child and, more widely, of adults over children as a social category. It is an exhortation used not solely to control specific behaviour but also to symbolise something more abstract – that is, children *should*, as a matter of principle, do what adults tell them. Thus, apart from reflecting adult authority in general, the phrase highlights the ability, and often the wish, of adults to exercise control not only over their children but also over their childhoods. Such, then, is the focus of our concern in this volume: to explore and explain how children's behaviour and, consequently, their childhood social experiences are shaped and controlled by adults across four key social arenas of their every-day lives – in schools, in families, in relation to their health and in respect of the criminal justice system in contemporary British society.

It is apparent that control over children may sometimes be sought for reasons concerning their welfare. It is equally apparent, however, that control is also sometimes sought in order to pre-scribe some kinds of behaviour and to proscribe others, not on the grounds of welfare but simply on the grounds of conformity, as part of the process of bringing up children. 'Doing as one's told' becomes in this sense part of children's socialisation experience, a simple and yet very clear reflection of the process by which social order is maintained across and between the generations.

However, that adults have to tell children to do as they are told also draws our attention to another important feature of childhood and of children's everyday lives – that a child will often seek to do

3

as he or she wishes, even if this goes against what they have been told or taught to do. In this case, childhood appears less constraining of children's behaviour and becomes a social space in which children learn to explore their environment and to experiment with their agency. Inevitably, from time to time, children therefore test out their potential to act in ways that go against what they have been taught or told to do. In such circumstances the admonishment, 'Do as you're told', becomes an attempt by those in authority over children to stand up to the challenges that children, as relative newcomers, may make against the old social order.

It is, therefore, in the minutiae of these everyday interpersonal encounters, as much as in the broader sweep of social, political and economic processes, that what we are describing as 'the cultural politics of childhood' unfolds. Taking place both through processes of continuity as well as change, the cultural politics of childhood comprises, therefore, both the many and different cultural determinants of childhood and children's behaviour, and the political mechanisms and processes by which these are put into practice at any given time.

An illustration

At the time of drafting this book, in August 2002, horrific events were unfolding in the small market town of Soham in Cambridgeshire. On the evening of Sunday 4 August, two 10-year-old girls, Holly Wells and Jessica Chapman went missing. The girls were described as 'two seemingly sensible 10-year-olds'; Jessica's family described her as 'a "tomboy" with an inquisitive nature'; and everyone who knew them stressed how ' "out of character" it was for them to have disappeared without warning' (*The Independent*, 7 August 2002). A former teaching assistant at the school the girls attended, who was subsequently arrested in connection with their murder, said 'They are both bright kids. They wouldn't get into a car with someone they didn't know. They would have kicked up a right stink if somebody tried to get hold of them, they would have screamed out' (*The Independent*, 9 August 2002).

When they were first reported missing, both sets of parents appeared on television, highly distraught, asserting that their children were good girls and very obedient, that they knew the geographical limits of the neighbourhood in which they were allowed to play, that they always did as they were told and that they knew they had to ask permission before they went farther away – they had been taught what to do, they knew how to do it, and they did as they were told. Holly's father was reported as saying that 'It is out of character for them to do this'; Jessica's father pleaded for the girls to 'Come home, all is forgiven' (*The Independent*, 6 August 2002), while her mother said 'I don't allow her to go far on the streets at all. I don't understand why Jess didn't contact us to ask if she could go out' (*The Independent*, 8 August 2002). Within hours, however, it became clear that on this occasion, Holly and Jessica had decided, for reasons we may never know, to act in a way that was contrary to how they knew they should behave, for their images were captured on CCTV having ventured beyond the boundaries of their permitted play area without having sought prior permission from their parents.

For our immediate purposes their reasons for doing so are unimportant, even though these reasons may later prove to be central to understanding what happened to them and why. The significance of these events for us is, instead, that in spite of being good, obedient girls they *chose*, on this occasion, *not* to do as they had been told – they exercised their agency as individuals. What this event also illustrates, however, is the power of adults who have authority over children in various and different roles, in whom children place their trust and for whom children choose to suspend their agency – in this case with such dreadful consequences – for, as it transpired, it seems that Holly and Jessica had not been abducted by strangers but by an adult who was known to and trusted by them. And in the process of choosing to act and to trust, the girls set off a series of life-changing events for them and their families.

In the short term, the impact of these events on parents and children in Soham was immediately apparent – as one local resident commented, 'Everyone in the village is walking around with sad faces. It seems so quiet with no children playing about' (*The Independent*, 8 August 2002). Two days later, as another resident observed, 'Normally there would be children all over the place during the school holidays, but there is not one child about this week. Any children you see are with their families and they are being held on to tightly by their parents' (*The Independent*, 10 August 2002). And in the days after the discovery of their bodies, there was an outpouring of grief and sympathy, not just from residents of Soham but from around the country and across the world. In the longer term, therefore, if the events and the moral panic about childhood triggered by the murder of Jamie Bulger are anything to go by, the decision of Holly and Jessica not to do as they had always been told could well have an impact on the childhoods of future children – for example, by instigating specific changes in the law and the introduction of new social and welfare policies, by encouraging greater adult surveillance over and restrictions of children's activities, and by promoting an increased and more widespread concern about children's vulnerability and need for dependency.

It may be the case, of course, that this was *not* the first time on which Holly and Jessica had chosen to ignore their parents' injunction, although clearly any previous incidents of 'disobedience' had either passed undetected or had had no such life-changing consequences. What is certain, however, is that no matter how much adults seek to control childhood and children, each child has the capacity from the moment of its birth to exercise a degree of agency. And it is this capacity that parents, and adults more generally, seek to control through the introduction of particular kinds of social and educational policies in order not only to protect children but also to socialise them and thereby shape the pattern of their childhoods. Paradoxically, however, it is precisely the capacity of children to act independently that adults also have a responsibility to foster, since 'Do as you are told!' does not provide an adequate dictum for raising the next generation of independent minded adults! Understanding tensions such as these takes us, therefore, to the very core of the cultural politics of childhood, which aims to explore the links between the theories, policies, and practices through which childhood unfolds for children.

The cultural politics of childhood

By way of introduction to the rather complex set of arguments that unfolds throughout this book it is perhaps useful, at the start, to set out what we regard as the key elements that constitute for us the cultural politics of childhood. Three features can be identified at the outset as characterising our approach.

First, the cultural politics of childhood attempts to understand the cultural determinants of childhood. Importantly this will include both the social status to which children are assigned, as well as the influences children themselves might have over their position *as children* during childhood in any society. Of importance here are such social factors as family structure, the nature of kin and gender relations, the structure of the school system; conceptions of the educational process and of the child's health and welfare; secular or religious discourses about what children are or should be; and the economic and political conditions which underpin such discourses as, for example, those which exclude children from the world of adult work and confine them, instead, in the school room in the role of non-producers. All of these will vary, in different combinations, between cultural settings.

A second key feature of the cultural politics of childhood is the identification of the processes by which these cultural determinants and discourses are put into practice at any given time, in any given culture, to construct 'childhood' in society. Here, we shall argue, that the key mechanism is that of Law, broadly conceived of as processes of social ordering. These range from the implicit habituations of custom or the routinisation of tradition, through to their encapsulation and expression in the form of social policies, to their encoding within the frameworks of more formal legal systems of different kinds. Of especial interest here is the way in which, in Western societies in particular, social policy facilitates the regulation by the state of the relations between the various different cultural determinants and discourses, identified above. It is these that surround 'the child' and shape 'childhood' for children. This, then, is 'politics' with a small 'p'. However, in addition – and most importantly – all of this needs to be recognised as subject to the influences of specific, national politics with a large 'P' – that is, the narrow, vested interests and persuasions of particular political regimes. For this reason, in the final chapters of the book our discussion is framed by the politics of New Labour in the UK.

The third key element of the approach to understanding children's lives, which is embraced within the idea of the cultural politics of childhood, is an examination of the ways in which children themselves experience these cultural determinants, the processes of ordering and control and the regulatory framings of who they are. Important here is the question of the extent to which children themselves can influence the form and direction these take. That this will occur differentially amongst children, and be experienced variously by children in different cultural contexts as well as within a single setting, underlines the extent to which 'childhood' is both united by a set of common and shared experiences and yet, at the same time, is fragmented by the diversities of children's everyday lives. A cultural politics of childhood thus engages with and tries to capture this important dimension of childhood.

These three elements constitute, then, the core of the project that we have, ambitiously, set for ourselves in this book – to try to explain the changes and continuities in childhood over time and the particularity of its form in any social space. To tackle such a task requires us developing, therefore, some rather robust but specialised tools to work with and these are forged in Part I of the book. In Chapters 1 and 2 we introduce the key concepts with which the book engages. We outline the issues these raise within childhood sociology and the challenges they make to more traditional understandings of childhood. In addition, we indicate the ways in which a cultural politics of childhood takes us to the heart of the matter in childhood studies – to an understanding of the ways in which structure and agency combine during childhood in the process of social and cultural reproduction.

Chapter 3 extends this discussion of social theory through a close detailing of the way in which childhood is reproduced within the social order, looking here at the role that Law plays in this process. In doing so it offers a generalised theory of childhood change, indicating the conditions under which social policy may work to shore up and maintain particular forms of childhood by controlling what children do. Similarly, it identifies why and how childhood may change, indicating the lynchpin role which Law has to play in this process too. In Chapter 4 this argument is extended through an examination of the role of international law in shaping childhood and in particular, the workings of one of the main contemporary regulatory framings of childhood for children – the United Nations Convention on the Rights of the Child (UNCRC). As a supposedly universal piece of legislation, designed to serve the needs of all children, globally, the UNCRC is shown to be problematic in a number of regards, not least in its attempt to regulate childhood across time and space, irrespective of the diverse cultural determinants which mark out children's lives differentially. Chapter 4, therefore, underscores the importance of an approach that engages with the *cultural* politics of childhood.

Part II of the book becomes our testing ground, with the last four chapters providing us with empirical illustrations of how this politics unravels for children themselves in the context of contemporary British society. Each chapter engages with one discrete area of social policy – education, health, crime and the family – and demonstrates the ways in which childhood is currently being constructed under New Labour. In each arena it becomes possible to see how social policies of different kinds engage with particular discourses of childhood, respond to social events and embody specific ideological stances, combining to reproduce a particular form of childhood for children. And in turn we see how children engage with these policies in their everyday lives, sometimes responding obediently to the controls which are placed upon their actions, while at other times refusing to do what they have been told. In this way, children themselves – through their own actions – might be said to help instigate some of the changes and continuities that are characteristic of childhood, albeit often unintentionally. Herein lies the politics of the politics of childhood.

CHAPTER 1

Constructing Children, Childhood and the Child

In the contemporary media, all kinds of images and representations of children's childhoods are to be found. In the world of advertising and marketing, for example, children constitute a rich and abundant pool of new consumers. They can be targeted as customers not only of traditional children's toys, pop music and computer games but, as has occurred more recently, as health-conscious dieters and drinkers of bottled water (*The Independent*, 21 April 2002). They are an audience to be wooed and enticed, not only for what they represent now, but also in their immanence as the next generation of adult consumers.

For the current UK government, by contrast, children seem to represent an ever-present danger to the moral fabric of contemporary British society, as a social group in need of control and containment. In April 2002, for instance, not only were policemen introduced to patrol school playgrounds (*The Independent*, 14 April 2002) but new measures were also announced by the Home Secretary, David Blunkett, to lock up more 'young offenders', defined as those young people, aged between 12 and 16 years of age, who repeatedly commit crimes while on bail. And, in the same month, parents were accused of fostering cycles of disrespect amongst their children, attitudes that manifest themselves at school in ill-disciplined pupil behaviour (*The Independent*, 25 March 2002). Meanwhile, a strong public sentiment focused on the innocence and vulnerability of children continues to pervade the pages of the press: the compassion and sadness expressed over the violent death of the young boy, Damilola Taylor, in

November 2000 was followed 2 years later by the public outcry and mass mourning for the murder of two little girls in Cambridgeshire.

Such contrasting and contradictory images of children have a long history, harking back to at least the 17th century (James *et al.* 1998). They reveal a deep-rooted ambivalence about the nature of childhood and, by implication, of children themselves. It is an ambivalence, however, which does not simply manifest itself in words and pictures. As we explore in this book, it is also present in the many and various laws and policies through which children's lives are governed and controlled, laws which, ironically, often ignore differences between children's experiences by riding rough-shod over the diversities of childhood with which we are all so familiar!

This is one of the conundrums with which this book engages in its exploration of the cultural politics of childhood: the tension between the changes and continuities of childhood across time and space. Put simply, then, the cultural politics of childhood asks about the outcomes for children, who may live very different lives and whose everyday experiences may be quite diverse, of inhabiting a unitary 'childhood' that is regulated and ordered by sets of laws, policies and social practices that work to sweep aside any differences between them.

Unravelling the complexities of this process and the implications and outcomes these have for children is the aim of this book. As outlined in the introduction, this will involve demonstrating the importance of the cultural determinants and discourses of childhood (including the influence children themselves have over the social status of childhood) and an attempt to identify the political mechanisms and processes through which these are given expression at any given time. Taken together, it will be argued that these cultural determinants, political mechanisms and the discourses they produce work to construct childhood and thereby control, or at the very least constrain, what children do. Such an approach to childhood does not, therefore, just pose a series of challenges to traditional understandings of children and childhood through its avowedly social constructionist framing, it goes on to offer a new perspective – the cultural politics of childhood. From within this, as we shall show, all children and their childhoods can be analysed and understood, whatever the cultural context.

In this first chapter, we begin by outlining some of the key issues and debates with which this approach must engage. We must be concerned, for example, not just with the fact that childhood is socially constructed, but with the precise ways in which this occurs in any society and the specificity of the cultural context to that construction. We must also explore the changes and continuities in the particularity of that construction and be attentive to the implications these have for children, for their childhoods and for the societies in which they live. We need, too, to seek out the extent of children's own contribution to the construction of childhood and to remain alert to the diversities as well as the commonalities that give shape and structure to children's everyday experiences. We need, therefore, also to be quite clear about the conceptual tools we employ and the theoretical contexts within which this discussion takes place. We shall begin then at the beginning – with the social construction of childhood.

Childhood as a social construction

It was Aries (1962) who first highlighted the socially constructed character of childhood in his historical research into children's lives from the Middle Ages onwards. Through his assertion that 'in mediaeval society childhood did not exist' he argued that, although younger members of the species clearly existed in the Middle Ages, they were not granted a special or distinctive social status (1962:125). Once weaned, they participated in society according to their abilities just as adults did. Aries argued that such practices existed because of the lack of any awareness that children might require a different and specific kind of social experience. This awareness, he suggested, only gradually emerged from the 15th century onwards. In his view, therefore, the dawning consciousness of children as being 'different' and 'particular' is marked out, over time, in the gradual social, political and economic institutionalisation of the idea of children's needs. This can be illustrated for the UK in the late 19th century by, for example, the rise of universal schooling (Hendrick 1997b) and the development of paediatrics and specialist children's clinics (Armstrong 1983).

Though the precise details of Aries' claim have been, and still are, subject to critique (see for example, Wilson 1980; Pollock 1983), the broad framework of his argument remains foundational to childhood studies. Notwithstanding some serious objections to both his methods and his interpretation of the historical record, Aries' thesis, as Heywood (2001) argues, at least provided scholars with a platform from which to 'mount a radical critique of thinking about children in their own society' (2001: 12). What Aries offered, above all, was a taste of cultural relativity across time. This alerted researchers to the diverse, rather than universal, nature of conceptions of childhood.

Core to this are two key propositions. First, that 'childhood' cannot be regarded as an unproblematic descriptor of a natural biological phase. Rather the idea of childhood must be seen as a particular cultural phrasing of the early part of the life course, historically and politically contingent and subject to change. Second, Aries' thesis underlines the point that how we see children and the ways in which we behave towards them necessarily shape children's experiences of being a child and also, therefore, their own responses to and engagement with the adult world.

In sum, therefore, what has been central to the development of childhood studies is also central to the cultural politics of childhood – that is, the twin recognition that 'childhood' is, at one and the same time, common to all children but also fragmented by the diversity of children's everyday lives. That is to say, childhood is a developmental stage of the life course, common to all children and characterised by basic physical and developmental patterns. However, the ways in which this is interpreted, understood and socially institutionalised for children by adults varies considerably across and between cultures and generations, and in relation to their engagement with children's everyday lives and actions. Finally, and most importantly, as we shall see later, childhood varies with regard to the ways in which concepts of child-specific 'needs' and 'competencies' are articulated and made evident in law and social policy, as well as in the more mundane and everyday social interactions that take place between adults and children. Here, then, is the social construction of childhood, depicted as the complex interweaving of social structures, political and economic institutions, beliefs, cultural mores, laws, policies and the everyday actions of both adults and children, in the home and on the street – and herein, therefore, lie the essential ingredients of the cultural politics of childhood, the nature of which is developed through the chapters of this book.

Childhood, children and the child

With the socially constructed character of childhood firmly in mind, we turn first to consider with more precision what is meant by the terms 'childhood', 'children' and 'the child' and to making clear the analytical distinctions between them, since these terms are so often used almost interchangeably in everyday discourse. But why does this matter? After all, we all can easily recognise a 'child' and know well enough who amongst us are 'children'. In the course of our everyday conversations we apply these descriptive labels without too much difficulty, often using visual clues such as size and sexual immaturity as evidence upon which to make our judgments. Our views can then – if there be any further doubt – be firmed up using more culturally based evaluations, such as young age, immature behaviour or necessary exclusion from the world of work. But given that 250 million of the world's children (aged between 5 and 14) are estimated to be economically active, the inherent difficulty in trying to apply these more culturally based criteria for the purposes of analysis, or even more generalised description, becomes immediately apparent. Since we wish to use these concepts, therefore, we need to be clear what – or who – exactly we are talking about.

Moreover, it is also the case that the terms 'childhood', 'children' and 'child', actually *do* represent rather different concepts and raise rather different analytical issues.[1] Thus, although we shall flesh these out in more detail throughout the course of this volume, we need, right at the start, to provide some initial points of departure. Put simply, in our view 'childhood' is the *structural* site that is occupied by 'children', as a *collectivity*. And it is within this collective and institutional space of 'childhood', as a member of the category 'children', that any *individual* 'child' comes to exercise his or her unique agency.

Thus, the common – but uncritical – use of the term 'the child' in social science literature and government policy is, we suggest, misleading, while yet, of course, being highly revealing of concepts of and attitudes towards childhood through its misuse! A singular term, 'the child', is often used to represent an entire category of people – 'children'. This happens in a way that would *never* occur in relation to adults, except ironically, in other politically marginalised groups such as 'the elderly'. Indeed the idea of a concept – 'the adult', which could be used to speak of adults, *in general* – contradicts the very notion of the individual that, in the UK and in many other societies, is a fundamental constituent of adulthood itself. For young people, on the other hand, such generalisations are, traditionally, seen as unproblematic. Children, it would appear, can be united under a singular umbrella term 'the child', their individuality dismissed and disregarded. Such a formulation thus not only dismisses children's uniqueness but also, by collectivising children in this way, reduces their significance as agents with individual contributions to make. And that this usage is seen as unproblematic – viz. the United Nations Convention on the Rights of *the Child* – is precisely because of our strange obsession with the physical and developmental stage through which, as we shall go on to explore, 'childhood' itself is most often conceptualised.

That these subtle distinctions are not only analytically important but have practical implications for children themselves can be illustrated by considering the Children Act 1989[2] in the UK where careful attention to this differentiation allows us to locate two of its most important elements in rather different contexts. (As we shall go on to explore in detail in Chapter 8, this is of considerable importance to children themselves in terms of the kinds of decisions adults make about their lives.) Central to the Children Act and the discourse that surrounds it is, first, the principle of the paramountcy of the welfare of *the child* and the associated phrase, 'the best interests of *the child*', which between them identify children's welfare as being the fundamental concern of the Act. Second, the text of the Act embraces, in principle, the idea that *the child's* wishes and feelings should be listened to and taken account of.

Analytically, what is occurring here is a great deal of conceptual slippage. The concept of 'the child' is being used metonymically – one part standing for the whole, in this case the social collectivity that is '*children*'. The effect of this, however, is to suggest that principles such as 'best interests' – which are, in fact, structural and culturally specific and refer to the collectivity of children – can be applied, unproblematically and always, to *the* (individual) *child*. The use of the singular term 'child' stands in, as it were, for children, with 'the child's best interests' collectivised and constructed by means of reference to what is held culturally to constitute a 'normal', or even an 'ideal' childhood. One stands for all and all for one.

However, precisely because the concept of 'best interests' is formulated in this manner within the Children Act 1989, when the family law system does have to address the wishes and feelings of any *particular* child – for example, the crying child who stands in the welfare officer's or solicitor's office – problems may arise. Adult practitioners dealing with children whose parents are separating or divorcing may find themselves having to confront the problem of what happens when a *particular* child's wishes and feelings go against what they, as adults and social workers, judge from their perspective to be in that child's best interests – interests defined by them, however, on the basis of their experience and the collective case-histories they have encountered during their working lives.

An example here would be the child who expresses a wish to live with his father but for whom the courts decide, on the basis of a generalised view of what is good for children, that he should live with his mother, together with his siblings, since this is (usually) in 'the child's best interests' (see James *et al.* 2002). In such a situation, therefore, there can be very practical consequences of the conceptual slippage between these different terminologies, a fact which may go some way to explain why, as other commentators have noted (for example, Lyon 1995; Lansdown 1996), the principles embedded in the UK Children Act are fine in theory, but often difficult to apply in practice.

In our view, then, it is important that the term 'child' should only be used to refer to the individual social actor, to the young person one meets on the street or in the schoolyard. Although as a purely descriptive label the term 'child' does, of course, also connote a young person's developmental position in the life course and his or her potential membership of a collective category, unlike the terms 'childhood' or 'children', the term 'child' is primarily descriptive, rather than analytic. Thus, as we shall explore through this volume, although our day-to-day encounters with any individual child are necessarily informed by our broad understanding of the analytical concepts of 'childhood' and 'children', the term 'child' is not – and indeed *should not* be – necessarily dependent upon them, nor regarded as co-terminous with them. The diversities that distinguish one child from another are as important and as significant as the commonalities they might share, especially to the individual children concerned!

The importance of this can be underlined by looking at another facet of the idea of 'the child'. Whilst, as suggested above, the term 'child' is used to refer to a life course category, the same term is also used to indicate kinship relations – my child, her child, his child. Here, a child is being described, not in relation to developmental stage, but in terms of its genesis, to which the idea of uniqueness, rather than commonness, is paramount. To suggest to a proud parent, for example, that their child has nothing that is unique or distinctive about them, that their child does not deserve special consideration, would be to tread a very dangerous path indeed! Thus, while on the one hand 'the child' is simply one generalised instance of a category, when it is viewed through the lens of kinship as 'my child' it assumes a unique and highly individualised identity. The question this raises, which is one of the concerns of a cultural politics of childhood, is how do children themselves manage these different, sometimes conflicting and competing interpretations of their 'selves'?

As we shall show in our account of childhood as it unfolds through this book, only if children are acknowledged as social agents – as people who combine their uniqueness as individual boys and girls, as sons and daughters, with their membership of the wider collectivity of children – can their active contribution to changing the nature of childhood be recognised. And only by incorporating an agency-focused perspective can the more structurally determined accounts of childhood change, offered by historians of childhood and the family, by developmental psychologists, social policy specialists, socialisation theorists and others, be given a sensible and sensitive actuality. This child – the one who stands in front of us – we recognise as an individual and as a child. However, in that same moment, this child – the one who stands in front of us – also helps shape more general ideas of 'childhood' and our expectations of what all children might or might not do.

However, as just a single instance of the generalised category 'children', *this* child does tell us something, although clearly not everything, about *all* children. Furthermore, *this* child – the one who stands in front of us – may, or may not, through his or her actions, lead to shifts in our thinking about what children are and what childhood is like, thus also shaping our responses, as adults, both to that child and to children more generally. In this process of identification (Jenkins 1996) there is therefore a continual dialectical interplay between these various conceptions – of childhood, children and the child – and it is this interplay that is at the heart of the ongoing cultural politics of childhood that we seek, in this book, to uncover.

Childhood as a 'natural' temporal space

Although, as we indicated above, a cultural politics of childhood is very much concerned to explore children as active social agents in the shaping of their own lives and to see childhood as socially and culturally constructed we do, nonetheless, have to acknowledge the limitations within which such theorising can take place. One of these is the commonality of childhood itself – that is, that it does constitute a particular phase in the life course of all members of all societies. This has to be taken account of in two ways.

First, the very materiality of the biological base of childhood is a cultural universal. Childhood is a phase in the life course of all people everywhere, and a period marked by rapid and common physiological and psychological development. In this way, therefore, the embodied reality of child development might be said to work as a kind of 'structural' constraint on action-centered theories of childhood: children's competences and skills are, to some degree, shaped by the 'facts' of their ongoing physiological and psychological development, despite the cultural context in which this takes place. Thus, as much as we might wish to regard children as authors of their own histories, we do have to acknowledge their shared experience, as children, of processes of maturation.

This said, however, as Woodhead (1996) has suggested, the ways in which these biological 'facts' are interpreted in relation to ideas about children's needs *do* vary between cultures and account for the wide variety in the kinds of social discriminations and legal differentiations made – or not made – between children and older people in any society. He argues strongly therefore that

> Those involved in early childhood development must recognise that many of their most cherished beliefs about what is best for children are cultural constructions.
>
> (1996: 10)

An instructive example of this is the idea of children's needs, a concept that is, as we shall see, fundamental to the cultural politics of childhood. Woodhead argues that 'needs' form a spectrum from what might be called 'fundamental needs' which have biological roots and therefore *are* universal – such as the need for food and water – to those needs that are more socially constructed and therefore particular. These latter kinds of 'needs' are situational and culture-bound in that they are 'as much about the culture and society into which the child is growing as they are about the child' (1996: 11).

An interesting example of this can be seen in the assumption by Western planners that children 'need' a certain amount of play-space and that 'overcrowding' is detrimental to their social development, leading to aggressive and non-co-operative behaviour (Woodhead 1996). Regulations are therefore in force in England to ensure maximum density levels in the design of nurseries and play groups. However, as Woodhead argues, citing evidence from study of a South African nursery carried out by Liddell and Kruger, this is not a universal biological 'need', but a socially constructed one, for the study demonstrated that the 'children were functioning effectively in the South African township nursery in conditions that produced adverse reactions among British children' (1996: 48). In part this was due to the children's own experience of living in large families in crowded townships and in part due to the attitudes of the care-givers who were experienced in working with children under such conditions.

For Woodhead, it is therefore the 'universalist aspirations of developmental psychology' that underpin the Euro-American models of quality child-care embedded in many of the social development programmes used in non-European contexts that, in his view, account for the repeated failure to deliver 'quality' and effective care. As he argues,

Children do not grow up in a vacuum, nor do childcare programmes function in isolation. Both are embedded in a dynamic social context of relationships, systems and cultural values.

(1996: 10)

As we shall see in Chapter 4, however, in relation to the implementation of the UN Convention and its assertion of the universality of children's needs, rights, shared skills and competences, in practice there is often considerable difficulty in making judgments about what *is* in fact in children's best interests in a particular culture for, in any particular context, what is to be regarded as 'social' and therefore relative, and what is more fundamental and intrinsic, may be hard to disentangle. Exploring and explaining these kinds of difficulties is also central to a cultural politics of childhood.

Childhood as a generational space

A second important material fact about children is that, eventually, all children do grow up and, in doing so, leave their 'childhood' behind them. In this sense 'childhood' is, as Qvortrup (1994) reminds us, a constant structural feature of all societies: 'childhood is perceived as a structural form or category to be compared with other structural forms or categories in society' (1994: 6). At the very least, therefore, we must acknowledge childhood as a universal feature of the life course, which all societies deal with through the imposition of structures, rules and laws of different kinds that separate 'children' from 'adults' in one way or another. This is why, for example, Qvortrup (1994) argues for the use of the concept 'the childhood', rather than childhoods in plural, arguing that 'children who live within a defined area – whether in terms of time, space, economics or other relevant criteria – have a number of characteristics in common' (1994: 5).

However, notwithstanding Qvortrup's observation, although all today's adults have been, and remember having been, children and will thus have some of experiences in common, the 'childhood' of the current generation of children will undoubtedly be different from that remembered by their parents. Thus, although 'childhood' as a social space *does* remain and is, as Qvortrup rightly argues, both a constant and a universal, its temporal location in generational history means that its character, nonetheless, changes over time, shaped by changes in the laws, polices, discourses and social practices through which childhood is defined.

A simple illustration of this would be the way in which concepts of 'age' have been variously used, over time, to delimit the structural boundaries between children and adults in English society, boundaries that in turn have shored up conceptions of childhood itself. The historian Gillis (1996) argues, for example, that in the pre-modern period, schooling was not something just associated with children, as it was to become in modernity. In the early 19th century, the perception encapsulated in the concept of 'school children' – that only children need schooling, and that therefore 'schooling' should only take place when one is young – was simply absent. Instead, young men (for few girls were educated at this time) would go in and out of education over a protracted period of time until they were quite old, with work interspersing education as and when more communal or familial needs demanded it. By the end of the century, however, the process of industrial-isation, which had set in motion an increasing chronologisation across all aspects of the life course (Hockey and James 2003), ensured that schooling had become firmly associated with childhood alone. Thus, the 1880 Education Act decreed that all children between the ages of 5 and 10 years should attend school, with the result that children were excluded from the workplace and adults from the school-room, numerical 'age' being the key criterion and measure for selection.

Such separatist policies were not confined to education, how-ever. The later 19th century and early 20th century positively bristled with all kinds of reforms designed to protect children, measures that consolidated childhood as a distinctive structural *social* space in English society, to be populated by a distinctive group of people. The 1889 Prevention of Cruelty to Children Act, for example, protected children against willful cruelty in the home and the workplace, working in tandem with the various Factory Acts of 1864 and 1874 which had raised the age at which children could work and limited their working hours. And, by 1908, a Children Act was in place, which consolidated all the previous legislation, established separate children's courts and made it illegal for children under the age of 16 years to possess tobacco.

The overarching reach of such institutional processes to define and separate children as a group apart emphasises the hegemonic control that concepts of 'childhood' – what is thought right and proper for children – exercise over children's experiences at any point in time. These processes are therefore also some of the cultural determinants that are central to a cultural politics of childhood, processes which largely work to oppose childhood to that more powerful and relational concept of 'adulthood' – in other words, children are what adults are not.

However, as Mayall (2002) notes, such exclusions are defined primarily by the adult world. This leads her to conclude, therefore, that the 'study of children's lives... is essentially the study of child–adult relations' and, furthermore, to argue that in order to understand childhood, 'generation' must be regarded as a key concept (2002: 21). The concept of generation forces consideration of the differential power relations that exist between adults and children and indeed, Mayall goes as far as to argue for a new con-cept of 'generationing', defined by her as

The relational processes whereby people come to be known as children, and whereby children and childhood acquire certain characteristics, linked to local contexts, and changing as the factors brought to bear change.

(2002: 27)

However, although this *is* a highly instructive and insightful formulation, it is also the case that even within one generation of children, in any one society, each child's experiences of 'childhood' will nonetheless be tempered by the particularities of their social circumstances. Other structural differentiations or cultural determinants – those of class, gender, ethnicity and health status for example – will combine with age so that the similarities between two same-aged children may be far less than the differences that separate them. Thus, accepting Qvortrup and Mayall's arguments that, respectively, concepts of age and generation are important keys to our understanding of childhood, in that they allow us to see childhood as a structural space occupied by children as a minority group, other factors have to be considered too.

Patterns of material and/or cultural deprivation, for example, will ensure that in any given society, 'childhood' is experienced rather differently by different children. Thus, as James *et al.* note, 'being a child of a prosperous middle-class urban family in Rio is not the same as being a child of a poor share-cropping family in north-east Brazil' (1998: 130). Indeed such a middle-class child may have far more in common with her London counterpart. The potential age-based commonality of childhood, which structures children's experiences chronologically according to the idea of generation, is, therefore, open to fracturing by other structural processes which bring potential diversity to children's experiences of the social world.

For a cultural politics of childhood, therefore, we need to develop not only a relational concept of 'generationing' that allows us to examine the vertical relationships between childhood and adulthood and which permits the political status of children to be conceived of in terms of a collective 'minority group' (Mayall 2002 and see Chapter 3) but other concepts that will allow us to take account of the ways in which the child's generation has embedded within it the powerful differentiations which make for differences in children's everyday lives (cf. Christensen 1999).[3] All of this makes 'childhood', 'children' and 'the child' very slippery concepts indeed!

Arguably, however, the nature of children's childhoods is not simply the outcome of the particular structural conditions in which children happen to find themselves at any one point in time. Neither is it solely the outcome of sets of discourses produced by adults, seeking to preserve and recreate the childhoods they remember. Nor yet is it simply a function of the cultural determinants associated with, for example, class or kin relations. It is also a product of the everyday actions of children themselves. Through these, as Christensen (1999) suggests, childhood unfolds, empirically – through 'children's experiences, understandings and practices... [and the] multiple, different forces... that influence their lives (1999: 30). We turn now, therefore, to consider what a more agency-focused perspective can contribute to our discussions. This perspective, now commonplace in empirical research carried out with children, has enabled children's own views and opinions about their lives to be regarded as important sources of data (Christensen and James 2001). Here we consider some of the theoretical underpinnings of this approach and their import for a cultural politics of childhood.

Children as social agents

Listening to the voices of children has become something of a clarion call since the late 1970s, both within and outwith the academy, drawing attention to the pressing need to take into account children's own interests in and perspectives on the social world. Since the emergence of the new paradigm in childhood studies (Prout and James 1990), no longer can children be regarded as the passive output of child-rearing practices nor their social development envisaged as the product of a simple biological determinism (James et al. 1998). Instead, acknowledgement has to be made of the diversity of children's childhoods and of children's own part as social agents in shaping their childhood experiences. It is not, however, always quite clear what this, in practice, might mean.

While this rhetoric is often loudly proclaimed, as we have argued elsewhere in relation to specific aspects of social policy in the UK (James and James 1999, 2001), children's own interests may still be ignored. In their dealings with children, adults often take refuge in traditional and particular models of 'the child' and ideologies of 'childhood', models which, as we shall explore in Chapter 3, turn out to be of central significance in the production of social policies and the other regulatory mechanisms of childhood. All of these work to negate children's agency. Before exploring why this might be so we need first, though, to define what is meant by children's agency and the implications of the idea of children as social agents for a cultural politics of childhood.

To do this we return once more to the question of childhood's apparent universality. As noted above, this stresses the salience which the unifying experience of the common and shared life course position of children has for our comprehension of childhood. Notwithstanding this material fact, it can be argued, however, that children are not simply passive objects, the product of universal biological and social processes, but are active participants in their own social worlds and in those of adults. As Mayall argues, this stress on agency suggests not only that children are social actors – people who 'express their wishes, demonstrate strong attachments' and so on – but that children's 'interaction makes a difference – to a relationship, a decision, to the workings of a set of social assumptions or constraints' (2002: 21).

This important dimension, to which Mayall's distinction draws attention, is at the centre of our conceptualising of the social relationships and processes through which the cultural politics of childhood has to be understood. This is not to say, however, that children are necessarily powerful political actors who can take a major part in shaping their own histories, although there are indeed exemplars that can be pointed to, particularly in the context of the developing world and for the UK in the largely unremarked history of children as political actors in school strikes (Cunningham and Lavalette 2002).[4] Instead, it is to draw attention to their capacity to act and to recognise that these actions have consequences, consequences that are unintended as well as intended. These may be very mundane and insubstantial, hardly noticeable in the course of everyday life. And yet, incrementally, they do in time come to represent new and different ways of being a 'child' as becomes apparent, for example, in the domestic 'generation gap' that is acknowledged daily by parents in conversations and indeed conflicts with their children!

On the other hand, children's actions may also have more profound and more obvious consequences for themselves as well as for others in society and for the childhoods of children in the future. An example here in the UK would be the change in thinking about the relationship between age and children's competence which was instigated by what has become popularly known as the Gillick case (*Gillick v West Norfolk and Wisbech Area Health Authority and Department of Health and Social Security* [1985] 3 WLR 830), in which a teenage girl sought contraceptive advice from her doctor, unbeknown to her parents, setting in motion a whole series of legal (and social) debates and disputes (see Alderson 1993 and Chapter 6). Whatever the outcome, however, the conceptual repositioning of children as *agents* and not simply as actors allows us to take note of them as potential participants in childhood change.

This 'potential' can be illustrated by examining the changing historical emphasis placed on the regulation and control of children and the ebb and flow of concern about children's impact on social order. As James *et al.* (1998) note, history is patterned with changes in conceptions of children and childhood, images of the evil and innocent child alternating over time and made 'fact' through the different ways in which children's lives were ordered and regulated. Thus 17th century Puritanical regimes that controlled children through models of the 'evil' child were gradually replaced by less strict regimes designed to foster the child's natural innocence and to protect it in its vulnerability. In the UK this reached its heyday perhaps in the inter-war period when the child was the focus for the golden age of welfare (see Hendrick 1997b).

However, now at the turn of the 20th century, the 'natural' innocence of children is being questioned once more and children are becoming, subject to tighter regimes of surveillance and new forms of ordering, as the net of social control threatens increasingly to restrict children's everyday lives and activities (James and James 1999). If children were *not* agents and were simply passive beings, at the mercy of some social and developmental trajectory over which they had little control, then clearly the 'need' for such forms of ideological control and social intervention would disappear. That different kinds of control and interventions *are* put in place, however, reveals that children *are* agents, whose actions have consequences the effects of which adults might – and often do – wish to control.

At the most fundamental level, then, it is clear that neither the processes of maturation nor those of socialisation repress the agency of children, although they are the context within which it finds expression. On the contrary, both work to shape the form of its expression by providing the context within which particular kinds of agency are permitted to flourish while others are treated with more circumspection! Harnessing their increased physical and psychological competences to the knowledge and skills given to them via the socialisation process, children, it could be argued, acquire a vicarious experientiality. It is this that permits them to act – and often to act rather differently from how they were expected to act by adults! Thus, somewhat paradoxically, it is in part the common and shared characteristics of childhood that offer the very springboard for the varied and diverse practical articulations – by children themselves – of the idea of 'the child' in society.

Conclusion

That the ready recognition of children's agency took so long to be acknowledged, both within the academy and outside of it, may in itself reflect an implicit adult knowledge of children's potential as social agents to effect childhood change. This may also explain our adult reluctance to capture this potential in our social theorising about the role of children in society! As has been discussed in detail elsewhere (Prout and James 1990; James *et al.* 1998), traditional socialisation theory was, for example, modeled on a rather crude developmental psychological understanding of 'the child'. This not only embraced universalistic ideas of child development but also represented children as passive in the march of its progress. Stages of development were pre-determined and linked to age, leaving little room for children to assert any individuality, except as forms of deviance. Too much learnt too early was deemed precocious, while too little, learnt too late, was problematised as backwardness.

When this view of 'the child' was translated into the social arena, such theorising rendered explanations of children's acquisition of social skills as a similarly passive process. Socialisation was understood to take place in much the same kind of way for all children, regardless of the individuality of 'the child' or the specificity of the social environment. Children were rendered helpless against the onslaught of the socializing forces of the family, the school and the peer group, as helpless as they were in the face of those more natural forces involved in the maturation process. As Lee (2001) points out, the dominant discourse or 'regime of truth' about childhood, offered by developmental psychology and social-isation theory, emphasised the 'changing' (i.e. unstable) state of 'the child' en route to the stable status of adult. The child was regarded as 'becoming', rather than 'being', and it was the very materiality of childhood – the fact that children do grow into adults, physically, psychologically and socially – which permitted childhood socialisation to be conceived of as 'the way to give the desired shape and order to future adults and to future society' (2001: 43). However, what was clear – and by the late 1970s made such theorising in the end unsustainable – was that this depiction of 'the child' as 'passive' bore little or no resemblance to the every-day lives and actions of children which, as noted above, were either benignly or more hostilely often regarded as needing some kind of regulation and control!

What a cultural politics of childhood offers, therefore, as this chapter has begun to explore, is a way of theoretically harnessing this agency to the other cultural and structural determinants of childhood in order to understand how the social construction of childhood takes place. It allows us to see the individual child as a social actor in the collectivity of children and allows us to recognise both the uniqueness of his/her childhood as well as its commonality as a life course phase. A cultural politics of childhood will help us to see changes in conceptions of child-hood as the product of the relations that adults have with children, relationships that are themselves located within the broader social, political and economic frameworks that structure societies and which give shape to the institutional arrangements – work, schools, families, churches – through which children's daily lives unfold. And finally it will help us to position children as participants in those institutions – as part-time workers, school children, as family members and church goers – actions which, in turn, may have consequences for the shape that child-hood takes.

Notes

1 See Qvorturp (1994: 5–7) for a comparable, but rather differently focused discussion of the uses of the terms 'child', 'children' and 'child-hood' in relation to macro-level and comparative analyses.

2　The Children Act 1989 applies only to England and Wales, but there is equivalent legislation for Scotland and Northern Ireland.

3　Christensen in her discussion of childhood sickness draws on Laura Nader's (1981) work that distinguishes between horizontal and vertical perspectives in social analysis, describing the 'horizontal' level as the everyday and varied experiences of children and the 'vertical' level as the system of bio-medicine. Following Nader, Christensen argues that our analysis of children's lives has to explore the connections between these two. In this book we extend this argument, by exploring the diversities and commonalities of childhood present in *both* the 'horizontal' and vertical planes, seeing neither as necessarily more unified than the other (see Chapter 3).

4　An example here would be that of the South African boy, Nkosi Johnson, who, at the age of 12, spoke at the 13th International Aids conference in Durban and criticised his country's president Thabo Mbeki for his handling of the AIDS epidemic in South Africa (*The Guardian*, 2 June 2001). (See also Johnson, V., Ivan-Smith, E., Gordon, G., Pridmore, P. and Scott, P. (eds) (1998) *Stepping Forward: Children and Young People's Participation in the Development Process*. Intermediate technology Publications: London.) It is interesting to speculate whether the reason that the developing world most often provides the context for children as political actors is because of the absence of a powerful model of childhood dependency which in Western contexts relegates children more easily and more often to marginal social spaces within which their voices and actions are given little weight or credence (see Chapters 5, 6, 7 and 8).

CHAPTER 2

Key Constructs: Politics, Policies and Process

Globalisation has done more for children than make the hamburger available worldwide. It has revealed a great diversity in childhood experiences, both inter- and intra-culturally, with television and other media providing visual evidence of this on an almost daily basis. Differences in children's everyday lives are, in this sense at least, taken-for-granted, with some childhoods, however, becoming problematised as 'incorrect', as the public display of children as child workers, or as hunger stricken refugees or child soldiers in Africa, serves to sharpen ideas about what a proper childhood ought to be (see Ennew 1986 and Chapter 4).

Perhaps less publicly accepted and readily acknowledged, though, is the corollary of this diversity in children's experiences: that ideas of what *the child* is also vary across time and space. Indeed, it is the very concept of a universal child that allows us to criticise or feel angry about the childhoods of the poor and to distinguish between what is and what we think ought to be. And, as the previous chapter suggested, one explanation for this apparent unwillingness to engage with any notion of variation in concepts of 'the child', and thus to abandon the comfort and security that such a universal definition provides, can be found in the continued adherence to the explanatory power of developmental psychological models.

However, despite the powerful grip that such ideas have in public discourses about children, as the previous chapter argued, what is foundational to the cultural politics of childhood is the socially constructed character of childhood (James and Prout 1990). But, although from childhood studies there is by now much empirical and documented evidence of the 'growth' in and the 'development' of different concepts of childhood, questions still need to be asked about how, *exactly*, that takes place in particular places and why it occurs at particular historical moments. This is central to a cultural politics of childhood. Adopting such a perspective, however, immediately throws into disarray the supposed commonality of childhood. In what ways and under what circumstances is 'being a child' a shared and common experience and how much does it vary, and in what ways and why? Why is it that children's 'needs', nowadays increasingly regarded as 'universal', were – and still are – differently and differentially institutionalised in terms of a rights agenda in different cultural contexts and historical eras? And, why is it that, even *within* societies, the diversities in children's experiences are often masked, downplayed or indeed strongly regulated for the sake of emphasising commonality? What effect does this control over and silencing of their own perspectives have on children themselves?

These are but a few of the many questions with which a cultural politics of childhood engages! It is, therefore, clearly both a broad and a complex agenda for, in explaining such processes of change and continuity in childhood, we have not only to account for the socially constructed differences between adults and children, but also to enquire into – and perhaps even challenge – the very basis upon which cultural ideas of childhood's difference are built. With such a daunting prospect in view, this chapter paves the way by first sketching in the contextual background of the issues and debates within which a cultural politics for childhood must be situated, before moving on to identify some of the concepts and theoretical tools and perspectives that may prove useful along the way.

Politics, children and childhood

As a discipline, political science has been rather reticent in engaging with children or issues of childhood and so it is to sociology and anthropology – for example, the works of Coles (1986), Stephens (1995) and Scheper-Hughes and Sargent (1998) – that primarily we must turn to find some studies that focus explicitly on the ways in which political processes impact on the everyday lives of children. Commonly considered to be apolitical – in that they have no political rights of citizenship – in the past, children's interests have been assumed to be, unproblematically, congruent with those of their family (Qvortrup 1990). It was Robert Coles (1986) therefore who, in his book *The Political Life of Children*, became one of the first to retrieve children from their political exclusion by arguing strongly that, just because they have no vote, children are not secluded or sequestrated from political life and neither are they shielded, as children, against the fall-out from political processes. On the contrary, they experience its effects, both directly and indirectly and may, indeed, be more pervious to some political events or decision-making than adults are.

Later, Sharon Stephens took up this theme in her edited collection, *Children and the Politics of Culture*, where the exploration of children's rights constituted a shared agenda. Together, writers from many different parts of the world explored the ways in which children's rights and cultural identities are shaped by global and political processes and considered the effects, often negative, which these have on children's experiences in particular local contexts – in Japan, Turkey, Brazil, Norway, South Africa, Indonesia, Korea, Singapore and the USA. Later still, Scheper-Hughes and Sargent (1998) adopted a more strident rights-based agenda, making an emphatic distinction between the cultural politics of *childhood* – the inability of families and children to escape 'the slings and arrows of the world's political and economic fortunes' – and the *cultural politics* of childhood, which concerns the 'political, ideological and social uses of childhood' in the institutional framework of societies (1998: 1).

Such studies alerted us to the need for the debate and theorising in childhood studies to take on a more political dimension and, in recent years, this has occurred in a variety of different ways. Questions have been raised, for example, about the extent to which contemporary childhood is in crisis – socially and politically – and about the direct role that governments have to play in this regard (Jenks 1996b; Scraton 1997; Wyness 2000). Similarly, other theorists have considered the extent to which, as a result of social, political and economic developments, children are becoming increasingly excluded as a minority group from the adult social world through the tightening-up of generational boundaries (Zelitzer 1985; Qvortrup 1994; Alderson 2000; Mayall 2002). Others, meanwhile, have suggested that childhood in Western contexts may be fast disappearing in the face of rapid technological and social change (Postman 1983; Buckingham 2000).

However, although very diverse, what is significant about such studies is that each of them demonstrates that ideas about the status and rights of children are, in fact, incorporated into the thinking and social practices of nation states, albeit this often occurs indirectly, rather than explicitly. Nonetheless, the precise manner in which this occurs in each particular context will have particular consequences for children at the local level, working to shape their everyday life experiences and social relationships (O'Neill 1994). It is this subtle process to which Stephens points in her wry observation that 'a nation's politics becomes a child's everyday psychology' (1995: 3).[1] In this sense – at the very least – children *cannot* be regarded as excluded from the vagaries of political life. Their everyday lives are, inevitably and fundamentally, intertwined with it, as we ourselves go on to demonstrate via the case studies detailed in Part II of this book.

However, it is our concern in this book, through developing the idea of a cultural politics of childhood, to show not only *that* this process occurs, but to explain *how* it does – by uncovering the precise mechanisms through which childhood comes to be constituted in society in the particular form that it does and to explain how and why it changes. As we suggested in Chapter 1, and we go on to argue more fully in Chapters 3 and 4, for us a key social mechanism in this respect is Law, conceived broadly as an ordering and a regulatory arena that helps constitute – in the broadest sense – children's political position in society. While the precise ways in which this occurs, and the implications this has for childhood change, will be described later, it is useful at this juncture and by way of illustration to reflect on this proposition first in more general terms.

We do so in the next section by considering the institutionalisation of 'childhood' and 'the child' in Western society.[2] It is our contention that the particular and often exclusionary ways in which childhood comes into being are not simply a result of the messy and chaotic path of history and random chance, although that surely does also have a place. Nor are they the outcome of some deliberate Machiavellian strategy. Rather it represents the culminated history of the various cultural determinants and discourses of childhood being encoded in particular political policies and enacted in and through particular kinds of social practices. Thus we can ask: What kind of 'institution' is childhood? How has it been institutionalised? What does being consigned to childhood mean for children's experiences?

Childhood as an institution

One of the key problematics with which this book engages, as suggested in Chapter 1, is children's distinctiveness for, in part, it is the supposed differences between children and adults that underpin the institution of childhood. As Jenks has observed:

> The child . . . cannot be imagined except in relation to a conception of the adult, but essentially it becomes impossible to generate a well-defined sense of the adult, and indeed adult society, without first positing the child.
>
> (1996a: 3)

Indeed, as we shall go on to show, what Jenks calls 'the necessity and contingency of the relationship between the child and the adult, both in theory and in everyday life' lies at the heart of many of the societal practices that come to be formulated as child-specific laws and policies and it is these, we would argue, that have helped give childhood its special character as a social and conceptual space, both in the life course and in social structure (Jenks 1996a: 3).

It is, for example, through law rather than simply as a result of the ageing process *per se*, that adults achieve 'adulthood' and their accompanying personhood. In the UK their special social status is symbolised by the achievement of the 'age of majority' at 18, the voting age, and is accompanied by the assumption of 'adult' rights and responsibilities. 'Adulthood' thus represents primarily a particular *social* category in the chronologised life course that may, but need not, reflect processes of bodily maturation (Hockey and James 2003). As Hockey and James note, for example, the precise chronologisation of ageing in relation to life course identities is a relatively recent phenomenon of modernity, a by-product of the rationalisation and categorisation of all aspects of life that industrialisation brought with it. In pre-modern times, by contrast, numerical age played but little part in delimiting what people did and it was only from 1870 onwards that an acute age-consciousness emerged with the consequence that, as Gillis notes, 'so as not to appear unnatural, everyone did their utmost to "act their age" from birth to death' (1996: 84).

In this sense, therefore, the categorical stage of 'adulthood' (and therefore correspondingly of 'childhood') can be regarded

substantially as arbitrary, fixed first by the social practices of
custom and then the practices of law. It is therefore something
that is, potentially, susceptible to change over time. This is indeed
the case. Thus, for example, the age of majority in the UK was, until
the Family Law Reform Act 1969, set at 21 rather than 18 years of
age and as Fortin has observed, in spite of this change the current
law in the UK remains confused and there continues to be:

> [a] variety of inflexible age limits, below which [children have] no
> capacity and above which [they have] total freedom to perform the
> activity in question.

(1998: 84)

As Lee (2001) has recently argued, therefore, the idea of a
'standard adulthood' as completeness is but a fiction from the
Fordist era that is now becoming destabilised by changes in both
the economic and the intimate lives of adults. It follows then that
the social category of 'children' is also in many ways arbitrary and
not solely determined by the age and biology of children's bodies.

However, the consequences of artificially fixing – through the
law – a chronologised identity for adults within the life course has
been to establish, simultaneously, a set of age-based criteria for
children that single out children as rather different kinds of
people. And in marking out this difference, the law has conferred
on children the status of non-personhood, the status of minors,
making this another necessary, although not sufficient, condition
of being a child. Not having full social personhood, as we explore
in our later case studies, is thus in part what makes children children and ensures, in turn, that they are regarded as different
from adults.

Understanding and exploring the implications of what Jenks
calls the rather circular and 'binary reasoning' through which
childhood is institutionalised in society lies, therefore, at the heart
of a cultural politics of childhood for it is through this that 'the
child' is *made* to represent 'difference and particularity' (1996a: 3).
And, as we shall demonstrate through the course of this book, it is
primarily through the framing of social policy and the regulatory
arm of the law that these culturally prescribed differences and
particularities come to be given a solid grounding in society,
locating children in 'childhood' and setting them apart from
adults in everyday life.

For example, it is largely on the basis of their age that children are sequestered into schools, playgrounds, children's hospitals and young offenders' institutions; that they are not permitted legitimate access to the adult spaces of the workplace and public house; that children's minds become the specialised territory of child psychologists and educationalists and their bodies the object of the paediatrician's gaze; and, finally, that the particularity of children's social needs are differentiated from those of adults, by making them the focus of specialised *children's* services in the welfare field. Such processes represent the institutionalisation of childhood in society, described by Qvortrup as 'adults' way of confining [children] in particular "islands" and "buildings", and thus a way of marginalizing or excluding childhood from adult society' (1994: 9).

But what is most significant about this process of institutional separation is that, for the most part, it is driven by adults on children's behalf. This raises questions central to a cultural politics of childhood, about the imbalances of power that exist between adults and children and about the ways in which Law and policy work empirically to ground, control and legitimate these as somehow 'natural' age-based, status differences and, in doing so, to make them more resistant to challenge and critique.

Children as citizens?

A further instructive example of this process of the political institutionalisation of childhood, which will be a recurring theme throughout this book, is how the citizenship status of children in the UK is articulated and given practical expression, when compared to that of adults. It was T. H. Marshall (1950) who first outlined the concept of citizenship, arguing that citizenship confers upon the individual full membership of a community. In this sense, therefore, citizenship is one aspect of personhood, although not co-terminous with it. Citizenship, according to Marshall, involves having three kinds of rights – political, civil and social. Political rights include the right to vote or to strike; civil rights, the rights to free speech, justice, property and personal freedom; and the concept of social rights embraces such rights as access to welfare and education. Within this understanding of citizenship, children were seen by Marshall as citizens *in potentia* only – as having no political rights and only limited civil and social rights.

As Cockburn (1998) has argued, in the UK this exclusion of children from full community membership as citizens became firmly institutionalised during the 19th century. It went hand-in-hand with the growth of modern conceptions of childhood and was given empirical grounding through the introduction of numerous social policies that were designed to remove children from areas of adult and public life under the guise of protection. Thus, as Hendrick (1997) argues, this laid the grounds for the emergence of the 'welfare child' in the later inter-war period. However, the apparent benevolence of these 19th century reforms and the establishment of children's rights to welfare and educational provision can be shown to have worked, ironically, to disable and disenfranchise children as citizens. These 'progressive' policies set children apart from the public world of adults and put in motion a very particular kind of age-based social exclusion. Children became largely confined to a state of dependency and to the social worlds of the school and the family (see Lee 2001).

What is significant, however, about this example is its continued pertinence for the cultural politics of contemporary childhood (see Part II). Today, for example, the classification of individual children as members of the social category 'children' continues to make them the targets for special welfare measures and renders them subject to specific legal constraints. While this process can, of course, be beneficial and benevolent, it does, however, ignore children's individuality and uniqueness through bracketing all children together and, in the spheres of education and criminal justice, it is still often the behaviour of a troublesome minority that is taken as the springboard for constraining action, just as Cockburn noted for the 19th century:

> Children came to the attention of the authorities largely as delinquents threatening security and property, as future workers requiring skills, as future soldiers in need of health and fitness or future mothers.
>
> (1998: 105)

If, following Donzelot (1979) and Rose (1990), it can therefore be argued that a 'caring' state actively works to control its adult members, both through regimes of surveillance of different kinds and through encouraging people to take on personal responsibility and self-regulation, it becomes important to ask whether the state's treatment of children in the 19th century in the UK and elsewhere, which led to the denial of their citizenship, represented a comparable process of governmentality in relation to children. And more importantly still, are the contemporary concerns of the British government simply a continuation of this process, and thus an integral part of the cultural politics through which childhood is constructed for children? As the case studies in Part II of the book will suggest, notwithstanding the new emphasis on citizenship education for children as a feature of the government's commitment to communitarianism, children remain marginalised and treated as non-citizens by the systems of surveillance and control through which 'childhood' is protected as a social space in the life course.

Childhood's structure and children's agency

Despite this apparent wish to deny or, at the very least to curb, children's agency, which is represented by children's lack of social citizenship, social status, personhood and opportunities for participation (as noted in Chapter 1), it is important for the cultural politics of childhood to consider the possibility that children themselves might contribute, as social agents, to processes of childhood change. This means asking questions about children's experiences of 'childhood' and about the part they might play in shaping the ways their childhood unfolds which, in turn, means incorporating an account of children's agency into our models and theories of childhood. And in part this process has already occurred – witness the growth in childhood studies over the last 20 years (James *et al.* 1998).

Moreover, through what Giddens has described as the double hermeneutic of social science, some of that theorising has percolated down to allow children's agency to be acknowledged as important within the social, political and economic realities of different societies. In many contexts, as Chapter 4 will document, this has involved rather dramatic changes in conceptions of both the nature of 'childhood' and 'the child' with, in the UK for example, children now apparently being prioritised on the government's agenda in their own right, and not simply as part of 'family' policy. Children's projects are, for instance, the focus for special provision under the Government's Children's and Local Network Funds and children's participation in the political process is currently being given some priority with the institutionalisation of a Youth Parliament. Considering that less than 20 years ago, prior to the Children Act 1989, it was still considered best that, as the old adage has it, 'children should be seen and not heard' these represent rather dramatic shifts in the collective thinking about children and childhood in the UK.

Such developments are indicative, therefore, that certain structural shifts in the thinking about the place and position of children have occurred in British society. However, in themselves they tell us little about how or why these changes have taken place. Nor, conversely, would a simple structural focus enable us to give a sufficient account of the resilience of discourses of childhood to change and, therefore, of the many continuities over time in thinking about what children are and what children need. We need instead to account for both these processes of change and continuity by exploring, empirically, the contribution made by people, individually or collectively, to the production and social reproduction of childhood in and through time.

The relationship between structure and agency is therefore central to our understanding of the production and reproduction of childhood, as we shall go on to demonstrate in Chapter 3. However, in discussions of cultural reproduction, few social theorists have considered the status and position of children; and fewer still have examined the potential of children themselves as the agents of social change, their roles being usually cast as its victims or, less commonly, its beneficiaries. Such a standpoint is, however, central to a cultural politics of childhood, as we have already suggested. Thus, although it is not appropriate here to analyse in detail the various theoretical debates around structure and agency and to assess their relative merits, it is important to consider how the issues raised by these debates within social science can illuminate our theoretical thinking about change and continuity in childhood. Two issues emerge as particularly significant.

First, as Tucker observes, in their attempts to unravel the relationship between structure and agency, theorists have turned their attention to time itself: 'placing time at the center of social analysis moves theory away from a view of individuals as separated from the social structures that they actively reproduce' (1998: 71). Thus, Giddens (1979) argues that there is a false dichotomy between structure and agency for, social action or agency and social structure presuppose one another *in the same moment*. This 'duality of structure', which is core to Giddens' theory of structuration, finds many parallels therefore with Bourdieu's (1971) concept of cultural reproduction in that both theorists see people's ongoing activity and creativity as that which, over time, reproduces society through all its cultural forms and which therefore accounts for both change in, as well as the persistence of, social structures.

As noted already in Chapter 1, childhood is itself a double temporal phenomenon such that the *transient* experiential temporality of childhood within the life course of individuals has to be understood, and indeed is only experienced, in relation to the structured *enduring* temporality of childhood as a social space, embedded within the fabric of society itself. This twin temporal framing of each individual who passes through 'childhood' has therefore to be taken into account, we argue, in terms of *both* agency and structure and as an ongoing and interwoven experience. It is not sufficient to focus simply on the structural changes which childhood undergoes, as if these were independent of the social relationships through which 'childhood' and 'adulthood', in social practice, come to be embodied in everyday life. It is people, after all, who breathe life into such structural concepts!

To do this, temporality – pace and rhythm – becomes a key feature to be examined.[3] We need, for example, to ask why and how do particular continuities remain in our thinking about children and childhood? When and how do turning points arise which may spark radical change in concepts of childhood and the way that social space is shaped and ordered? Is the pace of childhood change so imperceptibly slow that it is only when children grow out of it and, as adults, have children themselves, that the contrast between then and now becomes noticeable and 'change' can be remarked, or can we 'see' change taking place for children in and through their everyday activities?

A second important insight from the structure/agency debate of significance for our discussion relates to the nature of individual action. Central to Giddens' (1979) view of structuration is the reflexive individual who has a practical consciousness of the way the world works. Through his/her actions, the reflexive individual contributes to social reproduction, by both choosing to conform or to act otherwise through using the rules and resources available to him/her in particular contexts and in particular context-specific ways. Routinised over time, this social phenomenon takes on the reality that sociologists have reified by the concept of a 'thing' called 'social structure'. According to Giddens, however, this 'thing' is no more nor less than the culminated means and outcomes of people's social practices enduring over time.

For Bourdieu too, social structure is the outcome of people's practical engagement with the world and of their reproductive interactions that take place over time. Through sets of culturally specific dispositions constituted as the 'habitus', people unconsciously think and act to reproduce the power relations through which their everyday interactions are structured: 'the habitus imbues people with a tacit sense of how to become competent social agents, which is realized in practices that are constitutive of social life' (Tucker 1998: 71).

Notwithstanding the critiques of both these perspectives concerning the extent to which structuration theory does, in fact, dispense with some reified notion of structures working as external constraints on individuals, or whether the theoretical account of 'habitus' sits comfortably with what we know, empirically, about social change, what is important for our purposes here is that both theorists are attempting to explain social reproduction and change as the result of ongoing social action, manifested in terms of structures of different kinds ranging from social institutions through to mental dispositions. Both theorists therefore see social structure and the institutions through which it is constituted not as rigid forms, which constrain the individual, but rather as the more fluid social contexts through which social action takes place and acquires meaning in an ongoing and recursive manner.

In relation to the production and reproduction of childhood, this recognition of the 'ongoing' nature of social action as central to the constitution of society is an important insight because, as Chapter 3 will explore in detail, it allows us to consider both change *and* continuity as central features in the social construction and reconstruction of childhood. It also allows us to see this as potentially achieved through both the intentional and unintentional actions and interactions of children, as well as adults, as a feature of generational relations and as depending on any number of personal, social and cultural factors. What this perspective allows us to do, then, is also to account for the many diversities in children's experiences and the discontinuities that fracture the notion of a unitary 'childhood'.

Childhood change and continuity

The issues raised above underscore the complexities of our subject. The identity of 'the child' is, on the one hand, a transient identity for the individual, simply a passing-through en route to adulthood. On the other hand, through the institutionalisation of childhood it represents a potentially more enduring mode of identification that is informed by sets of continuities and discontinuities in the discourses and cultural determinants that have come to shape it. And, just to muddy the waters further, this twin referencing takes place both at the macro level of the collective, structural and institutional, as well as within the more micro context of everyday life – on a one-to-one basis, between parents and their children within the confines of the family.

As a way of grasping such complexities of social life and moving beyond the dichotomies of the structure/agency debate, Jenkins has recently suggested an alternative sociological approach to understanding both change and continuity that appears to transcend some of the difficulties encountered previously by social theorists working within the confines of the structure/action debate. For Jenkins, the human world is composed of three different orders: the individual order, the interactional order and the institutional order that are in continual process of change or movement, for human worlds are not static. Change is visualised as an ongoing feature of human society and, at any one moment, what factors will lead to which major social transformation is far from predictable:

> All actions are movement . . . and which will produce change is not necessarily clear at the time. That depends, at least in large part, on other people: whether they recognise what is happening, and how they respond to it. For change to occur old ways of doing things have to be stopped and/or new ways of doing things have to become established and recognised. In other words, change frequently involves institutionalisation (which, only apparently paradoxically, involves certainly in the first instance the inhibition of further change.)
>
> (Jenkins 2002: 77–78).

For Jenkins, then, the individual and collective always co-exist in the human world and it is the process of identification, via interaction, through which these are both simultaneously realised:

> Identification . . . refers to how we know who we are and how we know who others are . . . simultaneously a matter of behaviour (what humans do) and of how that is understood by ourselves and others (meaning)
>
> (2002: 68)

Identification, he argues, 'always involves how others identify me or us, and how we identify them' and it is through processes of interaction that this occurs; but, equally, interaction also depends, in large part, on processes of identification for 'without identification of self and others, interaction would be impossible' (2002: 68–72). Any change in identity is also, therefore, 'rooted in interaction and negotiation with others' although, as Jenkins notes, some are more resistant than others, in part depending on the extent to which they are institutionalised or not (2002: 72).

This perspective offers, then, a way to circumvent the either/or dichotomy of structure/agency in explaining the continuities and discontinuities of childhood for it encourages exploration of the interactions that occur between the different elements in society in order to locate the precise mechanisms and processes of change. Thus, although collective institutions or structures like churches, football clubs or childhoods endure and survive all kinds of changes, and in this sense transcend the agentic individuals who are their constituent members, nonetheless 'they are all sometime products of people, which require at least some maintenance work by other people if they are to persist and prosper' (Jenkins 2002: 76).

This perspective can be set alongside that offered by critical realism which, as Mayall (2002) suggests, also provides a useful way forward for understanding childhood in that it offers a relational account of society and social change through inserting an historical perspective. Bhaskar, in contradistinction to Giddens, does not acknowledge the duality of structure for, he argues, people do not 'create' society in the present so much as transform it:

> People do not create society. For it always pre-exists them and is a necessary condition for their activity. Rather society must be regarded as an ensemble of structures, practices and conventions

which individuals reproduce or transform, but which would not exist
unless they did so

(Bhaskar 1979, cited in Mayall 2002: 343)

This does not mean that critical realism therefore shies away
from seeking out explanations for why change does – or does not –
take place. On the contrary, it engages with this as a central issue.
However, it suggests that when attempting to identify 'causal
mechanisms', we have to see the real world in terms of the open
system that it is. That is to say, the world is not a closed system of
simple structures, which might enable us to offer straightforward and
unambiguous deterministic explanations of the kind 'A causes B'.
Rather, what we have to recognise is that, in the real world, 'A *may*
cause B', depending on the precise combination of circumstances
(Houston 2001). It may also not. To understand change therefore
requires us to be content with identifying a whole range of tendencies or influences, rather than causes, which might – or might
not – come together in different and highly complex ways to
produce or resist change, including in one and the same moment
the innate psychological mechanisms of individuals alongside the
broad sweep of a whole variety of different social mechanisms and
institutions.

Childhood as an interdisciplinary field

Given the theoretical, conceptual and empirical complexity of
the processes that the cultural politics of childhood attempts to
unravel – to identify the ways in which social, economic, legal and
political systems position children in society, and children's and
adult's responses to that positioning – it is clear that no single discipline could claim this topic as theirs by right. However, although
the virtues and virtuosity of interdisciplinarity are often held up
as a mantra of contemporary research, there remains, in practice,
a certain coyness within the academic community about admitting
the potential fecundity of such re-partnerings. Instead, difficulties,
obstacles and objections are often loudly proclaimed in the name
of academic purity and integrity by those clinging to particular
disciplinary life rafts, while the new opportunities for critical
reflection that interdisciplinarity can bring remain muted and are
downplayed. In this book, however, we intend to make the most
of the opportunities that the interdisciplinarity of childhood studies

embraces. Indeed, as will become clear, an interdisciplinary perspective is in fact *essential* if we are to grasp fully the nature of the socially and culturally constructed character of childhood, as it unfolds and changes in and through everyday life.

Through a deliberate act of academic promiscuity, therefore, we draw, as and when necessary, on the rather different perspectives offered by sociology, social anthropology, social history, social policy and socio-legal studies and, by doing so, reveal the subtlety of the ways in which childhood is culturally constructed for children and the rather different contexts in which this occurs. In particular, and by way of illustration, we focus on four case studies in Part II of this book to reveal the details of how this takes place in the health-care sector, through the education and criminal justice systems and, finally, within the family itself.

In contrast, then, to the fears expressed by Donnan and McFarlane (1997) that the eclectic mixing of disciplinary perspectives risks reducing 'culture' to a residual category, what this book reveals is the exact opposite. Drawing on the strengths of the different disciplines, we are able to reveal the intricacies of the social and cultural processes through which ideas of 'the child' and of 'childhood' come to be constructed for and on behalf of children themselves, in the course of their everyday lives and through children's own engagement with these processes.

Of particular importance to this endeavor, as we shall explore more fully in Chapters 3 and 4, is the value that an interdisciplinary perspective can bring to the study of social policy especially, by enabling us to think about the consequences that policies have for children, both as individuals and as category members. As Wright and Shore have argued for example, it is no longer possible for anthropologists – or other social scientists for that matter – to ignore policy or feign disinterest in it for,

> through policy, the individual is categorized and given such statuses and roles as 'subject', 'citizen', 'professional', 'national', 'criminal' and 'deviant'. From the cradle to the grave, people are classified, shaped and ordered according to policies, but they may have little consciousness of or control over the processes at work.
>
> (1997: 4)

As they suggest, such topics are in fact at the heart of the anthropological enterprise, not marginal to it. Moreover, in the context of the modern state, policy processes are in fact central to the ongoing reproduction of culture itself, through the making and re-making of law and through its application as policy in everyday life (cf. Bourdieu 1971). Thus, as we shall show, taken together, sociology, social policy, socio-legal studies and social anthropology can illuminate different aspects of processes of identity formation, at both the structural and the experiential level (Jenkins 1996). And, for our particular concerns in this volume, it is how the identity of 'child' is brought into being and an understanding of the ways in which 'childhood' is socially constructed and reconstructed for children over time, which will be our main focus.

In this way, this volume reveals policy-making to be fundamental, not merely to the fact of social categorisation but to the very particularity of any categorisation by, for example, setting out the cultural values and moralities associated with the social ranking of personhood and status (see Hockey and James 1993). Within any particular cultural context, therefore, policy works to delimit the conditions of possibility and the arenas of restraint through which meanings are given to social practice and, ultimately, to ideas of the person. Thus, one of the ways in which people come to know not only their own social place and selves but also those of others is, in effect, through experiencing the process and outcomes of policy as it shapes and reshapes the humdrum pattern of their everyday lives. And it is in these everyday encounters that people's identities as this or that kind of person are revealed, taken on, negotiated or rejected. As Jenkins has described,

> identity can only be understood as process. As 'being' or 'becoming'. One's social identity – indeed one's social identities, for who we are is always singular and plural – is never a final or settled matter.
>
> (1996: 4)

It is crucial therefore to consider the import for children themselves of the different conceptions of 'childhood' as a social space and 'children' as a collectivity that they, as individuals, encounter across the early part of their life course and on an everyday basis.

Conclusion

This chapter has been concerned to identify some of the key concepts and theoretical concerns with which a cultural politics of childhood must engage in order to explore the ways in which 'childhood' is constituted and regulated – and how it changes. In doing so it has indicated that law and social policy are important mechanisms to be explored. When these are, however, regarded as processes, rather than things, as both texts and discourses open to different interpretations, mediations and implementations (Ball 1994), it becomes possible to account for the discontinuities and differences of childhood, as embodied by individual children, as well as the structural similarities between them. This is to understand how and why a particular policy might have rather different, even contradictory, sets of outcomes and effects for different groups of people – one of the questions core to a cultural politics of childhood.

Thus, to take just one example, the law prescribes that children in the UK should go to school. It states when they should do so and for how long. It details what goes on in school – the kinds of curricula that are taught, the punishments that may be inflicted, the amount of playground space permitted and the meals provided. Thus, whenever they play, learn, or even eat their dinners, children indirectly find that the temporal pattern of their days, their experiences of learning and even the content of their school meals is shaped for them by the policies through which 'schooling' is ordered and policed. Such prescriptions are, however, subject to the shifts in thinking of politicians, over time, and to implementation by a variety of different policy-makers. Thus, in the case of 'schooling', exactly how that ordering process takes place depends – in large part – on cultural conceptions of what children are thought to need or ought to have, conceptions which may subtly change or be made to take on different hues within a local context. It is in this sense then that in the social and cultural construction of childhood for children, and of allocating social identity to any individual child, policy-making can be said to be an important *cultural*, rather than simply, political process. As Jenkins has argued,

> social identities exist and are acquired, claimed and allocated within power relations. Identity is something *over* which struggles take place and *with* which stratagems are advanced: it is means and end in politics.
>
> (1996: 24)

Thus, as the next chapter goes on to argue, regulatory mechanisms designed to implement and enforce social policies are forms of societal practice for the production and reproduction of social order. And it is through these that the political aspirations of the state are made manifest. These societal practices are, however, not uniform in their effects and outcomes, being variously and strategically used by people in terms of everyday social practices. Rejected and opposed by some, whilst being joyfully embraced by others, neither uniformity nor conformity can therefore be guaranteed. Disorder of some kind is thus, ironically, an inevitable by-product of this ordering process. In this way then, even within one society, whilst being subject to its rules, different children may experience rather different kinds of childhoods and as we shall see, it is precisely through the messy process of living out their lives as children that children themselves may contribute to the process of childhood change.

Notes

1 This can be encapsulated, for the contemporary UK, in the notion of the 'Thatcherite generation' (1995: 3). Having been born and brought up under the Conservative regime of the 1980s, this label identifies today's young people as having a selfish and uncaring attitude to others, Margaret Thatcher having famously claimed that there was no such thing as society.

2 This is not of course to suggest that there is only one childhood common to Western societies. As we go on to detail in Chapters 3 and 4 there are many important variations between, say, children's experiences in the UK and many of the Nordic countries, which have rather different conceptions of childhood. However, it is nonetheless the case that the *process* of institutionalisation has been an historical process common to both cultural contexts.

3 For Mayall (2002: 29–31) this is represented by the distinction between 'cohort' and 'generation'. However, for our purposes, employing these collective terms would imply too great an emphasis on the commonalities of childhood and down play the differences and diversities. See also Lee (2001: 53).

CHAPTER 3

The Production and Reproduction of Childhood

Given the variation between concepts of childhood and the variation in children's social experiences noted in previous chapters, it might be argued that childhood is always best understood in terms of its local diverse context; that it is no longer credible, as has often been the case in the past, to speak of 'the child' as a universalised and apolitical subject of the modern world or of 'childhood' as an unproblematic and universal feature of the generational order (see Chapter 1); and that, instead, we might best concentrate on exploring the local diversities and cultural variables which fracture the coherent sensibilities of the notion of 'the child' as a common and shared category status.

However, there is an inherent danger in overemphasising cultural differences and local diversity. In doing so we risk losing sight of those commonalities that *do* unite children (Qvortrup 1994; Mayall 2002). And to lose sight of these would mean dispensing with the political and policy agendas that might be brought into play to serve (or frustrate) all children's interests, both globally and within the context of a single society. There is, then, some ambivalence, both in the academy and in the 'real' world of practitioners and policy-makers, with regard to how to manage these twin aspects of children's experiences.

What this dilemma also draws attention to, however, is the fact that the theorising about childhood that *has* taken place to date has failed to specify adequately the mechanisms and processes through which childhood or, as we would wish to argue, culturally and politically diverse *childhoods*, have emerged historically. In this chapter we seek to rectify this situation by offering a generalised model of childhood continuity and change which will be of use in explaining the framing of children's experiences as 'childhood' within and across different locales.

As we shall demonstrate, central to this model is the role of 'Law'. We shall employ this, however, in a generic rather than simply in a narrow legislative or judicial sense. Used in this way, we take 'Law' to include not only the formal institutions of law (i.e. *the* law) – statutes, courts, judicial and other legal actors – but also the less formal processes and mechanisms of regulation that exist in all societies, both religious and secular. Thus we also include in our definition of Law the informal discursive processes through which morals, norms, expectations and behaviours are both framed and moderated, processes which inform social practices and social policies, become codified in *the* law and through which societies are ordered.[1]

Law in this formulation is taken as one of the primary mechanisms for social ordering, comprising a system of principles and practices that underpin the social construction of a wide range of behaviours, attitudes, beliefs and relationships. It is Law that defines the rights and responsibilities of, and therefore the relationships between, citizens in any given cultural and political context. It is Law, therefore, that also creates and sustains the regulatory frameworks that define 'childhood' as a particular kind of collectivity specific to a particular locale; *and*, therefore, it is also in and through the operation of Law that the everyday interactions that take place between adults and children are encapsulated, routinised and systematised (see also Qvortrup 1994).

We can think here, for example, of the use of concepts of age to delimit and regulate various aspects of children's behaviour, such as sexual activity between adults and children, as well as amongst children themselves. In order to illustrate such issues in more detail, Part II of the book offers a series of case studies that consider, *inter alia*, the relationship of age to various aspects of children's competence and the role of Law in defining this in the spheres of education, health, the family and criminal activity. These reveal the current thinking in the UK about what is appropriate in these very different locales, and suggest that similar analyses in different societies might be equally revealing.

As we subsequently illustrate, therefore, it is through Law, in its broadest sense, that children's everyday lives as children are constructed and regulated. In this way Law can be seen as an integrative social mechanism – it formalises and/or mitigates conflicts and facilitates social interaction by regulating the relationships between the differentiated parts of social systems (Roach Anleu 2000: 41). And since Law also comprises and reflects cultural knowledge, it is quintessentially normative, defining people's legal rights, freedoms and responsibilities, not only in relation to the State but also in relation to other citizens, be they adults or children.

Since, however, it does this at the same time as it seeks to *regulate* these rights and freedoms, the normative power of Law is further enhanced by framing our expectations of those others with whom we share social space – Law is thus a social mediator. Arguably, then, it is through the operation of Law that social order is produced and *re*produced, since the wide diversity of social realities within any given society means that these must be mediated through Law, by reference to the common principles that it both embodies and represents. This perspective reflects, therefore, that developed in somewhat different contexts by social theorists such as Parsons (1962, 1978) and Habermas (1996) who also examined the role of law in terms of the 'ordering' of the social.

However, Law (including *the* law) does not exist in a vacuum. Neither does it exist *sui generis*. Law, it must be remembered, is a product of what Jenkins calls 'the human world', a world 'full of real people dealing with each other and producing and reproducing their world, whether they intend to or not' (2002: 143–44). Thus, given the 'ordering' role that Law has, it therefore must also allow for and respond to the changes that the human world produces through the actions and interactions of embodied individuals. And it must do so while also ensuring a sense of continuity for the collectivity. Law therefore has to be dynamic and to be able to accommodate diversity and change, as part of the process of ensuring commonality. In this sense, Law mediates constantly between individuals and the collectivity we call society.

What we want to explore in this chapter, then, is the proposition that a key element in the cultural politics of childhood is the role of Law, be this religious or secular, in both mediating between, but also helping preserve, the boundaries between adulthood and childhood as they shift and change over time. This means therefore that the concept of 'childhood' – however and wherever it finds local expression – can be theorised in terms of the cumulative history of social practices and policies about children, expressed as Law, which have arisen in response to the activities of children in their ongoing engagement with the adult world and adults' views about those activities.

The model we outline therefore identifies Law as the key mechanism through which social structures (including the social space of childhood) and social practices (including the day-to-day interactions between adults and children that constitute the lived experience of childhood) are linked. However, while Law incorporates the principles on which social structures are founded, the law provides the means through which relationships between the State and citizens are ordered and conducted. Consequently, we also argue that it is through this linkage that both continuity and change are facilitated since, in ordering social relationships, Law sometimes facilitates change while at other times resists it. Thus, in the analytical model that we develop in this chapter, we show that it is Law that articulates the relationship between structure and agency.

Law and social change

In terms of our approach, Law is not therefore, as some theorists (for example, Teubner 1989; King and Piper 1990) would argue, an entirely closed and self-referential system (James 1992), since this implies a somewhat static view of the law. Like 'childhood', it too is a social and cultural construct and it must therefore also be located and understood in the context of social change. Law mediates between 'the State' and 'the individual' and, in doing so, its role is to manage and regulate the tensions between the collective expression of conformity and commonality on the one hand and the rights and freedoms bestowed by the law on individuals, to explore and express agency, on the other.

This tension – and it is a very real and practical one – is, we suggest, 'held' in the sphere of social policy in, for example, the promulgation of policies defining the rights and responsibilities of citizens in a secular society, or the promulgation of doctrines that define the rights and responsibilities of believers in a religious-based society. All such policies however, whether defined by the secular or the religious state, have their ultimate source in 'Law'. It is this through which the social practices of people in the social collectivity of the 'State' are ordered and regulated.

Importantly, of course, such polices change over time, in response both to internal and external pressures, and thus Law also changes along with the institutions – such as childhood, marriage and the family – that it serves to regulate. We would also contend, therefore, that Law is a dynamic mechanism, not only in the here-and-now but also over time. It articulates and mediates the many different kinds of social relationships that are involved in the ongoing processes of change that characterise the social and human world: between the individual and the State; between what is common and that which is diverse; and between social policies and the everyday social practices which are their focus for regulation. Thus the role of Law is to manage change whilst also providing continuity between pasts, presents and futures; continuity of childhood as the space within which children grow up to comprise the adult population; and continuity of the relationships between 'childhood' and 'adulthood' as separate but contingent spaces within the generational order.

In our view, therefore, Law is of fundamental importance in the process not only of 'managing' social change but also of mediating between structure and agency. At the macro level, regardless of historical or cultural specificity, it is the acceptance by people of the *Rule* of Law that is of fundamental importance in the creation and maintenance of social order. By this, we mean accepting the primacy of, and compliance with, a body of ideas and principles that are rooted in and specific to that society and which serve to organise social behaviour. The Rule of Law is thus the legitimated means by which social structures and hence 'society' are maintained. At the heart of the concept of the Rule of Law, therefore, is the idea that social behaviour is contained and regulated within the framework of a legal system and laws, which embody and regulate normative expectations. It is these that therefore serve to maintain social order.

Such concepts and analytical tools are too coarse, however, to help us to understand people's daily lived experiences. Thus, in order to begin to achieve such understanding, it is necessary to deploy a rather different range of tools to analyse social practices at the micro level of people's interactions with one another. As self-conscious, self-determined individuals, their actions are informed by a common sense, almost implicit understanding of the laws and systems that exist in every society for securing and enforcing justice and the modifications of these that are wrought by custom and practice.

To adopt such an analysis requires, therefore, a model of law and social change that embodies a reflexive and recursive approach to understanding the interaction between concepts and praxis – for example between structure and agency, between the rule of law and the operation of judicial systems, or between particular laws and their application through custom and practice. Recent research by Ewick and Silbey (1998) provides powerful empirical support for such an approach. As they argue, law, or what they refer to as legality, is:

> an emergent feature of social relations rather than an external apparatus acting upon social life . . . It embodies the diversity of the situations out of which it emerges and that it helps to structure . . . Legality is not sustained solely by the formal law . . . Rather it is enduring because it relies on and invokes the commonplace schemas of everyday life.

(1998: 17)

Indeed, as they go on to argue, legality is constructed through and comprises everyday actions and practices. Thus:

> the law does not simply work on social life (to define and to shape it). [It] also operates through social life as persons and groups deliberately interpret and invoke law's language, authority and procedures to organize their lives and manage their relationships. In short, the commonplace operation of law in daily life makes us all legal agents insofar as we actively make law, even when no formal legal agent is involved.

(Ewick and Silbey 1998: 20)

We must therefore also incorporate into our approach a slightly more sophisticated understanding of the relationship between law and custom and practice and to do so we build on Mary Douglas's (1973) grid/group approach to social analysis. Douglas argues that the nature of any given society is a product of the interaction between the grid – the structures/thoughts/ideas that bind people together and the group – the way people organise themselves and are organised (Figure 3.1).

This model can be adapted to produce a matrix that enables us to explore the varying relationship between the Rule of Law, as an

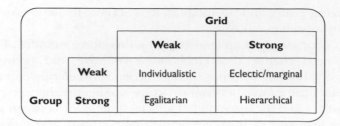

Grid		
	Weak	**Strong**
Weak	Individualistic	Eclectic/marginal
Group **Strong**	Egalitarian	Hierarchical

Figure 3.1

Rule of Law		
	Weak	**Strong**
Social **Weak**	*Repeal of laws* – law outdated, unenforceable as a result of changes in custom and practice	*Intensification of enforcement* – law still valid and relevant but ignored in practice, better enforcement seen as just
Response **Strong**	*Relaxation of enforcement* – law no longer valid or needed, enforced but seen as unjust	*Pass new laws* – response to changes in custom and practice, need to enforce or resist change

Figure 3.2

expression of structural determinants, and the social response to it, as a reflection of the exercise of agency and social action (Figure 3.2).

In this matrix, the Rule of Law as a concept is equated with the Grid (the structures, thoughts and ideas that bind people) and the Social Response is equated with the Group (the way in which people are organised/organise themselves). The concept of the Rule of Law reflects the idea that social behaviour is contained and regulated within a framework of a legal system and laws that serve to maintain social order. However, by considering the Rule of Law alongside and in relation to the social response to it – that is, the way in which persons and groups deliberately interpret (or misinterpret) and invoke (or choose not to invoke) law's language, authority and procedures to organise their lives and manage their relationships – we are able to consider the impact on law of everyday social behaviour and to consider the customs and practices which structure our daily lives. These also incorporate our common sense or lay understanding of various laws, the details of which are unknown to most of us. We can also, most importantly, use this model to consider the relationship between law, agency and social change.

If, for example, there is only a weak social commitment to maintaining the rule of law in a given area of social life, the laws that regulate this particular social arena may be defined as outdated, or as unenforceable as a result of changes in social priorities or custom and practice. If the State is not anxious to enforce such laws and there is no strong public demand that they should be, they may be repealed or allowed to lapse. A small example of this in England and Wales is that cyclists are still legally required to show lights on their bicycles during the hours of darkness (white to the front and red to the rear) and yet in practice, a large number do not. There are, however, very few prosecutions for breaches of this law. There are also many long-established local bye-laws that remain on the statute books but have not been repealed.

If, however, there is only a weak social commitment to maintaining the rule of law in a given area of social life but a government wishes, for political or social reasons, to change the social response in that area, it may react by intensifying enforcement. It may argue that existing laws can and should be enforced more vigourously but that no new legislation is needed. In England and Wales, for example, there has been a recent resurgence in demand from politicians, both nationally and locally, for a stricter enforcement of the laws relating to the disposal of litter in public places and the non-attendance of children at school, as part of a response to wider political and social concerns.

If, on the other hand, there is a weak commitment to the rule of law in a given area of social life, accompanied by a strengthening social commitment to developing or maintaining an emergent set of social practices and customs, there may be a relaxation of enforcement. In this case the law is redefined as being 'out of touch' with the social changes that have occurred and therefore, if and when it *is* enforced, it is seen as unfair because it is so commonly disregarded. Thus, for example, in spite of recent expressions of concern about children's apparently increasing consumption of alcohol in the UK (see Chapter 6), the laws that prevent under-age drinking in public houses are currently not rigorously enforced. Similarly, the social response to the use of cannabis in the UK has undergone a substantial change in recent years, as a consequence of which the laws relating to personal use are much less rigorously enforced than they were a decade ago and, when they are, this is commonly regarded as unjust.

Finally, if there is a strong or renewed commitment to the rule of law in a given area of social life that is also accompanied by a strong or growing social commitment to maintaining or strengthening social practices and customs, existing laws will continue to be enforced vigorously. Or, if customs and practices have changed in a way that is not reflected in the law, new laws may be passed. Thus recent political concerns in the UK about weak or feckless parenting have led to various changes in the law in order to require parents to behave more responsibly regarding their children's school attendance or delinquent behaviour (see Chapter 7).

In the UK and, we suspect, in many other parts of the world, there are numerous examples of the differential enforcement of laws as a result of either changes in custom and practice or discrepancies between legal provisions and social (although not necessarily universally held) attitudes, which are and have been differentially enforced at different points in history, reflecting clear shifts in the social response to such issues over time. Viewed from the perspective we have depicted in Figure 3.3, law therefore becomes a pivotal mechanism in terms of mediating both the nature and the pace of social change. As Ewick and Silbey argue:

> Because law is both an embedded and an emergent feature of social life, it collaborates with other social structures ([e.g.] religion, family and gender) to infuse meaning and constrain social action . . . Legality operates, then, as both an interpretive framework and a set of resources with which and through which the social world (including that part that is known as the law) is constituted.
>
> (1998: 22–23)

What is crucial to this perspective is the idea that social structures, although they are often perceived and depicted as external and coercive, do not exist apart from our collective actions and thoughts. In this sense they are 'more appropriately understood as ongoing processes rather than as sets of immutable constraints' (Ewick and Silbey 1998: 41). Viewed in this way, Law *is* social action, albeit

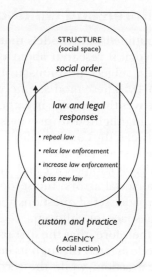

Figure 3.3

with varying degrees of codification. Thus, every time an individual interprets some event or analyses some situation in terms of legal concepts or terminology, legality is produced and 'repeated invocation of the law sustains its capacity to comprise social situations' (1998: 45).

The significance of this for childhood, of course, is that concepts such as rights, responsibilities, duties, protection and welfare are deployed on a daily basis in the various discourses surrounding children. In this way, the laws that comprise childhood are constituted, reiterated and *re*constituted through the everyday actions and practices that comprise, and which take place in the context of, the relationships between adults and children. As Ewick and Silbey note, however, 'societies are collections of many practices and multiple structures that draw upon common schemas and resources. In short, legality shares schemas and resources with other social structures' (1998: 49). And so the processes that drive social change and reflect the evolution of social practices, from generation to generation, mean that these common schemas and resources are both adopted and adapted. Such an analysis has profound implications for a cultural politics of childhood and for our understanding of the theory and practice of childhood change, to which we now return.

Theorising children and childhood

James *et al.* (1998) outlined four models that, they argue, inform contemporary sociological research about children and suggest that these offer four subject positions from which to theorise childhood (Figure 3.4).[2] These models emerge out of two particular research perspectives that engage in rather different ways with the tricky problem, highlighted in previous chapters, of how to manage the gulf between the commonality and diversity of childhood and that between structure and agency. The first perspective asserts strongly children's competence and stresses the importance of seeing children as social actors; the second addresses, equally strongly, a rather broader set of questions about how childhood is structured as a social space for children.

It could be said, therefore, that the first pays more attention to diversity in childhood research through its emphasis on children's individual and social action, while the second, by emphasising

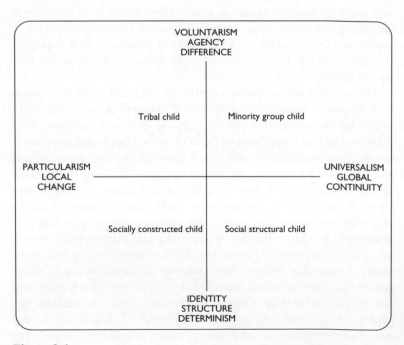

Figure 3.4

structural issues, works towards an exploration of what is common for all children. However, despite their apparent diametric opposition to one another, each approach does recognise, implicitly, the necessity of acknowledging *both* the commonalities and diversities of childhood.

Turning first to the perspective of the child as social actor, James *et al.* (1998) note that this embraces two rather different models of childhood, which they term tribal and minority group. In both models children are positioned as competent social actors, as people with an informed and informing view of the social world. But for those working with a 'tribal' model most attention is paid to the ways in which that competence is acknowledged and expressed, or how is it disguised and controlled, in and through children's everyday relationships – with each other, with their family and with adults. Within the 'tribal' model the commonalities of childhood are downplayed and instead the diversities in children's experiences – those wrought by age, gender, class, health and ethnicity for example – are highlighted (see, for example, Corsaro 1979; Thorne 1993). Seeing children as competent means exploring the ways in which children themselves, in and through their own social relationships, actively construct a child's world, distinctive and unique in its form and content. Children's own culture, their local play traditions and language are thus key foci for researchers working with this model of childhood.

This positioning of children as active learners and socialisers also marks the second agency-focused perspective – the 'minority group' – but here finds translation through engagement with what is common to *all* children. Children's competences and concerns are here regarded as being shared by all children within the social space of childhood, rather than as a child-specific set of abilities that are simply of and about the concerns of some children. In this way children are visualised as taking on the characteristics of a minority group vis-à-vis the adult population, separated and often discriminated against by the very institution of childhood itself (see, for example, Alderson 1993; Mayall 1996). Research in the context of this model explores the ways in which children are united as members of the social category 'child' by factors such as young age, lack of citizenship status and lack of political, economic and social rights. Within such a perspective, then, children as social actors are understood against the backdrop of an overall and shared commonality, a feature characteristic of all minority groups.

Turning to the second perspective on childhood, which examines how childhood is structured as a social space for children, we find two further subject positions identified. Once again, the differences between them centre on the extent to which the particularity or diversity of children's childhoods, as revealed in children's everyday actions, is acknowledged within the more overarching paradigm of the commonality of childhood as a social space. Thus, James *et al.* (1998) suggest that the third model – the social structural child – explores the ways in which the social space of childhood is marked out for children in society, seeing this as a constant and recognisable component of all social structures. Beginning from the assumption noted in Chapter 2 that 'children' are common to every social system, this model focuses on the shared commonality of 'childhood'. The status identity and subject position of 'the child' is examined in its inter-relationship with others – adolescence, and adulthood for example – as a structural feature of the life course and, therefore, as a more general feature of the social system. Such a perspective on childhood permits work to be carried out at a national and a global level through the adoption of a comparative framework within which the status and subject position of 'the child' is taken as read and is not, in itself, made a matter of dispute (see Qvortrup 1994).

A final model of childhood – the socially constructed child – explores the diverse ways in which 'childhood' comes to be constituted in society for children. In contrast to the previous one, rather than taking the subject position of 'the child' for granted, this radically relativistic model examines the discourses through which the idea of both 'the child' and 'childhood' is produced. It asks what is 'the child' in the local context? How is the status of 'the child' understood locally? What features of 'the child' are highlighted as important and attributed with significance? There is no assumption, within this model, of a set of naturalised competencies which allow us to define 'the child' from the outset and, in this sense, it is diametrically opposed to the perspective offered from within developmental psychology, while nonetheless being focused on the social structures and concepts through which ideas of childhood are articulated (see, for example, Stainton-Rogers and Stainton-Rogers 1992; Jenks 1996a).

In summary, each of these models, represented diagrammatically in Figure 3.4, offers rather different subject positions for children along evaluative axes. One defines children's social status as (more or less) able and active participants in the social world. The other defines the extent to which childhood, and hence 'the child', is to be understood in terms of local particularities or, alternatively, as encompassed by a more universalising and global perspective. However, as heuristic devices, what these models also point to, we suggest, are four different facets of children's experiences as children. Taken together they constitute and reflect the totality of the childhoods lived by children throughout the world and, from the perspective of the individual child, it is these same four positions that, in varying proportions, at any given time and in any particular social situation, combine to shape their daily lived experiences. Viewed in this slightly different way, what Figure 3.4 allows us to do, therefore, is to hold 'the child' and 'childhood' constant at any given historical moment but, at the same time, to vary the perspectives from which we view them.

Children, childhood and social order

Such models are, of course, simply models and in this sense they are, sociologically speaking, ideal types. Nonetheless, they are useful pointers to the ways in which we might begin to unravel the complexities of the cultural politics of childhood and account for the commonalities and diversities that unite and fracture 'childhood' for children and which are core to the cultural politics of childhood. For example, by focusing on the child as social actor within the tribal model of childhood, we are able to see children exercising their agency within local contexts and in response to local particularities. And in doing so, we might see how it is that this exercise of agency creates some of the diversities that are just as much a part of childhood as are its commonalities.

As Bluebond-Langner (1978) has so graphically described, for example, the prospect of imminent death serves to give children an experiential confidence and competence in dealing with the adult world that would in other circumstances not be theirs. The dying or chronically sick child's childhood represents, therefore, one kind of diversity. Alternatively, we might explore how the common social space of childhood positions children as members of a minority group, united as actors in a shared and particular space within the social structure, and how, as a consequence of such perceptions of commonality, exceptions emerge in the course of everyday life – for example, the child, who exceeds expectations of an age-based competency, the child carer, or the child who works to support their family (Hockey and James 2003).

What is significant about such exceptions, however, is the rather different consequences they can have, over time, for the way in which 'childhood' is understood. On the one hand they can serve to reinforce existing local models of 'the child'; on the other, they can provoke reconsideration. Change and continuity in thinking are thus both possible as outcomes. We contend that the question of *which* will occur, however, is shaped by the prevailing social, political and cultural conditions realised in and through social action of rather different kinds, since not all change produces radical transformation. As Jenkins has observed:

> Change in the world of humans does not simply mean alteration: it is alteration that is noticed and recognised as significant by the people concerned. It is alteration to which human meaning is attached.
>
> (2002: 80)

It might be postulated, for example, that the changing regulation and control of children's actions and agency, which as noted in Chapter 2 has over time patterned adults' relations with children, will vary in its intensity and that it will do so in relation to adult perceptions of the priority to be given to the status quo by maintaining, reinforcing or altering the existing ordering of these. This is implicit in our analysis above in relation to childhood change and continuity (see Figures 3.1 and 3.2 above).

A recent example from the UK would be the demand made for new forms of control over childhood and, indeed, the emergence of new constructions of children's nature and competences that followed in the wake of the James Bulger case in 1993 when two 10-year-old boys murdered a younger child, after abducting him from a shopping precinct in Bootle (see James and Jenks 1996). From the stepping up of controls over truanting, stricter regulation of children's access to videos and the setting up of a 'Mum's army' to assist with primary school education through to the lowering of the age of criminal responsibility to ten, this new version of childhood was no longer a 'once-upon-a-time story with a happy and predictable ending' (James and Jenks 1996: 316).

This was, however, a rather 'local' phenomenon. In Trondheim, Norway, around the same time a small child was also killed by two other children – but with a rather different response. The Norwegian case led to no reconceptualisation of childhood and no changes in the regulation of children or calls for an increase in their control. Instead, the Norwegian child killers were regarded as the 'victims', rather than the perpetrators of violence and there was no public debate about the nature of childhood similar to the outcry and calls for retribution and revenge that so marked out the UK case. The exercise of agency can thus give rise to either continuity or change.

We are not, of course, suggesting that in either of these cases there was any self-conscious exercise of agency by the children who committed these crimes. They surely did not intend to influence social change. In this sense, therefore, the un-self-conscious exercise of agency by individual children is, of course, quite different from the self-conscious exercise of collective agency that might be seen in situations where children combine to act with the specific intention of effecting change (such as, for example, child workers in the Bangladesh garment industry in the early 1990s – see Boyden and Myers 1994). What we have here, however, is an illustration of how, depending upon local models of the child, there might be very different responses from adults, and therefore divergent impacts on childhood.

At a theoretical level, then, we envisage the relationship between change and continuity in childhood as a reflexive, flexible and evolutionary process in which 'childhood', as a social space inhabited and experienced by individual children, is continuously located within and shaped by successive generations of adults and children. It is a process that can occur as a result of the unintended impact on adults of the exercise of agency by individual children, or as a consequence of the impact of *collective* expressions of agency by children who act with the specific intention of achieving change. The extent to which such actions do or *do not* result in change, however, will be determined by the range of institutional mechanisms, processes and structures that constitute 'the social' and through which the collectivity of 'childhood' is made 'real' within the social order.

What we need to add to this analysis, then, is an explanation of why and how this happens, for it is by understanding this that we can begin to unravel the cultural politics of childhood and central to this process is, we suggest, the regulatory mechanism provided by law.

The role of law in constructing childhoods

As we have argued above, Law is a key element in the process of social change. It is thus integral to the production, regulation and the reproduction of childhood over time. In particular, we need to appreciate how it works to shape particular ideas of the child; its partiality and significance as an agent of social change; and the way in which it works differentially, according to varying cultural and political parameters. As James *et al.* argue, the late 20th century has witnessed a growing public concern for and about children:

> with an intensity perhaps unprecedented, childhood has become popularised, politicised, scrutinised and analysed in a series of interlocking spaces in which the traditional confidence and certainty about childhood and children's social status are being radically undermined.
>
> (1998: 3)

Childhood change appears, therefore, to be a key issue of public concern and one in which, as later chapters detail, the law is increasingly being used to construct particular childhoods as a form of social ordering and reordering. As Freeman has argued, legislation, as one expression of Law, becomes 'a potent symbol of legitimacy. It has the ability . . . to set new standards of what is right and wrong' (1998: 345). Once incorporated into a formal and explicit system of rules and regulatory mechanisms, the law therefore represents a highly specialised system of thinking about social realities and their regulation.

As we go on to argue in Chapter 4, globally, legal codes, in whatever legal tradition they might be constructed, work to institutionalise childhood by defining, for example, key aspects of the relationship between adults and children (see Chapter 2). These same legal codes also incorporate and reflect some of the social practices that reveal how adults and children are differentiated between cultures; and it is to these codes that we can also look in order to see how nations not only define but also regulate children and childhood, whilst also seeking to protect the rights of children.

In developing this theory we refer back to the different models of childhood described earlier and summarised diagrammatically in Figure 3.4. Through offering a range of different subject positions and social contexts, this analysis of childhood and the child permits children's agency to be explored at the same time as the context and condition of contemporary childhood can be explicated across its many contemporary sites – be these the school, the family, the street, the workplace or other kinds of social, cultural or institutional settings. And, for children, of increasing importance in all these sites is the role of Law as a reflection of social policy. This has a central part to play in the construction of childhood and of children's different experiences and subject positions, yielding differential impacts, effects and consequences (Figure 3.5).

A first point to note from the introduction of law into the diagram is that the law's focus, *inter alia*, is on the *social-structural child*: generically, Law deals with childhood as a universal, but specific, social and legal category which is, and needs to be, distinguishable from adulthood. As we have argued above, however, Law is also an important element in the *social construction of childhood* in that, because it is constituted through everyday actions and practices,

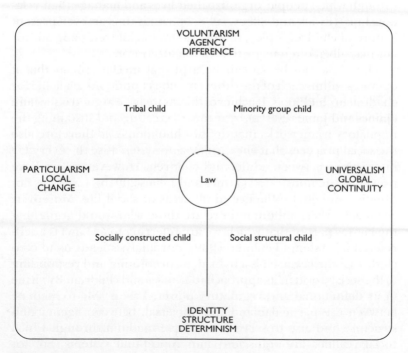

Figure 3.5

it defines the key parameters of childhood – the age of majority, age of consent to sexual relations, age of school leaving – in any particular social and cultural context.

In addition, what Law also does in many cases is to provide a mechanism whereby children in difficulties can be protected. It does this by articulating both the principles and procedures through which the issues raised for individual children and their widely differing selves and circumstances can be addressed. In this sense Law also works with an implicit model of the *minority group child*. Finally, and again used in the generic sense described above (i.e. as an implicit means of ordering and regulating social behaviour), Law is even of fundamental importance to an understanding of the *tribal child*. The ways in which rules of play, for example, are formulated and enforced by children themselves can be understood as one aspect of the internal regulation of children's own social worlds which can be compared with the regulatory systems found in the adult world (see, for example, Corsaro 1997). Law, as 'an emergent feature of social relations' through which people 'organize their lives and manage their relationships' (Ewick and Silbey 1998, op.cit.) is thus an ever-present feature of children's play, made evident in children's appeals for fair play albeit often made to an adult arbitrator.

Thus Law can be said to be a pivotal mechanism in that it operates within each of the different subject positions available for children in childhood. It achieves this, as we have argued elsewhere (James and James 2001a), by means of creating and sustaining the regulatory frameworks that define childhoods *and* therefore also the social practices that encapsulate and systematise the everyday interactions between adults and children. However, as we have previously demonstrated (James and James 2001b), Law does not exercise an equal influence in all areas of social life. Moreover, as noted earlier, although there are those who would argue that the law (as part of that which we are referring to as Law) is a self-referential system (Teubner 1989), our analysis leads us to conclude that the law itself is a hybrid, incorporating and responding to the social world in its approach to families and children. By virtue of its definitional and regulatory power, Law is able to mediate between the particular and the universal, between agency and structure and also to serve as a unique medium through which social realities are translated into conceptual systems. So, for example, through Law, 'children' and 'families' are translated into a series of general definitions which provide the building blocks of a system of family law, which are then used, recursively, to define, legislate for and thus to regulate 'our children' and 'our families', thereby producing a particular kind of local social order.

However, as Figure 3.6 suggests, the reach of Law is both partial and particular. Insofar as it is concerned with codifying the particular structural characteristics of any given society or culture, the law is an important source of defining and understanding a variety of socially constructed phenomena, including adult relationships with children. And insofar as it is concerned to recognise agency and to provide a framework within which this can continue to be exercised – for example, through the provision and protection of rights – it is much more active as a regulatory mechanism when dealing with those who belong to minority groups – the abused, the exploited, the deprived – than when dealing with others. Importantly, children constitute such minority group.

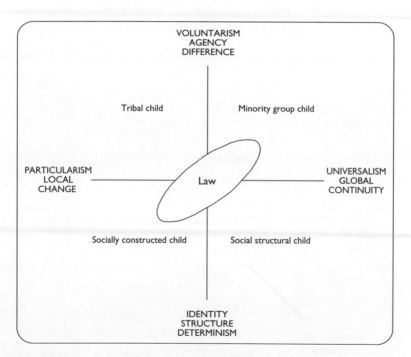

Figure 3.6

This observation leads to a further refinement in the analysis: to the extent that Law not only reflects social definitions but also, through *the* law, defines and regulates social realities, it is evident as we have argued above that it has a strong normative function. It is this that produces social order and that therefore ensures continuity. Law does change, however, in response to changing social realities. This can be seen, for example, in any analysis of the history of family law. To explore how this occurs we therefore need a more dynamic three-dimensional model that can include a temporal continuum (Figure 3.7). This will allow us to incorporate both continuity and change (although change is, of course, not always continuous or unidirectional) into our analysis and to consider also the role of Law (and the Rule of Law) in providing a normative brake on social change.

A dynamic model such as this allows us, for example, to understand and trace out the ebb and flow of the debate about the relationship between the family and the state and the role of Law in defining the family through the institution of marriage and the position of children within the family. What is still missing from

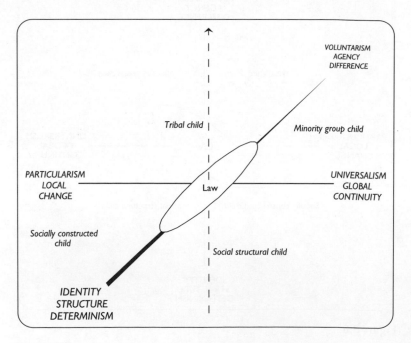

Figure 3.7

this analysis, however, is an account of the many perspectives on childhood that inform the way in which the law is framed, and which therefore, in turn, influence the way in which children and childhood are regulated and social order is produced. These allow for both the continuities and the changes in childhood over time. And of central importance here is the recognition of children as social agents who themselves influence the shaping of childhood.

Such a model is depicted in Figure 3.8. Here, for example, it is clear that the subject position of the child as 'the tribal child' incorporates children as social agents, exercising their agency within local contexts and in response to local particularities. It is these that create some of the diversities that are just as much a part of childhood as are its universalities. It is also these that can, in time, create pressure for the greater regulation and control of children, in order to reinforce the social order and a particular construction of childhood as a particular kind of social space.

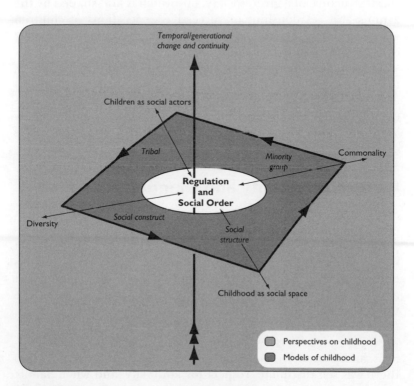

Figure 3.8

The creation of this common social space of childhood serves to locate children within the social structure, a subject position that is consolidated and reinforced by legal regulation. However, one consequence of such perceptions of commonality is the inevitable emergence of exceptions – the non-conformist child – whose presence produces the subject position of 'the minority child', the child who must be protected by new laws and regulations in order to reinforce the existing social order. Over time the existence of such minorities and their activities as social agents may, however, lead to changes in the law as response to their need for both protection and regulation.

What Figure 3.8 depicts, therefore, is a reflexive and evolutionary process, one that is driven forward by the interaction between different perspectives on childhood and subject positions for children, regulated by the Law in the production and reproduction of social order. Such a process sees the gradual evolution of childhood as a social space, one that is continuously located within the social structure of a given society, but which is also shaped by the actions and relationships of successive generations of children who succeed in creating diversity within the common socially constructed category of childhood.

In summary, therefore, what our theoretical model enables us to do is to explain how children are not only shaped by culture but also help shape it, a view which is at the heart of a cultural politics of childhood and one that reveals how commonality and diversity are simultaneously at work in *all* children's everyday experiences of childhood.

History, continuity and change

Such a theoretical model does, however, require testing against empirical evidence, of which there is a considerable if widely dispersed body. Of particular interest though, given our concern with continuity and change, is Pearson's (1983) historical analysis of the history of 'respectable fears' in relation to the criminal and anti-social behaviour of young people. Pearson advances the thesis that in spite of commonly held and expressed views about the moral impoverishment of modern life in comparison with previous generations – when there was a shared set of social standards and morality, when the streets were safe to walk, when there was self-discipline, respect for authority, and when 'family values' were understood and respected – such images of some bygone 'golden age' are the stuff of fiction, or rather mythology, as opposed to fact. Nonetheless, these are important ingredients in shaping the responses of adults to the children and young people of today, in the same way that, as Pearson demonstrates, the adults of yesteryear responded to the behaviour of the children and young people of that time.

So, just as the Conservative party, in the run up to the 1979 general election, waxed loud and long about the threat to law and order from soccer hooligans and relished calls for the reintroduction of the birch and the flogging of young offenders, so it was with the Conservative Party Conference at Blackpool in 1958, when similar issues were anguished over: the 'lack of parental control, interest and support' and the fact that young people 'were no longer frightened of the police' were bewailed (Pearson 1983: 13), and similar solutions were suggested (Pearson 1983: Chapter 2 *passim*). In particular, Pearson focuses on the impact of and reaction to the emergence of 'Teddy Boys' in the 1950s and, importantly, in terms of our analysis he argues that:

> What was (and is) totally submerged in the conventional understanding of the Teddy Boys was that their style and demeanour was by no means unprecedented ... [but] is better understood as a continuation of earlier forms of gang life in working-class neighbourhoods – rather than a sudden departure from tradition ... the Teds had borrowed large parts of their supposedly unprecedented cultural equipment from earlier youth cultures.
>
> (Pearson 1983: 22)

What Pearson offers is a detailed analysis of historical evidence over several generations that supports the model we have developed. His analysis reveals that within the age-specific social space of youth, as with that of childhood, there are continuities as well as changes. It is clear that the actions of those in a particular historical social space, be it youth or childhood, shape and create the uniqueness of that space and those experiences, as well as providing continuities across generations. Thus the lived experience of the Teddy Boys was very different from those of their Victorian predecessors, the Hooligans, as was the social, political, economic and cultural context in which they emerged; yet their behaviour, and the exercise of their agency, was just as important in shaping the responses of adults, who sought once more to define and redefine this particular social space.

And so it was in the run up to the 1997 election and during the early years of the New Labour government, which introduced a wide-ranging programme of measures designed to provide tough responses to young offenders and neglectful parents. This was in response to the perceived 'growing problem', not only of crime but of a more diffuse social disorder which was seen threatening the very fabric of civic society, a view that, as Chapter 7 will go on to explore in detail, was clearly reflected in the provisions of the Crime and Disorder Act, 1998. This established a clear link between youth crime, education and parenting and also reflected the view that tackling youth crime required action to deal with some of the other underlying causes of youth offending, such as truancy and school exclusions. Alongside such developments, a range of other measures was also introduced to increase the surveillance of young people in general, both in terms of the school/home nexus and the community. These were intended to regulate and control young people's behaviour in order to ensure the next generation of productive and pliable workers. However, it is important to note in the context of these particular developments that, to the extent that their aim is on the prevention of offending and not just *re*offending, crime control is focused on children and young people as an *entire* social category, and not on just young offenders (see James and James 2001b).

However, although the adult response to concerns about anti-social behaviour by children and the depredations of youth crime has often, in times past, been one of calls for stricter control, tougher action by the police and the courts and the passing of new laws extending the powers of the courts, and thus of the community, to control wayward youngsters, this has not invariably been the case. This underlines the importance of the temporal context of such developments in terms of the prevailing social, political and cultural ethos. As Pearson notes, therefore, in the inter-war years in Britain, there was a counter-movement to the oft-articulated feelings of cultural deterioration and criticisms of the leniency of the law:

> so that, particularly in response to rowdyism and lawlessness amongst the young, there was an unusual degree of sympathy towards offenders ... in a typically maverick comment on the matter, Baden-Powell thought

that if there had been an increase in juvenile crime, then this was "rather a promising sign".

(Pearson 1983: 34)

As Pearson notes, to Baden-Powell, such delinquency reflected not so much behaviour to be suppressed but a spirit of adventure and initiative that, if it could be harnessed and turned in the right direction, could make such youngsters useful men. And nor were such views unique to Baden-Powell, for a number of commentators at the time argued that the line between mischief and crime was not easily drawn and that:

A fair deal for youth is what is advocated, informed by a recognition of the ease with which boisterous youthful energy can make itself objectionable and even dangerous to others, linked to the necessity of not allowing its troublesome character to dull the awareness of the natural and even positive qualities of youthful misconduct.

(Pearson 1983: 42–43)

Thus the actions of children and young people do not always elicit the same responses from adults since such actions are historically as well as structurally situated. In this particular case, not only was there an awareness amongst adults of the impact of the First World War on the younger generation but there was also sympathy for the problems caused by the mass unemployment of the inter-war years, linked with the widespread view that crime was an almost inevitable consequence of poverty.

Pearson's historical analysis illustrates clearly, therefore, how the social space of childhood continues to exist, over many years and generations, even though it is occupied by different children; and how the actions of the children in each generation shape their childhoods – by their behaviour and by the responses that this elicits in adults, which is reflected in the resulting social policies and the associated legislation. Thus, for example, if we consider his account of the phenomenon of the Teddy Boys, through the subject position of the tribal child we are able to emphasise the differences between the culture of their working class youth and that of other young people, whilst the minority group subject position alerts us to broader concerns about the behaviour of young people in general and the supposedly adverse impact of consumerism, libertarianism and the decline of the family and moral standards more generally on children.

Pearson's analysis also allows us to consider childhood or, in this case, youth-hood, as a social construct, by examining the discourses through which the ideas of 'youth' but also, by the same token, 'the child' and 'childhood', are produced. It thereby allows us to consider what being a 'youth' or a 'child' means in the local context. Simultaneously, however, it also highlights the subject position of childhood as part of the generational order of social structure through focusing on the activities of young people in terms of their inter-relationship with other status categories such as children or adults. Importantly, therefore, what Pearson provides us with is empirical evidence to support our contention that continuity and change, and therefore time, are crucial elements to understanding both the commonality but also the diversity of the social space of childhood.

Conclusion

At a theoretical level, we have argued that there is a highly dynamic and symbiotic relationship between the conceptualisation of childhood as a particular generational and cultural space, and children's actions as the occupants of that space; that children are social members of the category 'child' who, through their interactions and engagement with the adult world, help to form both the categorical identity of 'child' with which they are ascribed *and* the generational space of 'childhood' to which they belong; and that this relationship delineates the 'how' of the socialisation process. In this sense, discourses of childhood are never simply discourses; they are, and indeed have to be, enacted, to be given practical realisation and material form through the minutiae of the everyday social practices that take place between adults and children in the home, at school, in the community, or in the doctor's surgery. Moreover, such discourses do not stand alone or emerge from nowhere; they represent the culminated history of social policy-making and Law. They incorporate, for example, measures intended to provide for the protection of children and for their welfare, through policies both predicated upon and helping to promote particular ideas of children's needs, as well as ideas of what children are or normally should be (see Stainton-Rogers and Stainton-Rogers 1992; Hendrick 1997b).

This, however, raises a key question that, as we suggested earlier, requires us to draw on other disciplines if we are to explain and understand more fully the relationship between children, childhood and the adult world. If the categorical identity of 'child' and the social and generational space of 'childhood' to which children belong *are* created through their interactions and engagement with the adult world, is it sufficient to see these as simply the product of everyday social practices, or does such a process require the specification of a more powerful institutional mechanism than this which can explain how this takes place over time? Our answer must be that it does and that the clue to understanding this mechanism lies in both the threats and potentialities which the commonalities and diversities of childhood bring to and for children, and adults' responses to these, since it is through the combined effect of these that both the changes and continuities of childhood arise.

We have argued in this chapter that Law is this central mechanism: that, in its effect, it is the law that constructs childhood. Law also, however, provides a highly significant institutional mirror, one that reflects social policy and thus those adult perspectives on childhood that underpin the law. And since the law is an institution created by adults to regulate society and to ensure the existence of social order, it is inevitable that it will also seek to regulate and control children and childhood, as part of the adult response to the challenge of imposing order on the threats and potentialities of childhood. As such, it will – indeed, it must – fail to take account of, or seek to delegitimize, or at best retain close control of the contribution children themselves make to the construction of childhood.

However, since the law concerns itself first and foremost with articulating those general principles that serve to define childhood in any given social or cultural setting, and since it comprises the socially and legally defined images of childhood that are constructed by adults, or those which are inferred by adults from their location in relation to the social space occupied by children, the law must continue to regulate and control childhood, even as this changes. With all of the diversity that children as social agents bring to this process, the law will always therefore struggle to cope with the agency of children where this challenges those images.

Our analysis therefore raises fundamental questions about the relationships between adults and children. In particular, we might ponder whether, and if so to what extent, the formal machinery of law acts as a brake on change, either by default – that is, as a result of inertia – or by intent – that is, through the passage of proactive legislation to implement social policy aimed at achieving social change. We might also consider the extent to which it can be used to provide a site that facilitates the clarification of important social issues by exercising a *neutral* influence such as when, through changing customs and social practices in relation to childhood, laws are not enforced or are enforced less rigourously, as part of a process of facilitating social change. Since, viewed in this way Law is very much a social construct, such an approach also prompts us to question whether the legal system and the codified body of laws that comprise the formal institution of the law, *accurately* reflect the way in which any society might actually wish to structure its relationships between adults and children.

What our analysis does suggest, however, is that Law is a centrally important mediating influence in the social construction of childhood, the influence of which is neither temporally nor conceptually static. As we have argued, the processes that drive social change reflect the evolution of social practices and the modification of these as, from generation to generation, the common schemas and resources that are central to social practices and therefore to Law are both adopted and adapted. There may, of course, be other mediating influences and structures, which have yet to be identified and explored in the way we have sought to explore the influence and reach of Law in this chapter, which will further refine and increase the explanatory power of the approach we have outlined. It is clear, for example, that both economics and politics, as bodies of knowledge and as powerful structural determinants, also play an important role in the construction of childhood.

Nonetheless, however, in the light of our analysis we contend that the mechanism of Law is also likely to play a key role in the exercise of these or any other influences, not only at a national level but also, as we go on argue in Chapter 4, internationally. We therefore intend to use our model to underpin the remaining chapters of this book as we seek to develop further our understanding of the social construction of childhood. In particular, in Part II we offer a series of case studies that illustrate the complex inter-relationships between children, the agency they exercise within the social space of childhood, and the social policies that attempt to shape these; and the ways in which law mediates between these by acting as a conduit between structure and agency, thereby facilitating both continuity and change.

Notes

1 Throughout this chapter, we have sought to differentiate consistently between our usage of the terms 'the law' and 'Law' in order to reflect this distinction.
2 For comparable schema see Mayall (2002).

CHAPTER 4

The Universalisation of Law?

In addition to the hamburger, albeit perhaps not yet with quite the same degree of impact, the increasing reach of international law has also resulted in some significant changes in the discursive construction of childhood around the world. Central to this essentially political process, we would argue, are the institution and institutions of the law, since it is through the law that nation states, be they secular or religious, exercise their authority and, as argued in Chapter 3, it is through the law that some of the key aspects of childhood, such as the age of majority, are defined. In addition, however, we can also observe shifts in contemporary notions of childhood through the relationship between national and international law, as this mirrors the continuous interaction between the child and the state.

As Van Bueren notes, 'the development of the international laws focusing on children reflects the evolution of the concept of childhood which has occurred since the beginning of the twentieth century' (1993: xv). She goes on to list four global international child instruments, as well as numerous international and regional human rights instruments that contain provisions relevant to children, including recommendations and resolutions adopted by global, regional and inter-governmental organisations. She also notes the significance of a number of non-binding declarations, many of which have later found their way into binding agreements. As Van Bueren observes, although such developments do not constitute a universal definition of childhood, they do reflect the gradual development of a more coherent approach to children's issues.

It is also, as Halliday and Karpik (1997) argue in the context of their historical overview of the contribution of the legal profession to the growth and defence of political liberalism, difficult to separate national changes from transnational developments since these were and are 'parts of more global transformations...across all continents' (1997: 349), with national lawyers' movements concerned with liberal politics being part of the process of political and legal globalisation.

Important evidence of the increasingly global reach and influence of law is, they argue, to be found in the fact that:

> International legal institutions and forms of dispute resolution have sprung up...and these in turn have had significant effects on national legal and regulatory systems. Some even see the emergence of a global legal culture, with its supranational organisations, international law, international treaties, and the global diffusion of legal and organisational innovation.
>
> (Halliday and Karpik 1997: 367)

Halliday and Karpik describe the globalisation of law as a trend towards universality, albeit not necessarily reflecting a smooth or unilinear process. Indeed, they argue that it is a trend that frequently encounters reactions to reverse, or contain, its universalising tendencies. However, in an analysis that is reminiscent of Teubner's (1989) development of a constructivist epistemology of law (in which information produced by one discourse is 'reconstructed' and incorporated into another to produce a 'hybrid' discourse), they go to argue that:

> national politics domesticate the general mechanism of globalization and through resistance, conflict, translation, and innovation produce either variants on global themes, or original syntheses of global and local models.
>
> (Halliday and Karpik 1997: 361)

What this analysis draws our attention to, therefore, and what we shall seek to explore in greater detail in the course of this chapter, is the reflexive and dialectical relationship between the 'universalizing tendencies' of law and the relative conservatism of national cultures and politics, and how these affect the cultural politics of childhood. Implicit in this is an appreciation of the nature of law and legal discourse which:

> must reduce the complexities of the modern world to manageable proportions by imposing simple (and simplistic) concepts. From this flows ... for example, the need for the law to reduce behaviour to rights, duties and responsibilities, or to culpable and innocent conduct – those normative, moral judgments that, where they are not made explicit, lie just below the surface of formal legal pronouncements.
>
> (King and Piper 1990: 26)

Important though the law is in helping us to understand changing definitions of childhood, however, we must guard against making the assumption that, even within the relative coherence of a single jurisdiction, there will be a single clear model of the child in law, for as Fionda (2001) argues,

> legal concepts of the child help us, on the one hand to understand the treatment of children within [a] legal system, but at the same time highlight contradictions and nonsensical paradoxes. The conception of childhood adopted within any area of law can ... impact significantly on the way that the child is treated or their needs and interests responded to.
>
> (Fionda 2001: 16)

This should come as no surprise, of course, given that the law must engage with complex social realities. As Fionda (2001) points out, given the varied constructions of childhood to be found in *non*-legal disciplines (see Chapters 1 and 2), the plurality of approaches to the construction of childhood that can be seen in law is not only to be expected but is fully justified. Nonetheless, the universality of childhood as a life-space, in conjunction with the 'universalizing tendencies' of law, has, in recent years, triggered a profoundly important international discourse about childhood which, we would argue, may yet match or even exceed the reach of the hamburger in terms of its impact on the cultural politics of childhood.

In this chapter, therefore, we shall consider in some detail the impact of the United Nations Convention on the Rights of the Child (UNCRC) on the emergence and framing of a cultural politics of childhood, particularly in the context of the UK. This is not simply in order to provide readers with a case study of the tensions that can be generated for the domestic law of nation states by the adoption of such international instruments; nor is it simply to illustrate the importance of the Convention in terms of the increasing global influence of a westernised model of childhood. More than this, our purpose is to build on the model we developed in Chapter 3, by exploring the role of international law in mediating continuity and change in childhoods, both nationally and globally.

Children, childhood and international law – the UNCRC

Such 'universalizing tendencies' in relation to childhood have been evident since the early part of the 20th century, with the promulgation in 1924 of the Geneva Declaration on the Rights of the Child, followed by the UN Declaration on the Rights of the Child in 1959 and a plethora of subsequent international statements and declarations of varying levels of scope and significance, including the three Hague Conventions of 1980, 1993 and 1996. Arguably, however, in terms of its impact on the international discourse about children and childhood, the most important amongst these, even though – or maybe because – its focus was aspirational rather than operational, was the adoption in 1989 by the UN General Assembly of the Convention on the Rights of the Child (hereafter UNCRC). All of these developments reflect the globalisation of child law but, as Lansdown has argued in relation to the UNCRC,

> The incorporation for the first time in an international treaty of the recognition of children's civil and political rights makes this Convention particularly significant, and the ratification within four years by 177 countries is further testimony to the importance now attached internationally to promoting children's rights. No other Convention in the history of the UN has achieved that level of support within such a short time scale.

> (1996: 57)

By 2002, 191 countries had ratified the Convention, the only countries not to have done so being the United States and Somalia. Indeed, Somalia became the last country in the world to sign the Convention at the UN General Assembly Special Session on Children in May 2002, although, like the US, it has yet to ratify it.

The introduction of the UNCRC has not only attempted to create for the first time a truly international vision of childhood, it also established mechanisms for the review of its implementation by signatories, which sought to provide encouragement to governments to legislate, in order to give legal effect to the provisions that lie at the heart of the Convention in jurisdictions world-wide, although evidence that we shall consider later in this chapter suggests that these are not particularly effective (see also Lansdown, 1996). This has, of course, raised a number of very difficult issues, precisely because childhood has hitherto been constructed quite differently in different economic, political and cultural contexts. Nonetheless, the UNCRC, by attempting to articulate the *rights* associated with childhood as a single and undifferentiated collective social status, provides the first ever framework within which discussions about the nature of childhood and the rights of children around the world can take place.

In particular, as John points out, Article 4 of the Convention

> stresses that children are to be seen as equals in that it gives children and teenagers the status of human beings with full rights, giving them the same value as adults. The fact that they are valued and that childhood itself has a value, independent of it as an apprenticeship period to the adult world, is underscored by the rights . . . embodied in the convention.
>
> (1996: 6)

What this draws attention to is the important implicit linkage in the Convention between children, the universal concept of humanity, and the universal rights associated with the value and status of human being, independent of chronological or generational considerations. Whilst this represents a hugely important step forward in terms of the way in which we think about children and childhood, it may also, in the final analysis, prove to be a fundamental weakness in the philosophy behind the Convention since, in spite of its attempts to eschew any *particular* philosophy of children's rights, many adults (and especially adult politicians) may find the political implications of such a perspective ultimately impossible to reconcile with the cultural politics of childhood within their own societies. As John argues, however, the Convention, because of its aim of universal ratification and universally applicable standards, has been highly important in focusing the debate as to whether human rights norms are capable of this sort of transcultural generality or whether they are inevitably relative to each individual society.

(1996: 8)

Nonetheless, in spite of according children and young people the same rights as adults, the continuation of their 'special' and *non*-adult status, which recognises their need for protection, is reflected in the fact that the Convention also has as one of its central themes the 'best interests principle'. This, according to Article 3.1 requires that 'In all actions concerning children... the best interests of the child shall be a primary consideration.' This principle is, however, extraordinarily difficult to define as a generality, partly because it refers to the best interests of the *individual* child but also because, and stemming from that fact, the best interests of each individual child will, in large part and as a matter of necessity, be determined in the light of the cultural context in which each child lives (cf. Chapter 1). Thus whilst not reflecting any *particular* philosophy of children's rights, through the articulation of this principle, the Convention, both implicitly and in practice, is able to accommodate a multitude of culturally determined philosophies. However, as John argues in relation to Articles 12 and 13, which provide the co-ordinating framework in relation to the voice of the child:

when attention is turned to the best interests principle as a primary consideration in providing for children, it is rare to find the voice of the child in the debates surrounding what those interests are.

(John 1996: 7)

What the provisions of Article 12 *have* done, however, as Griffiths and Kandel have put it so succinctly, is to open up 'an international legal "sound space" for the child's "voice"' (2000: 161).

The nature of children's rights

There is a huge literature discussing children's rights from both philosophical and legal perspectives (see, for example, Fortin 1998; Archard 2001), which can only be touched upon briefly in the context of this chapter. As Wringe (1996) argues, however, discussions about children's rights tend in practice to be about, or at least rooted, in *abuses* of rights. Thus the UNCRC is about rights of freedom, rights of protection and needs-based or welfare rights, the first two of which reflect 'traditional doctrines of Natural Rights' (Wringe 1996: 20). Needs-based rights, however, are not rooted in the right to be let alone but in the right to receive certain necessities of life that are defined as being necessary to the particular social status to which those rights are accorded – in this case, childhood.

The problem is that such needs-based rights are rooted in a perception of the developmental needs of children and thus are particularly susceptible to being defined, or at least moderated, by political and cultural considerations. Therefore, unlike 'Natural Rights', they are not fixed and universal but are highly contextualised. An additional complication is that even the most extreme kinds of needs have not traditionally been regarded as sufficient to justify a right. Nonetheless, Wringe argues that in addition to the right to protection from gross harms, which is also partially needs-based, there *are* minimal welfare rights the meeting of which provides 'the condition of our obligation to obey the law and respect the rights of others' (1996: 22). This assertion is important, for without it such rights would be entirely context-specific and culturally determined. Given that one of the purposes of law is to protect the vulnerable and those living on the margins of society, the *raison d'être* of the UNCRC was to articulate those rights that were seen to be universal and central to the process of moving children from the margins to the centre of society. By making children's rights explicit in this way, social power is potentially redistributed since rights can, in principle, be secured through the working of law and the legal process.

As Roche (1996a) argues, the UNCRC therefore provides us with a useful yardstick by which to measure progress on the condition of childhood, one that provides a basis for considering the impact of public policy and legislation on different childhoods. Critically, however, as he points out,

> once we genuinely allow children to exercise their right to speak and be heard, we might have to participate in different conversations... there is no single voice of childhood... Yet any commitment to children's rights... is part of a larger project regarding citizenship.
>
> (1996: 33)

This is particularly important in the context of, for example, post-communist states (see, for example, Ondrácková 1996) and countries in Latin America (see, for example, Petit 1996), in which the protection and the promotion of the rights and needs of children, particularly in relation to education, are regarded as being fundamental to the process of civic and political reconstruction.

As we argue in Chapter 5, however, insofar as rights to resources such as education are concerned, we should not necessarily be sanguine about the extent to which this will empower children. Articles 28 and 29 of the UNCRC recognise the child's right to education, which should be directed at developing the child's personality and talents, preparing the child for active life as an adult and developing respect for the child's own cultural and national values and those of others. This suggests that in addition to the explicit intrinsic importance of education to the individual child, there is also a deeply embedded recognition of the important role of education in reinforcing the structural components of childhood and the place of children.

Thus, although the Convention identifies education as a key component of the global childhood and the right of children around the world, it simultaneously, reinforces the roles of education policy, education law and educational practices as the hand-servants of the State and the primary means by which different childhoods are produced and imposed upon children in different cultures, in order to produce tomorrow's citizens. It is therefore a key component of the cultural politics of childhood. As Hart argues:

> Many western nations think of themselves as having achieved democracy fully, though they teach the principles of democracy in a pedantic way in classrooms which are themselves models of autocracy.
>
> (1992: 5)

It is through processes such as this that children's agency is denied and they learn not only the power of the status quo and the limitations of democracy, but also the nature of the relationship between adults and children and of the structural location of childhood within a given social and cultural context. This they may then carry into and replicate within their own subsequent adulthood. As Franklin argues, children in all societies are still denied the right to make decisions about their affairs, which we as adults take for granted, including the right to a voice in deciding the nature of educational curricula (Franklin 1992 – cited in Griffith 1996). We will return to such issues in Chapter 5.

The UK and the UNCRC

The UK Government ratified the UNCRC in September 1991 but in doing so it entered a number of reservations – viz. that it would not, unlike many other European Member States, provide any protective employment legislation for 16–18-year-olds; that it would continue to place children and young people in custody together with adults where there was no suitable alternative accommodation or if it was considered beneficial to do so; and that it would retain the right to apply UK immigration and nationality legislation, regardless of whether it contravened the principles in the Convention.

In addition to States having the right to enter such reservations, it is also clear that ratification and implementation are quite different propositions. Thus, although the Convention also established the UN Committee on the Rights of the Child to monitor signatories' progress on implementing the provisions of the Convention, this provides few if any guarantees of implementation. The UK Government delegation that in 1995 presented the first report produced by the UK after it ratified the Convention was described by the Committee as 'uncooperative and arrogant' (Harvey 2002b: 4). In response to the report, Lansdown noted that the findings of the Committee 'represented a searing indictment of the Government's record in promoting children's rights' (1996: 70).

Quite apart from the fact that, in spite of having a duty to promote the Convention to both adults and children, the UK has done little in terms of shouldering this responsibility, the Committee also criticised, *inter alia*, the high levels of child poverty and homelessness in the UK; the physical and sexual abuse of children; the continued use of corporal punishment, both at home and in schools; the administration of juvenile justice; and the lack of attention given to Article 12 – the child's right to express and have their views given due regard in all matters that affect them. Writing a year later, Lansdown concluded that:

> There is a long way to go in order to achieve full implementation of the provisions contained in the UN Convention ... None of its principles and

standards are fully respected for all children. The UK is not a society which places sufficient value on its children. Until there is a willingness to recognise the extent to which these breaches are occurring and until all policy and legislative proposals are scrutinised with a view to considering their implications for children's rights, breaches of the UN Convention will continue and children will continue to be failed.

(1996: 72)

So how much progress has been made since then? The picture is complicated to some extent by the fact that, as a consequence of devolution, there have been different developments in the four different jurisdictions in the UK. Thus, for example, although the office of commissioner for children and young people has already been established in Wales, Scotland and Northern Ireland, in England, there is no similar independent human rights body for children.

In England, early signs of progress were evident in the appointment of a Minister for Young People. This development was particularly significant since, as recently as 1997, the Government expressly ruled out this possibility (Lansdown 1998). It should be noted in passing, however, that he was also the Minister of State for Crime Reduction, Policing and Community Safety at the Home Office (see also Chapter 7). Most recently, and more momentously, the appointment of the first Minister for Children, Margaret Hodge (Minister in the Department of Education and Skills), was announced in June 2003. Pressure is also gathering for the appointment of a children's commissioner in England as a result of the positive impact of the creation of such a post in Wales, although this would still fall short of the appointment of a children's ombudsman, following the lead taken by Norway and other countries (see Flekkøy 1991).

The Government has also been particularly active in developing a range of initiatives to encourage and enable the participation of children and young people. This process has been given considerable impetus by the establishment of the Children and Young People's Unit, a specialist unit within the Department for Education and Skills charged with advising the Government on the development of policies in relation to children and young people. Of particular significance was the publication of *Learning to Listen: Core Principles for the Involvement of Children and Young People* (Children and Young People's Unit 2001), a document giving guidance to government departments about how they could increase their involvement in policy and service design and delivery. This has culminated in a policy requiring all government departments to develop and introduce polices to enable the participation of children and young people in their policy-making processes. Such initiatives at central government level have also been mirrored in many local government areas, a development underpinned by the development of a strategy for increasing the involvement of young people in local government, built around a clear statement of key principles and supported by comprehensive standards (Wade *et al.* 2001).

The reasons behind such developments have, it might be argued, been less to do with the rights of children *per se* and the impact of the UNCRC and much more to do with the growing concern at all levels of government about the participation of young people in democracy and, in particular, the declining numbers of young people voting, whether in national or local elections. Nonetheless, a recent survey by the Institute of Public Policy Research (Combe 2002) found that nine out of ten of councils responding said that involving young people was important to their local authority and that more than seven out of ten were currently working to involve young people (see also Green 1999). Less than three out of ten local authorities had, however, evaluated the impact of policies to involve young people. In the absence of careful monitoring and evaluation, it is too early to conclude whether such initiatives are simply rhetorical flourishes, or whether they indicate a more significant shift of attitudes on the part of the local and central government.

Whilst there has been a considerable amount of activity aimed at increasing the political participation of young people, however, the impact of this to date has been largely symbolic. There was, for example, an almost total lack of participation by children and young people in the preparation of the Government's 1999 report to the UN Committee (House of Lords/House of Commons 2003: para. 15). In addition, there is also some evidence that children are far from happy with the progress that has been made overall. When, for the first time in the history of the UK, a group of children and young people appeared before the Joint House of Lords and the House of Commons Committee on Human Rights to express their views on the need for a children's rights commissioner for England, they strongly endorsed such a development, arguing that someone was needed to promote Article 12 of the Convention. They were also highly critical of the Government's education policy for its continued failure to educate children on their human rights and the fact that this had not been included in the national curriculum, despite, as Chapter 5 explores, the emphasis on citizenship education (ChildRight News 2002).

In 2002, the UK Government was again due to report on the progress it had made in implementing the Convention to the UN Committee on the Rights of the Child. As part of its preparations, the Government consulted with non-governmental organisations (NGOs) and a report was produced by the Children's Rights Alliance for England co-ordinating the responses of a wide range of such organisations. As Willow (2002) reports, in each of the areas criticised in the previous UN report (outlined above), there continue to be 'major children's rights issues requiring immediate and concerted Government action' (2002: 8). As she comments, although the Children and Young People's Unit appears to have

> an excellent record so far in promoting children's participation ... there is little sign yet that it – or the Minister for Children and Young People – feels equally at ease in promoting all the other rights in the CRC for all children.

> (Willow 2002: 8)

On 19 September, a 'far more cooperative delegation', led by Althea Efunshile (Director of the Children and Young People's Unit) met with the Committee to discuss the second report from the UK Government. In spite of recognising that some significant steps had been taken by the Government, however, overall the Committee was again highly critical of the UK's performance. The report itself was described as 'unduly confusing, complicated and chaotic' (Harvey 2002b) and the Government was criticised for failing to meet its *duty* under the Convention to implement the concluding observations made by the Committee in 1995. Indeed, the Committee highlighted the attitude of the UK Government and the lack of a rights-based approach as a particular obstacle to the implementation of the Convention.

In the Committee's view, the fact that 75 per cent of children in the UK have not heard of the Convention exemplifies the Government's lack of concern with children's rights. The same lack of concern is evident, in the Committee's view, in the failure of the Government to take action to abolish corporal punishment (although it has already been outlawed in Sweden, Norway, Finland, Denmark, Austria, Croatia, Cyprus, Latvia, Israel and Germany). It was also critical of the fact that, not only has the Government not *raised* the age of criminal responsibility as the Committee had recommended in 1995 but, in effect, lowered it (see Chapter 7). In these, and in other areas, it is clear that the Committee felt that the Government bows too readily to public opinion, emphasising that this did not, and should not be allowed to, override the UK's obligation to implement and protect children's rights (Harvey 2003). In spite of this criticism, however,

> the UK delegation said that the Government had no intention of incorporating the CRC into domestic legislation as it did not believe that some of the rights contained therein could be justiciable.
>
> (Harvey 2002b: 3)

It is interesting to note, therefore, the subsequent recommendations of the Joint Human Rights Committee of the House of Lords and the House of Commons that, *inter alia*, the age of criminal responsibility should be raised to 12;[1] that the Government should act on the recommendation of the UN Committee in relation to abolish the defence of 'reasonable chastisement' and thereby, in effect, abolishing the use of corporal punishment; and that the post of children's commissioner should also be established in England. Importantly, the Committee also commented, albeit somewhat guardedly, that:

> We do not accept that the goal of incorporation of the Convention into UK law is unrealisable. We believe the Government should be careful not to dismiss all the provisions of the Convention on the Rights of the Child as purely 'aspirational', and that children will be better protected by the incorporation of at least some of the rights, principles and provisions of the Convention into UK law.
>
> (House of Lords/House of Commons 2003: para. 22)

The international response to the UNCRC

The point of this detailed account of the progress of implementing the provisions of the UNCRC in the UK is not to offer a critique of the efforts of a particular country's government and its achievements from the time since it signed and ratified the Convention, justified though this might be! It is, instead, to point to the potential for significant slippage between the act of signing up to the principles that inform the Convention and the process of implementing them within any particular economic, political and cultural context. Importantly, what it also highlights, as we argued in the previous chapter (see, in particular, Figure 3.3) is the significance of culturally determined and accepted customs and practices in shaping the social order in any given society, the social space of childhood, and the reflexive relationship between structure and agency in that construction – that is, the cultural politics of childhood. As the Joint House of Lords/House of Commons Committee on Human Rights observed in the context of a discussion of the '[m]eaning of "children"',

> Since our views on what capacities children develop at what ages are culturally conditioned, different cultures assign different responsibilities to children for different actions at different ages.
>
> (2003: para. 5)

We should therefore also consider, in the light of this account, the extent to which there is evidence of a significant change in attitudes of governments at an international level.

As Griffith observes, in his discussion of empowerment and the global citizen, 'the rhetoric of empowerment abounds' (Griffith 1996: 201). However, in spite of numerous examples of the supposed empowerment of children, of which the UNCRC is perhaps the most prominent, he argues that 'there is still a gulf between the international and the national rhetoric, and the reality of practice' (Griffith 1996: 202). Thus, by way of illustration, even in Norway, where public discourses and projects connected to the promotion of children's rights as citizens have featured prominently on the political agenda since the mid-1980s, government ambivalence is evident. As Kjørholt (2002) comments, in spite of such developments and the fact that the UN Committee recommended in 1994 that the Convention should be incorporated into Norwegian domestic law, 'we can reflect on the paradox that the Norwegian Constitution did not include the CRC in the Human Rights Bill that was adopted in 1999' (Kjørholt 2002: 78). However, the UN Committee repeated and underlined this recommendation again in 2001 and, as a result of subsequent debate, the Norwegian government has now decided to accept the Committee's recommendation.[2]

The recent proceedings of the UN Special Session on Children, the holding of which was agreed by the UN General Assembly in 1996, also revealed the shallowness of even the international rhetoric. Designed to bring together heads of state, NGOs, children's advocates and young people from around the world, the Special Session on Children was held from 8–10 May 2002. A follow up to the 1990 World Summit for Children and the first time the General Assembly had held a meeting devoted solely to all aspects of children's lives, the Special Session was an opportunity for governments to review progress on children's rights and take action to fully implement the UNCRC.

Uniquely, more than 300 children were delegates to the conference, which was preceded by a Children's Forum from 5–7 May 2002. In the course of this, children made it clear that 'they wanted to be treated as partners and they wanted their views to be taken seriously by the adult delegates' (Child Rights Information Network 2002: 10). Sadly, they were not. As one observer put it,

> children's voices and demands were lost among the bickering of States, who attempted to protect their national interests at the expense of the best interests of the child.
>
> (Harvey 2002a: 3)

In the words of a child who was present:

> Although there was a high number of children and young people at the event, many of us felt we had little real influence. My impression was that the adults had their own ideas about how they would allow young people to participate: issues were predecided . . . and there was very little and poor dialogue between the 'adult meetings' and those of the 'youth delegates'.
>
> (Children's Legal Centre 2002: 20)

More succinctly, in the words of an under-18 delegate from the UK, 'We spoke, but it feels like no-one listened' (Harvey 2002a: 3).

Amongst the key issues of contention in drafting the conference declaration, *A World Fit for Children*, were: opposition from the United States and a number of governments linked closely to

Christian and Islamic interests to any references to abortion, sex
education, family planning and reproductive health; attempts by
the same countries to limit references to children's rights, on the
basis that it is the parents' job to bring up children; countries with
religious affiliations (including the Vatican, even though it is not a
member of the UN) opposing any references to 'family' with any
other meaning than mother, father and children; and opposition
from the United States to any references seeking to limit the use of
corporal or capital punishment (Children's Rights Information
Network 2002a).

It is perhaps ironic that, subsequently, Michael Dennis of the
US State Department accused other governments of watering
down the draft conference declaration, arguing that 'many states
are more interested in protecting their own national priorities
than in the general welfare of children' (Children's Rights Information Network 2002b). Describing the US as a global leader in
child protection, he said that his government had promoted a
number of specific recommendations during the Special Session
negotiations, such as limiting the role of children in armed conflict, but that other countries had favoured generalisations. These
countries, he argued, insisted on talking only about child rights in
the context of the UNCRC, which was detrimental to children's
interests because the Convention was weak in certain areas, such
as trafficking, prostitution, the sale of children and pornography.
The US had, he argued, taken a lead in adopting protocols cover-
ing these areas, whereas European countries had weaker laws and
therefore favoured the generalised language of the Convention.
Although the Convention provided an important standard for
legislation on the rights of the child, he said the US would not
accept it as the only one.

In contrast, the Child Rights Caucus – a coalition of more than
100 NGOs from the US and around the world – argued that the
United States was largely to blame and stated that they were:

> deeply disappointed in the position that the United States has taken
> during the negotiations on the outcome document for the Special
> Session related to the Convention on the Rights of the Child, sexual
> and reproductive health education and services, and the death penalty.
> These positions neither reflect the reality of children's lives, nor the
> international framework of children's rights that has developed over
> the last twelve years. By rigidly maintaining its positions on these

issues, the United States is putting the success of this Special Session in jeopardy.

(Children's Rights Information Network 2002c)

Of particular interest in this context is the powerful but perhaps less obvious role of NGOs in shaping such international debates about the nature of childhood, a role that reflects their pivotal importance in monitoring and reporting on government performances in terms of the implementation of the Convention. In the event, over 3600 NGOs were invited to participate in the UN Special Session, including many large-scale organisations with international networks. That there were so many, however, also reflects the significant number and influence of smaller NGOs, many of which have much narrower and more culturally specific origins. Thus throughout the world, in the run-up to the UN Special Session there were preparations involving governments and NGOs at regional level in countries as far flung as Jamaica, Thailand, China, Egypt and Africa. Such meetings spawned their own agreements, such as the 'Berlin Commitment', that addressed children's issues across Europe and Central Asia, and the 'Rabat Declaration', which sought to articulate the needs and requirements of children and societies in the context of the Middle East and North Africa (Children's Rights Information Network 2001).

Even at the level of NGOs, therefore, it is evident that there are tensions between international and regional and/or national interests, which reflect differences between international and national constructions of childhood. Thus although national NGOs are clearly important as pressure groups, and it is evident that since the inception of the UNCRC they have played a significant role in heightening awareness of children's issues in the countries to which they belong, they are also products of the same historical forces and social processes that have created the governments they seek to influence. They are therefore rooted in the same civil societies with the same cultural politics. This became evident, for example, during the Special Session: 'some Islamic groups and Christian fundamentalist organisations showed that . . . they were prepared to break up NGO meetings if their demands were not met' (Children's Rights Information Network 2002a).

As a consequence, the Outcome Document published at the end of the Special Session was

weakened by the horse-trading, back-tracking and damaging stances
of a number of States, [and it] was not met enthusiastically by many of
those who attended (apart from the USA, which described the Special
Session as 'immensely successful'!)

(Harvey 2002a: 3)

It is difficult to reconcile such political manoeuvrings with the
very real concerns about child poverty and health or the sexual
exploitation of children world-wide, or with the rhetoric of
empowerment and global citizenship, and it is all too easy to
understand them as part of a fight to preserve different models
and understandings of childhood – that is, as part of a local
cultural politics of childhood. Thus, for example, whilst some
attention was paid to protecting children from abuse, violence
and exploitation, governments were left with little or no account
ability for fulfilling their commitments to children. Nor was the
opportunity taken to strengthen the work and role of the Committee on the Rights of the Child. Overall, therefore, the Special
Session missed the opportunity 'to change the way the world
views and treats children' (Harvey 2002a: 3).

The UNCRC has also spawned variants, such as the African
Charter on the Rights and Welfare of the Child, which adopts a
similar approach to that of the Convention in terms of submitting
periodic reports to a Committee of Experts on the Rights and
Welfare of the Child as part of compliance-monitoring processes.
Although adopted by the Organisation for African Unity (OAU)
in 1990, however, the Charter only came into force in 1999 after
the fifteenth country ratified it. Even by 2000, more than half of
the members of the OAU have still to ratify it and the monitoring
Committee was not established until 2002 (Children's Rights
Information Network 2000, 2002). As with the UNCRC, some
countries have also been selective in the constraints they would
agree to. Thus, although the Egyptian Parliament approved the
African Children's Charter in 2001, some parts, such as the provisions relating to adoption and setting the minimum marriage
age for girls at 18, were rejected as being contrary to Islamic Law
and Egyptian tradition (Children's Rights Information Network
2001: 1).

Such then are the dynamics and the political realities that lie
behind the rhetoric of empowerment and children's rights. The
UNCRC and related agreements and declarations are, in the final

analysis, political products and, as has often been observed, politics is the art of the possible. Such international instruments are ultimately the product of a process of negotiation and accommodation that becomes progressively more distant from the image of the child as global citizen. In effect, therefore, they produce little more than the lowest common denominator, into which can be fitted the multitude of childhoods produced by the economic, political and cultural diversities of countries around the world.

Law and social policy

Although the UNCRC is clearly important in providing a basis for the reconceptualisation of childhood around the world, it is also clear that for such a discourse to effect social practices, there must be change at the level of individual governments. Our contention is that for such changes to become tangible, there must be changes in the law and in the social policies that underpin the law. It is for this reason that Article 4 imposes an obligation on governments to implement all of the rights in the Convention through 'all appropriate legislative, administrative and other measures'.

This inter-relationship between law and social policy is illustrated by developments in England relating to children and childhood. As Flekkøy and Kaufman (1997) note, children have had rights in law for some time and common law determined a range of rights of parents and duties towards their offspring. These rights were not easy to enforce, however, because, until the 19th century, the law did not make provisions for intervention by a superior authority when parental care fell short of the required standards, even had these been clearly defined. As they point out, however,

> [t]he nineteenth century was to become the period when legislation concerning children was introduced in many countries, very often in connection with child labour and education, but also in acknowledging a public responsibility toward orphans and other destitute children.
>
> (1997: 19)

This flurry of legislative activity reflected the fact that such measures were considered necessary and acceptable by the lawmakers, whilst their incorporation into law was also a recognition of the fact that politicians believed such measures to be acceptable to, and required by, the general public – that is, the electorate.

Several important points arise from this all-too-brief sideways historical glance. The first is that rights that are not known to the holder of those rights are of little value or significance. Second, it is clear that without recourse to legal remedy when rights are denied or abused, rights are of little value. Third, it is also clear that to make rights meaningful there must not only be mechanisms in place to monitor the extent to which rights are accorded in practice, but powers must also be given to 'a superior authority' to enforce rights where these are withheld or abused. Fourth, the granting of legal rights and, crucially, the extent to which there are associated powers of enforcement and legal remedies depend upon their political and therefore their social acceptability.

As this analysis makes clear, therefore, in order for children's rights to become a social as well as a legal reality, they must be firmly rooted in social policies that command the support of the adult population. It is, however, clearly possible for legal rights to be given to a status group such as children, which may serve a political function but which, in the absence of widespread social support, have little or no social function. As we argued in Chapter 3 (see Figure 3.3), law, social policies and social practices are separable but intertwined. How much easier is it, therefore, for governments to sign up to an international convention bestowing a range of 'rights' on children, secure in the knowledge that in the absence of public interest or support (or in the presence of active opposition) and without effective means of enforcement, the political price will be minimal and the impact on social practices non-existent? Thus as Fortin (2002) is able to observe in relation to the UK response to the UNCRC,

> It was hoped that the obligation on ratifying countries to produce periodic reports to the UN Committee and the knowledge that they would be subjected to criticisms would encourage states to implement to UNCRC effectively ... Unfortunately, the overall impression created by the UK's first and second reports to the Committee on the Rights of the Child is that the Government is relatively untroubled by fear of criticism by the UN Committee. A cynic might argue that a casual approach to the UNCRC will continue until there are improved enforcement procedures.
>
> (Fortin 2002: 19)

Indeed, the Children's Rights Development Unit (CRDU) (1994) went further, describing the response of the UK Government in its first report to the UN Committee as illustrating not progress but complacency. In the view of the CRDU, it was:

> dishonest by omission, highlighting particular laws and statistics that indicate compliance, without adequate recognition of gaps, inconsistencies and blatant breaches. It does not give a true picture of the state of our children. In itself, it breaches Article 44 which sets out detailed requirements for reports which must "contain sufficient information to provide the Committee with a comprehensive understanding of the implementation of the Convention in the country concerned".

> (CRDU 1994: xii)

A similar report by the Children's Rights Alliance for England (CRAE) (2002) is equally critical of the Government's second report to the UN Committee (Department of Health 1999). Whilst acknowledging that there has been progress in some areas, the CRAE report observes that the Government 'has so far failed to get to grips with its human rights obligations to children' (CRAE 2002: 1) and is critical of both the content and construction of the Government's response, pointing out that:

> The Report fails . . . to "indicate factors and difficulties affecting the degree of fulfilment of the obligations under the Convention", being mainly descriptive and selective of positive aspects of government policy, and failing to acknowledge many breaches of children's rights, several of which existed at the time of the Government's examination on its Initial Report and were noted by the Committee.

> (CRAE 2002: 2)

This stands in marked contrast to the European Convention on Human Rights and Fundamental Freedoms (ECHR), signed in 1950 and now incorporated into UK domestic law by virtue of the Human Rights Act 1998. Although not specifically concerned with the rights of children, as Fortin (2002) observes, the ECHR quickly became enormously influential, since it was the first international instrument of its kind to provide the mechanisms – viz. the European Commission on Human Rights and the European Court of Human Rights – for its own interpretation and enforcement. The fact that the ECHR was very adult orientated and concerned with *human* rights rather than solely the rights of children has not prevented it from being used in relation to and having a considerable impact upon some important children's issues in the UK and throughout Europe (see, for example, Fortin 1998).

Such a contrast underlines two important points. The first is that although Article 4 of the UNCRC defines children as equal to adults in their rights and value, by identifying them as a distinct category and seeking to differentiate between their needs and those of adults, the Convention implicitly highlights children's *lack* of equality and power, and the many boundaries between childhood and adulthood that are constantly being reinforced by adults on a daily basis throughout the world. Thus, as Pupavac (2001) argues in relation to recent developments in England,

> proposals to empower children through children's rights . . . does not represent a move towards children having greater self-ownership. Rather the enshrinement of children's rights means state officials or authorised professionals, instead of parents, deciding what is in a child's interests . . . The paternalism underlying the children's rights approach is underscored by the recent trend in legislation to impose more regulation and protective measures on young people, rather than granting them greater freedoms.
>
> (Pupavac 2001: 9)

A further possible understanding of the apparent ambivalence of many adults about children's rights is offered by Pupavac when she argues that '[t]he development of a special category of children's rights represents the infantilisation of citizens' (2001: 20).

As we go on to illustrate in Part II, it is clear in relation to a number of areas of social policy in England and Wales such as health, education and youth justice, that policy-makers believe that many parents are not themselves competent and require further education and direction on how to bring up their children. In such a context, in which 'the state is increasingly determining the nature of the day-to-day care of children' (Pupavac 2001: 21), it is not hard to see why there might be a certain lack of enthusiasm for the genuine empowerment of children by giving them *real* rights.

The second important point highlighted by the contrast Fortin draws between the UNCRC and the ECHR is the centrality not only of law, but also of the mechanisms and institutions of law in the effective implementation of social policies and the process of social change, since legal *systems* can allow for the interpretation and adaptation of substantive laws. Thus as Beveridge *et al.* (2000) argue in relation to Europe, for example, the European Court of Justice

> is also seen as having a key role to play in relation to social policy . . . by providing concrete mechanisms through which the adherence of reluctant Member States can be secured.
>
> (Beveridge *et al.* 2000:145–46)

Similarly, McGlynn (2000) argues that in spite of the lack of a distinct legal basis for the regulation of the family in the European Union, the European Court

> has constructed a "model European family" in which the rights and privileges of Community law reside . . . that of the heterosexual married union, in which the husband is the head of the family and principal breadwinner and the wife is the primary child carer . . . which reinforces the notion of children as dependents.
>
> (McGlynn 2000: 224)

What this discussion also highlights, however, is the fact that although the language of children's rights may have become global, the relationship between international conventions such as the UNCRC and the actions of governments in terms of the development of social polices and the introduction of legislation relating to the rights of children, which between them might facilitate social change in relation to the construction of childhood in different countries, is neither clear nor straightforward. Thus, for example, as Todorova observes in the context of recent developments in Bulgaria, although the Bulgarian government enthusiastically ratified the UNCRC, this 'remained only a political token' (2000: 138). Regardless of the incorporation of the Convention into domestic law, in the absence of an institutional infrastructure and proper mechanisms for implementation, it 'still remains no more than a moral document' (2000: 138). Interestingly, as she also comments, the most significant reason for the failure of the debate about implementation was the absence of professional communities, such as lawyers, who could press for reform of the law.

Similarly, as Fortin observes with particular reference to developments in Europe, the UNCRC and the ECHR are enormously important international human rights documents but they promote the interests of children in very different ways:

> Despite its weak enforcement mechanisms, the UNCRC remains the Convention which will nudge the Government into ensuring that children's lives are improved by better services. Now that the ECHR has become part of domestic law, it may have a more practical and immediate impact on the legal principles applying to individual children on an everyday basis.
>
> (Fortin 2002: 23)

Therefore, whilst the UNCRC might offer a global model of the rights of children and, arguably, of childhood itself, the development and application of that model will be largely dependent upon the operation of domestic policies and law, both of which are heavily bounded by the parameters of culture. Thus, it is a process that, as long as it is dependent upon governments being 'nudged', offers few certainties.

Such problems are compounded by the fact that the political realities of achieving change mean that it is an adult-driven process, in which children themselves have little say and are able to exercise little agency. As Wyness has argued, 'children's relationship to the political world in western cultures has traditionally been a marginal one' (Wyness 2001: 1) and although the discourse surrounding children's rights is making an increasing impact, there remains a tension between the concepts of children's needs and children's interests. Whilst the dominant needs-based discourse leads to the political exclusion of children, because their 'lack of political status is rooted in children's lack of social status' (Wyness 2001: 2), the discourse concerning children's collective interests and rights as a status group generates pressures towards their political inclusion. However, these rights-based pressures also reveal the tensions between 'children's rights to welfare and their rights to self-determination' (Wyness 2001: 3), since they serve to highlight the problematic nature of children's rights for the adult world. As Wyness observes:

> the former strengthens the hold adults have over children because it works on the assumption that those in authority have an obligation to

ensure that those rights ... are met on children's behalf. The
latter, on the other hand, are far more controversial. Rights to
self-determination take certain responsibilities and powers away
from adults as children have a right to make decisions for themselves
that could potentially go against adults' claims that they are acting in
the child's "best interests" ... Drawing on the language of rights, there
is a strong tendency towards child saving with children's rights to provision and protection, having priority over their rights to participation'.

(Wyness 2001: 3–4)

At the heart of this difficulty, both in the UK and elsewhere,
lies the way in which the cultural politics of childhood are constructed, for:

Over the decades, a range of government policies have constructed
young people as dependent children or as independent adults...
These policy constructions of youth, whether coherent or not, are
clearly likely to impact on the lives of young people.

(Jones and Bell 2000: 1)

This then identifies the centrality of social policy in both framing
and reflecting the social practices that define the cultural politics
of childhood. In the dynamic inter-relationship between childhood and law, social continuity and change,

Policies provide the institutional basis for the construction of dependence and independence in youth and define the threshold between
childhood and adulthood.

(Jones and Bell 2000: 4)

As Jones and Bell go on to argue,

the current policy emphasis on social citizenship, empowerment, participation and consumer rights is not matched by policies which allow
young people real power ... The emphasis on participation often
appears little more than window-dressing in the face of the somewhat
rigid expectations of government that young people will conform, and
should be penalised if they do not.

(Jones and Bell 2000: 54)

In this context, the announcement of the appointment of Margaret
Hodge as the very first Minister for Children in the UK in the

summer of 2003, and the associated transfer of responsibility for a number of areas of social policy relating to children and families to the Department for Education and Skills, where the post is to be based, is of particular significance. This is because the Minister for Children will be responsible for implementing the substantial agenda for the reform of services for children that is expected to be outlined in the Green Paper, *Children at Risk*, the publication of which was expected at the time of writing. This, it is widely anticipated, will be a key document in terms of framing the shape and direction of future social policy for children in England and Wales.

Daniel and Ivatts also argue that children's lives are shaped to a considerable extent by social policy but point out that in the study of social policy, they 'have remained relatively "silent and invisible"' (Daniel and Ivatts 1998: 1). As their review of UK social policy since 1945 suggests,

> while children may frequently be invoked by politicians for their symbolism and power to arouse emotions, the reality is that "the cause of children" rarely makes it on to the political agenda.
>
> (1998: 3)

Indeed, the UK is only just beginning to create a policy framework for family issues (see Chapter 8) compared with a number of other countries that have developed much more explicit policy frameworks for addressing children's issues (Daniel and Ivatts 1998: 4).

Viewed in this context, given that in terms of social policy children are, for most purposes, defined by their membership of and thus subsumed within the family, it is almost inevitable that in those countries that have been slow to develop family policies for fear that these might be seen to be interfering with the autonomy of the family (such as the UK and the USA), children's interests have been neglected. Given their status as non-citizens and the fact that their social status is derived primarily from family membership, children have only a minimal footprint in terms of social policy, with the exceptions of education policy (see Chapter 5), which is predominantly concerned with their future as adult workers and voters, and youth justice policy (see Chapter 7), the concern of which is to control those children who are reluctant to conform and behave as future citizens should!

Law, social policy and the cultural politics of childhood

As we go on to argue in the remaining chapters, in the context of the UK and England and Wales in particular, such discrimination is a reflection of the dominant cultural politics. We would also suggest, however, in the light of the theoretical analysis we have offered in the preceding chapters, that an analysis of social policies and practices in *any* state, whether it be religious or secular, will reveal the extent to which childhoods are, and historically always have been, rooted in, constructed by, and experienced through the lens provided by the culture of a given society. By focusing the international spotlight on the rights of children, however, the UNCRC represents a challenge to the dominant cultural politics of childhood in each and every country. As Woodhouse argues,

> The recognition of new rights always involves a dialogue between culture and law. It is often hard to tell whether cultural change is pushing the law, or the law is pushing change in the culture of the family.
>
> (Woodhouse 2000: 426)

Thus although the precise dynamics of this relationship between law and culture are not always clear, that there is such a relationship, and that the law and social policy play central roles in the social construction of childhood, is beyond dispute.

As Daniel and Ivatts (1998: 17) also observe, social policy in the UK differs from the UNCRC in terms of certain key philosophical elements. Not only does the Convention place considerably greater emphasis on State as opposed to family responsibility, children are also not only visible but central to its philosophy – they are regarded as people with inalienable human rights, who have a right to special assistance and whose views should be given due weight. Such differences apply to many other countries besides the UK, however, for as Leach (1994) points out, not only are children the largest minority group but the one that is 'most subject to discrimination and least recognised as being so' (Leach 1994: 172 – cited in Daniel and Ivatts 1998: 219).

We would also contend, therefore, that the lack of agency of children (in the sense of their ability to effect change) reflects their minority group status. It is, of course, evident that the actions of children, either as individuals or as groups can *cause* or result in changes in social policy and law. It is also evident, as we shall demonstrate in subsequent chapters, that over a period of time, such changes can change childhood and that in this sense, a range of social institutions are shaped or even constituted by childhood itself. Thus, as the behaviour of children changes, so do adult notions of childhood and as these alter, so too do the patterns and mechanisms of control that are designed to regulate children and childhood.

It is also clear, however, that in the absence of rights, citizenship and therefore of political power, children are not well able to effect change in the sense of self-consciously and, through the exercise of individual or collective agency, deliberately changing childhoods as they might wish to. Therefore, far from being a global phenomenon reflecting a status that is equal to that of adults, childhood, and within it the agency of children, continues to be differently constructed in each and every society according to the wishes and needs of the adult majority, rather than the wishes and needs of children. As Griffiths and Kandel put it, 'their role as creators and interpreters of culture and social norms is disregarded or devalued' (2000: 163). The laws that construct and define childhood, be they religious or secular, are culturally rooted – they are determined, enacted and enforced by adults, so the relationship between politics, law and culture lies at the very heart of the social construction of childhood.

Thus for example, to return once more to the UNCRC, beneath the rhetoric of the UK government's second report to the UN Committee, the reality of change is limited and a closer examination of many of the recent initiatives with regard to children and young people has revealed many areas of concern in relation to the status of children as citizens, as members of the community, and of the community's attitudes towards them. In spite of the UNCRC, therefore, and all of the political rhetoric in recent UK legislation on children and their rights to be heard, it can be argued that, in effect, these amount to little more than an artifice which conceals the real nature of the way in which mechanisms for retaining and increasing the control over children are being sustained and extended. This has created a wider net of social control, with an increasingly fine mesh that is permeating more areas of more children's lives than ever before (James and James 2001). As Freeman has pointedly observed, 'we have also to appreciate that ours is a culture that does not particularly like children. The adage that "children should be seen and not heard" has an authentically English ring about it' (1998: 342).

Conclusion

It is clear, as we have sought to demonstrate, that the UK is not on its own in its less than enthusiastic response to attempts to redefine childhood and the place of children in society. More broadly, however, and to the extent that we can increasingly speak meaningfully about the globalisation of law in relation to the production of childhood, it is also evident that the world-wide debate about children's rights is shaping a powerful discourse that is beginning to influence the politics of childhood around the world, and even to some extent within the UK. Law and culture are reflexively and temporally bound and bounded – they can and do change over time, as do the social structures and institutions they define and produce. So will the nature of childhood change. In this respect, the UNCRC marks only the beginning in the process of changing the cultural politics of childhood, albeit an important one. As Freeman (1995) has also observed,

> the lives of children will not change for the better until the obligations [the Convention] lays down are taken seriously by legislatures, governments and all others concerned with the daily lives of children.
>
> (1995: 83)

Childhood as a social life-space seems likely to continue, however, and the more children are enabled to become directly involved in such discourses, as well as in the political and policy processes that shape them and through which childhood is produced and reproduced, the greater is the prospect that they will also begin to shape the nature of childhood as a social status, as well as their own experience of childhood as a life-space. More importantly, as they achieve the agency, rights and status of adulthood, they will take with them into their adulthoods a set of experiences and understandings of childhood that will, in turn, begin to alter adult views and definitions of childhood, setting in motion a process of inter-generational cultural change. As Green has argued, 'society will be richer for their greater involvement – not just in the future but also in the present' (1999: 221).

Notes

1 If acted upon, this recommendation would, of course, only serve to return it to its previous level, which the UN Committee had already recommended, in its first report, should be raised.

2 Personal communication, Kjørholt (2003).

PART II

Case Studies in the Cultural Politics of Childhood

Introduction

In the first part of this book, we sought not only to outline some of the key concepts and dimensions in the social construction of childhood, but also to locate these within a cultural politics of childhood. Although the UNCRC provides a context in which a transnational and transcultural discourse about childhood is developing, there is, however, no *universal* cultural politics of childhood as yet and, indeed, we doubt that one will be realised within the foreseeable future. Rather, as argued, each society produces its own version that is rooted in the political, economic, social and cultural fabric of that society.

In Part I, we also sought to outline a theoretical model that not only incorporates the wide diversity of childhoods, but also articulates and explains the processes through which both continuity and change can coexist within the construction and reconstruction of childhood. Pivotal mechanisms in the operation of the dynamics of this model are, we have argued, Law and the related policy processes and social practices that constitute the cultural politics of childhood, through which the law is made a social reality and social realities are incorporated into the law. It is this that becomes a part of the daily lives of both adults and children and, as we have argued, it is through Law and social policy that the State seeks to regulate children and their childhoods. Our model also, however, acknowledges another important social reality – that children are not only constructed by the cultural politics of childhood but also help in its construction, by virtue of exercising, directly and indirectly, the agency (both individually and collectively) that is inherent in the state of human 'being' but that is so often denied to children, either in terms of its existence or its practice, by adults.

This model emerged from our reflections on a range of areas of social policy that are of key importance in the social construction and regulation of childhood in England[1] – the areas of education,

health, crime and the family – and it is to these that we now turn
our attention in Part II, taking each in turn as a case study
through which to illustrate the way in which our model works in
practice. In the course of our deliberations, we became aware of
many remarkable commonalities between these areas that we were,
initially, hard-pressed to understand or explain. Amongst these,
the family caused us particular problems, since it is an area in
which there is clear evidence of children's agency but where this is
also intensely contested. It is also the most obvious site in which
the influence of the law is limited because of the constantly contested boundary, and the ambivalent relationship, between the
State and the family. Although we have focused on the family more
broadly in Chapter 8, it is for this reason that we have looked in
some detail at the particular issue of family breakdown and divorce,
since this is one area in which law and social policy have a firm
grip on the family and in which the cultural politics of childhood
in relation to the family come sharply into focus.

The case study on the family is also important as a counterpoint
to the other case studies because families are about difference and
it is, in part, the unwillingness of the family to conform to the
whims and strictures of Government that underpins the ambivalence of the State about trying to regulate the family. The family is
also important because within that context, children lose their
identity both as individuals and as a separate status group. They
become part of an institution that is structured and governed by
more fundamental social rules concerning kinship, in relation to
which the role of the State is minimal, unless and until the family
fails – by breaking down or by parents failing to control or protect
their children. If and when this happens, the State intervenes and
children become targets of 'welfare'. Outside of the family, however, when children venture into the community, the State seeks
to regulate them and it is in this context that policies relating to
education, health and crime become crucial mechanisms through
which the State seeks to impose varying degrees of normalcy,
standardisation and conformity in the construction of childhood
and is varyingly tolerant of difference.

In the context of our model, the similarities that we seek to
explore in each of the case studies we have included in Part II can
be explained for, in essence, the cultural politics of childhood is
about the process of ordering and control. In the context of the
UK, from where we have drawn these particular case studies, this

process is partly about the production and regulation of conformity which is, in turn, partly about the management of 'risk' – the risk of educational failure, the risk of poor health, the risk of youth crime, the risk of the decline of the family and 'family values'. More particularly, however, it is about the regulation and control of children and of childhood, as these are experienced within the community, since it is in the community that any deviation from the norm or ideal becomes seen as problematic. Thus 'the community' becomes a critical site in which the cultural politics of childhood are played out on a day-to-day basis.

For the purposes of our analysis of the cultural politics of contemporary English childhood therefore, these case studies must be located in the context of New Labour's search for a 'third way' in politics, which is set against the political ideologies of the past by placing the concept of community at the helm. As Driver and Martell (1997) argue, for New Labour:

> community will create social cohesion out of the market culture of self-interest. If communitarianism is New Labour's answer to Thatcherism, so too is it Tony Blair's rebuff to Old Labour. Community will restore the moral balance to society by setting our moral duties as well as rights.
>
> (Driver and Martell 1997: 27–28)

With its emphasis on duties and responsibilities rather than rights, this communitarian perspective involves, in effect, the reinvention of social democracy. Giddens, one of its major proponents, argues strongly that '[t]he fostering of an active civic society is a basic part of the politics of the third way ... [t]he theme of community is fundamental to the new politics, but not just as an abstract slogan' (1998: 78–79). According to Giddens, of particular significance is the view that the cause of so many political and social ills is civic decline, evidenced in 'the weakening sense of solidarity in some local communities and urban neighbourhoods, high levels of crime, and the break-up of marriages and families' (Giddens 1998: 78).

The solutions to such a decline seem clear. Investment in the education and training of children will lead, literally, to the growth of a more flexible, cosmopolitan labour force and, although Giddens acknowledges that equality and individual freedom may conflict, his vision of a third way in politics involves the search for a new relationship between the individual and the community, a redefinition of rights and obligations. One might suggest as a prime motto for the new politics, no rights without responsibilities. A second precept, in today's society, should be no authority without democracy.

(1998: 65–66)

Giddens' thinking echoes the communitarian perspectives developed by Etzioni (1996) and other American social theorists who, in seeking to resolve the conundrum of how to maintain both social order *and* personal autonomy in the same society, argue that this can only be achieved in communities that respond to the needs of their members. Etzioni's focus on communities as relatively undifferentiated social entities, however, obscures the significant fault lines and social diversities that fracture their structure and which work to exclude certain sections of the population from community participation. In this context, it is clear that age and generation work to exclude rather than include people from belonging to the community (O'Neill 1994).

In trying to understand the cultural politics of contemporary English childhood through the following four case studies, the question of children's citizenship is therefore critical. We must consider, for example, the extent to which, in each domain, children are currently being defined and constructed as members of the community or whether they are still being set apart from adults? Are children being expected to be responsible, without being given any substantive rights? How far are adults being encouraged to continue to exercise authority over children without any overall increase in the rule of democracy?

If, according to Etzioni, a key feature of the notion of community is 'a commitment to a set of shared values, norms and meanings, and a shared history and identity – in short, a shared culture' this is problematic in the context of a pluralistic multi-cultural society for a hegemonic consensus actively works to exclude certain sections of the population from participation (1996: 5). Moreover, in relation to children, this problem is exacerbated because any such consensus masks the extent to which, as we have argued, there may be plural childhoods, shaped and differentiated by the inequalities of class, gender and ethnicity.

In his exposition of communitarian ideology, Etzioni (1996: 3) notes the fundamental contradiction between a society's need for order and an individual's quest for autonomy, a contradiction that complicates the realisation of a communitarian agenda. In the particular case of children, however, this difficulty is compounded. Communities have a responsibility to provide socialising structures that will both foster children's autonomy, as well as their ability to conform. Part of the 'problem' of children is precisely that they are still in the process of acquiring values, norms, meanings and identities. By definition of their youth, they do not, as yet, have a fully shared history and therefore cannot be assumed to be acquiescent to the values of the community. Children have therefore to be encouraged to explore their agency, their difference, and their individuality, but only within the broader, common societal framework (James 1993).

It is clear, therefore, that childhood constitutes a prime site for managing the tensions between conformity and autonomy, and thus also for identifying and working out the internal contradictions of communitarianism over time. But in doing so this may give rise to censure for, as Etzioni himself points out, community censure represents 'a major way that communities uphold members' commitments to shared values and service to the common good – community order. And indeed, community censure reduces the reliance on the state as a source of order' (1996: 5). Perhaps it is no wonder then, that, as we shall explore through these case studies, the net of social control has increasingly tightened around childhood in England during the 1990s, since it is through the regulation and control of children in the present that a particular kind of future, adult community can be produced (James and Prout 1990). In this sense, the state's current interest in childhood is very much out of self-interest.

All these case studies are, of course, drawn from England and Wales and, through the similarities they reveal with respect to children's lack of opportunities for participation and the regimes of control through which children's lives are regulated, serve to illustrate the prevailing cultural politics of childhood in the UK. Thus, to the extent that these are rooted in British politics at the start of the 21st century, as we have depicted them above, our specific observations and interpretations will not necessarily be reflected in other countries and cultural contexts. Our model is not, in itself, culturally specific, however. What we have identified in Part I is a dynamic model, one that describes a process that links structure and agency, social space and social action, and the formal mechanisms through which social order is achieved and maintained with the informal behaviours that constitute custom and practice. This, we believe, is a model that will be mirrored in some shape or form in most, if not all, societies. Consequently, we suggest that similar analyses, focusing on the role of Law and its relationship with social practices, could usefully be conducted in any political and cultural context and although we are presently unable to test this assertion for ourselves, we sincerely hope that others will be tempted to do so.

Notes

1 The reference here to English childhood is important since, while some legislation covers the UK as a whole, in the areas dealt with by the case studies – education, health, crime and the family – there are a number of important differences between the different countries in the UK, following on from the separate legislation and policies that exist in England, Wales, Northern Ireland and Scotland.

CHAPTER 5

Education

In his now classic account of the framing of educational knowledge, Bernstein (1971) showed that over and above the 'knowledge' that they acquire in the classroom, children learn their social place via the class inequalities perpetuated in the educational codes through which schooling is encrypted. This suggestion that a hidden curriculum of cultural values is imparted alongside formal knowledge was echoed by Bourdieu (1971) who argued that the school is a system for cultural reproduction *par excellence*. Through schooling, the State ensures its own continuity through the transmission of particular sets of values and patterns of thought, and, Bourdieu argues, because these are those of the educated and ruling classes the State is able to maintain its cultural hegemony, and the scope working-class children have in order to make the best use of the education they receive is restricted. In Bourdieu's view, then, schooling can be seen as an essentially conservative, rather than a liberating force, which works simply to reproduce and preserve the *status quo*.

Notwithstanding other critiques of Bourdieu's theorising about the nature of cultural reproduction (see, for example, Jenkins 1992), what this overly structural perspective also excludes, however, is any real acknowledgement of and engagement with children as social agents who receive and participate in the educational process as pupils in the school system. It simply positions them as the passive receptors of implicit and subtle messages about identity inscripted in the educational process and the policies through which schooling takes place.

More recently, however, such a view of children's experience of schooling has been challenged by Montandon with Osiek (1998). They suggest that children's perspectives on education correlate with the kinds of socialising experiences and rapport with adult children themselves are able to establish both at home and at school. Thus, they argue, single variables, such as social background or gender, do not invariably determine the ways in which children relate to and experience the educational process. On the contrary, what children learn through schooling is dependent upon the dynamic and complex interplay between a whole configuration of different variables, which may be unique for each individual child. In this way, given the same structural conditions children may nonetheless have rather different schooling experiences.

Embedded within this critique, then, is an illustration of the cultural politics of childhood that we are seeking to explore in this volume: a process that examines childhood continuity and change. As our model suggests, this is not simply the outcome of structural shifts at the level of law and government policy, it is also produced by children, as agents of change, through their everyday experience of and engagement with the policies through which childhood is defined and refined. Beginning with these observations about children's encounters with schooling, drawn from the sociology of education of the mid-1970s, this chapter explores, therefore, some of the ways in which contemporary education policy is constructing childhood through its particular positioning of children within the schooling process. At the same time, it considers how children themselves respond to the power, authority and value systems through which their position, as children, is being shaped within and through these social structures and societal practices and thus how 'childhood' is also, in this sense, being constructed by children too. And in outlining these processes, the chapter suggests that New Labour's commitment to develop a 'third way' in politics, which is being heralded as able to bring about a cultural and political revolution based on the principles of communitarianism (see James and James 2001), is potentially at risk of excluding children from this endeavour through a reinforcement of particular ideologies of 'childhood' that emphasise children's marginality as citizens, despite the recent introduction of citizenship education.

The chapter focuses, in particular, on some of the practices reflected in the framing and teaching of the National Curriculum in English schools which are, we suggest, currently regulating children's everyday lives at school in accordance with a rather particular model of 'the child'.[1] Policies surrounding the setting and sitting of standard attainment tests (SATs) for children, the removal of children from mainstream schools into pupil referral units, and the designating of some children as having special educational needs all work to classify children in particular ways and to audit their behaviour in accordance with a standardised model of 'the child'. However, as we show through our analysis, these three particular 'textual interventions into practice' combine with 'policy as discourse' to form a broader social and educational ideology which, at its core, is constituted by two conceptual tensions (Ball 1994: 18). These revolve around the place, placing and placement of children in contemporary English society.

The first tension is that between children's present status as non-citizens, and their future rights and responsibilities *as* citizens. This distinction is, for example, implicit in the Final Report of the Advisory Group on Citizenship which, in promoting the new citizenship education introduced into schools in 2002, recommends that it should cover, *inter alia*, 'the duties, responsibilities, rights and *development of pupils into citizens*' (DfEE 1998: 22 emphasis added). This statement not only confirms the present non-citizenship of children by highlighting the requirement that they *develop* into citizens but also, more importantly, illustrates the role of 'policy as discourse', as a mechanism for agenda setting and for framing the context within which thinking about children and childhood takes place.

Thus, for example, the Advisory Group on Citizenship Report (DfEE 1998) provides a significant part of the discursive framework within which the political aspirations of the Government are to be achieved – that is, to attempt 'a shift of emphasis between, on the one hand, state welfare and responsibility and, on the other, community and individual responsibility' (DfEE 1998: para. 2.5). This framing has particular significance for children who, as non-citizens, already lack an influential voice. However, as Ball rather ominously notes, 'policy as discourse may have the effect of redistributing "voice", so that it does not matter what some people say or think, and only certain voices can be heard as meaningful and authoritative' (1994: 23). Thus, it is questionable whether the proposed shift of emphasis away from the state to the individual, which lies at the heart of communitarianism, will make much difference for, or to, the place of children.

The second, and more fundamental tension, is between 'childhood' as a social and conceptual space and the activities, desires, feelings and experiences of 'children' who are the temporary occupants of that space and thus party to its construction (see Chapters 1 and 2). As we shall suggest, it is a tension which means that the universalising intentions of current education policy to produce and maintain a commonality in English childhood is at risk of disruption from the diversities of children's everyday lives and experiences at home and at school. And, we suggest, the consequences of that risk, for some children, is a tightening of state control over their lives as they come, rather abruptly, face-to-face with the common place of law as a powerful regulatory mechanism (see also James and James 2001). As such, therefore, this discussion of aspects of contemporary English state education provides a first illustration of our model of Law at work in the regulation and control of the social space of childhood.

Schooling the school child

The expressed intention of citizenship education in English schools is to instruct children in the art of 'active citizenship' so that, literally and metaphorically, children will, as they grow up, come to know their place:

> Active Citizenship is based on the principle that young people learn to be effective citizens through meeting real needs in the school and wider community. Active learning in the community becomes part of the mainstream curriculum. Young people develop social responsibility and political literacy through becoming actively involved in the school and wider community
>
> (Britton 2000: vii)

Such a view is, however, nothing new. The history of childhood can be mapped out through a series of iconic images which, over time, reveal that the changing nature of the transitory space of childhood is, in part, the outcome of contemporaneous policies brought in by successive governments to regulate and order children's lives (Hendrick 1997b). And in this trajectory of childhood identities being shaped by social polices and societal practices, Hendrick locates the emergence of the schooled child as occurring first in the late 19th century. This he sees as directly related to the simultaneous identification of delinquency as a primary characteristic of the young, citing as evidence the many social commentators of the period who saw education as an effective instrument of social control and change through which the dangerous classes might be made less so.

As Hendrick notes, however, for education to pull off this conjuring trick required a major reconceptualisation of the special nature of 'the child' and the particular place of children in society. Central to this process, Hendrick argues, was an attempt to construct, for the first time, 'a truly *national* childhood, one that ignored (at least theoretically) rural/urban divisions, as well as those of social class' (1997b: 46). And it was through the education law and policy that shaped the instruction of children in the new space of compulsory schooling that this childhood was to be constructed:

> on a daily basis through teachers and school attendance offices [the school] was able to impose its vision upon pupils ... and upon their parents ... This construction was intended to directly involve all children and was meant to be as inescapable as it was visible, for in denoting them as 'pupils' the school was a constant and omnipotent reminder of who they were.
>
> (1997b: 47)

However, the extent to which such a process of reconceptualising 'the child' and 'childhood' is, in practice, realisable for *all* children through such societal practices and prescriptions was then – and still is – questionable, notwithstanding a seemingly continual commitment to try to make it so! The national school child, who first appeared in the later 19th century, has been successively, but not necessarily successfully, conceptually reinvented and reschooled at regular intervals ever since.

In 1862, for example, a national test for children over the age of six was introduced. This set in motion a centralised system of control over the curriculum, an education policy that was, however, gradually amended such that, by the 1944 Education Act, concern over the content of the curriculum had for the most part been displaced by a concern for the relationship between age and aptitude. By the 1980s, however, the testing of young children and a national curriculum was back on the agenda, becoming law through the Education Reform Act 1988 (Pollard *et al.* 1994). And by the late 1990s, the call for the reinstatement of a 'national' childhood, which such policies implicitly embrace, had gathered such momentum that, as Ball (1994) notes, equality had become replaced by an ideology of classlessness.

This was to be achieved through recourse to ideas of 'a community of the past' and deference to 'the best of all that has been said and written', described by Ball as a curriculum of the dead (Ball 1994: 46). Thus, for example, in her speech to the Party Conference in 1987 Mrs Thatcher was quite clear about the place of children in society and about what *all* children need, regardless of the particularities of their social experiences or the diversities wrought by social context:

> Too often *our* children don't get the education *they need* – the education *they deserve*. And in the inner cities – where youngsters *must* have a decent education if they are to have a better future – that opportunity is all too often snatched from them by hard-left educational authorities and extremist teachers. Children who *need* to be able to count and multiply are learning anti-racist mathematics – whatever that may be. Children who *need* to be able to express themselves in clear English are being taught political slogans. Children who *need* to be taught to respect traditional moral values are being taught that they have an inalienable right to be gay.
>
> (cited in Ball 1994: 33 emphasis added)

Set out here is one particular politically, and also historically and culturally, specific version of the educational needs of children. It is, in essence, a societal prescription of what children need in order to secure their future as adult citizens. Rendering children collectively as 'our', any diversities between individual children's experiences are played down, making it possible to say that *all* children need an education that consists of being able to count, to speak English and to respect traditional moral values. And indeed, it is education that will be the tool to be employed precisely to eradicate differences between children, whether in relation to language, political education or sexuality. The Thatcherite vision was that all children are or, more correctly, *should* be the same, commonality being made to champion diversity through corrective policy measures. The placement of children themselves within such a construction of childhood was as recipients of, rather than consumers of or participants in, the education process. This effectively worked to curb their potential for agency, a feature that remains central to the contemporary cultural politics of childhood

in England, occurring systematically across a variety of other
domains (see Chapters 6, 7 and 8).

Most recently, however, and reflecting the political complexion
and agenda of New Labour, the common needs of children are
being defined in a slightly different way – in terms of children's
transition from their present place in society as non-citizens, to
the achievement of future citizenship status in adulthood. The
Citizenship Foundation makes the socially marginal or excluded
position of children quite clear in its response to the White Paper,
Excellence in Schools:

> [w]e believe that citizenship has a clear conceptual core which relates
> to *the induction of young people into the legal, moral and political arena of
> public life*. It *introduces pupils to society* and its constituent elements, and
> shows how they, as individuals, relate to the whole.
>
> (cited in DfEE 1998: para. 2.7 emphasis added)

Within this policy formulation children are, as children, placed
outside of society and public life;[2] they inhabit a conceptual space
that lacks the legal, moral and political values to which adult citizens
supposedly subscribe. And it is through education, through literally turning 'children' into 'pupils', that they can be introduced
into society and come to understand how, as adults, they will find
their place within in it. But the inclusionary message of the 1980s,
which during the 1990s became ever more strident, is nonetheless
like that of the 1870s, in practice, also massively exclusionary.

As we shall show, through its envisioning of a 'national'
childhood, English social policy since the 1980s has continued to
ride rough shod over the social diversity amongst children, marginalising the significance of children's own everyday encounters
with the 'childhood' being constructed for them. Moreover, in its
positioning of children as being conditionally and generically 'in
need', the policy of creating a 'national childhood' has, as noted,
rendered children progressively as the passive recipients of the
educational process, rather than as active participants in it. Thus,
despite there being an apparent ideological commitment in
citizenship education to children's rights of social participation,
somewhat ironically, it is only through *instructing* children how to
be 'proper children', and thereby effectively denying them those
very rights of participative citizenship, that a vision of a national
childhood has been able to be constructed and maintained over

the last 20 years. One of the unforeseen consequences of this political vision has been, therefore, that some children are, effectively, deemed improper, with their place in society rendered more, rather than less, marginal. Thus, the policies designed to construct a 'national childhood' have in the end, paradoxically, worked against, rather than for, the interests of *all* children.

The national curriculum for a national childhood

As indicated above, one of the ways in which a national childhood has been recently fostered has been through the development of the National Curriculum in the wake of the 1988 Education Act. This specified a subject-based curriculum for children, structured in terms of four Key Stages linked to the age-based school structure – Key Stages 1 and 2 map on to the infant and junior schools within the state primary education system in England and Key Stages 3 and 4 to those at secondary school. At the end of Key Stages 1 and 2 there are standard attainment targets (SATs) set which specify what children should be capable of doing in core subjects such as Maths and English by the age of 7 and 11. As children reach these ages they are 'tested' against these standardised targets. Leaving aside the fierce debates that have raged over the content of the curriculum, the appropriateness of the standards set and the administrative overload this system has placed on teachers (see Daniel and Ivatts 1998, for a useful summary), what we want to explore first here is the implications, for children and hence for the cultural politics of childhood, of this policy of age-based testing that accompanies the National Curriculum.

A first point to note is that, as Daniel and Ivatts observe, the current heavy emphasis on testing has been an important ideological shift in education policy in England:

> primary education at its best prior to 1988 was concerned to some degree with what education *is* rather than what it is *for*. By contrast the focus of the National Curriculum is on what children will have been equipped to become when they leave school.
>
> (Daniel and Ivatts 1998: 181)

More attention is now being paid to the importance of childhood as the preparatory stage for adulthood, rather than as a stage in the life course of value in its own right, and to establishing a set of predictive indicators that will reveal the contribution that children will make to society as future adults. By linking SATs explicitly to a developmental model of childhood (see Chapters 1 and 2) it becomes possible to identify those children who fall below the standards deemed appropriate. Ameliorative measures can then be put into place to help ensure that the maximum number of children achieve the threshold.

Thus, for example, following its introduction of compulsory literacy and numeracy hours in primary schools, baseline assessments of 4- and 5-year-old children and a trouble-shooting policy to identify failing schools, the government set a target that 85 per cent of 11-year-olds should reach the expected standard of literacy by 2002, with 75 per cent of them also reaching the standard set for numeracy. However, such a process of national and uniform target-setting sweeps aside the significance of the diversities potentially wrought by children's everyday experiences at home and at school and, at the very least, appears to downplay the variety of factors that can intervene to obstruct or discourage children's learning. That these *are* significant factors, however, is illustrated by the failure of this target being reached and thus, by 2003, the government's aspiration had had to be tempered a little. In the DfES report, *Excellence and Enjoyment: a strategy for Primary Schools* (2003) the targets remain the same but the time-scale has been altered. Now, the targets are to be achieved, rather more vaguely, 'as soon as possible' (2003: 5).

The above example provides, therefore, one small illustration of the politics of childhood, revealing how a change in policy occurred in response to children's agency and participation – albeit that in this case, it might be better construed as their apparent failure to participate in quite the way intended! In addition, while it is clear that testing and standard setting can have a place in ensuring educational quality and in encouraging children to aspire to success, the consequences of this policy for some children, as it is played out in their everyday lives at school, may be less than beneficial.

For example, the yearly publication of league tables of primary school SATs results, and those of the secondary school results in the General Certificate for Education (GCEs) and A-level-examination results, enables the rise and fall in the fortunes of different schools to be closely documented. In an era marked by parental choice in schooling, any school that is seen to 'fail' may witness a drop in its pupil enrolment and, spiralling down from that, a decline in its funding and teaching resource as staff leave for jobs in better schools. The children who do remain in such schools are often those who are already socially and economically disadvantaged, whose parents may not be able to exercise their right to choose. Ironically, therefore, it is precisely these children – those who would most benefit from additional and high quality educational resources to help them achieve – who are most likely to experience their schooling in poor conditions and to be taught by a series of temporary teaching staff. Despite special measures such as the Fresh Start schemes, introduced by the Government to try rescue failing schools, the notoriety of being labelled as such a school in need of 'special measures' has tended to make matters worse, rather than better.[3] In one London school,

> five years after the school went into special measures, the leadership of its head teacher was "excellent" and 60% of the lessons were either good, very good or excellent. And yet despite this the number of children at the school who scored five A to C grades at GCSE last year was only 5%. In the year before special measures, it was more than three times higher at 17%.
>
> (*The Guardian*, 15 March 2000)

Such examples reveal the importance, if social policies are to be successful, of acknowledging the very real contribution of children's agency to the achievement of desired outcomes. Increasing children's educational achievements is not simply a matter of manipulating structural conditions under directives from the DfES, but requires children themselves to be engaged actively with this process too. And yet the individual experiences some children currently have of schooling under the increasingly stringent demands of the national curriculum and its testing procedures offers little hope that this will happen. Thus, the 2003 policy document, *Excellence and Enjoyment: a strategy for Primary Schools* (DfES 2003) continues to be framed by a generalised and developmentally based model of 'the child', which imbues all children with the same potentialities and which the government believes can be brought to fruition by the best kinds of English schools:

> By offering *every* child – whatever their own individual characteristics – the chance to achieve their full potential, these schools achieve high

standards for *all* children, giving them foundations for future learning, and for success in life.

(2003: para. 1.6 emphasis in original)

The extent to which such ideal schools will be made available for *all* children remains, however, questionable, and, as we go on to explore below, this is especially significant in relation to those children whose needs cannot easily be met within the ordinary school system. There is therefore a considerable irony here, for it is only through individual children exercising their agency, as willing and able collaborators to the testing process, that the Government's charts and league tables of 'ideal' and 'best' schools can be constructed.

There is considerable evidence, therefore, that some children risk becoming alienated from the educational process by the policies and directives through which it is currently being managed. Leaving aside those children who take direct action and opt out of schooling altogether, or who are permanently excluded, other children's experiences of school life may also be more akin to being 'schooled' than to being 'educated', with individual aspirations being sacrificed at the alter of standardised educational targets. For example, as more time has been devoted to training children to pass the core curricula that are tested in SATs, so the curricula have narrowed, with 'primary school pupils starved of PE' (*The Guardian*, 28 February 2002) and Office for Standards in Education (OFSTED), the school inspection service, wanting 'music to be less fun' (*The Independent*, 1 January 2002).

And, as pupils have experienced this kind of hot-house schooling, so concern has grown about the 'test stress danger to pupils' (*The Guardian*, 19 April 2000). With ministers wanting to lengthen the school day through the introduction of homework clubs, Saturday schools and holiday revision classes, teachers announced that it was 'time to end factory farming and give our kids a bit of free range' (*The Guardian*, 19 April 2000). They warned that it would 'not be long before schools report test-induced pupil suicide', as is the case in Japan (see Field 1995) and foresaw increasing mental health problems among young people (*The Guardian*, 19 April 2000). By 2002, a poll of school children reported that 'worries about doing well at school [had] replaced bullying as their biggest fear during their school days' (*The Guardian*, 21 September 2002). Thus, by May 2003, in the face of such fears being expressed by children, as well as their teachers and parents, the Government had to revise its strategy and pledged to reform the testing for 7-year-olds. Charles Clark, the Minister for Education, restated government policy:

> Tests at 11 are especially important. They provide children with basic numeracy and literacy. At seven, there is a role for more teacher assessment in the process. We are not getting rid of them, but we are open to looking at ways of making the tests less stressful than they appear to be.
>
> *(The Guardian*, 16 May 2003)

Special needs and deviant children

A good illustration of the process of selective exclusion that is engendered by a focus on the assumed shared commonality of 'childhood' and 'children' (see Chapters 1 and 2) can be seen through an examination of the development and delivery of the National Curriculum, together with its associated assessment procedures (SATs), discussed above. This shows that the conjunction of various education policies has, since the 1980s, served to classify and then to exclude particular sections of the child population from participating in the very education system through which all children were supposed to be instructed into how to be 'proper' children.

Prior to the 1980s, children with disabilities or specific learning difficulties, and those who were unable to be taught in ordinary schools, were termed ESN (educationally subnormal) and were educated in special schools – that is, in places set apart from main-stream schooling. Following the recommendations of the War-nock Report (1978), however, which suggested that such schools only worked to stigmatise these children through their exclusion, ESN children were reclassified under the less pejorative label as SENs (children with special educational needs). These needs covered a wide range – from children with physical disabilities and learning difficulties through to those who had emotional and behavioural problems and for whom mixing with other children posed difficulties. By a reordering of letters – a (unintentional?) symbol perhaps of the desire to transform an exclusionary label into an inclusionary one – this new policy aimed to ensure that all children, regardless of their needs, might be taught together in mainstream schools. In this sense, this was another, albeit different, envisioning of a 'national childhood', this time with disability and difference, rather than social class, being downplayed. However, in order for a child to be classified as SEN, a series of 'tests', known as the statementing process, has to be undergone. This is a long, drawn-out process of assessment carried out to ensure that the particular learning support needed by any individual child can be identified and then provided for that child within the school. That the statementing process is, in practice, often difficult to accomplish speedily, because of the numerous assessments and checks that need to be made, has meant, however, that statementing and thus the label SEN is not acquired by children *as of right*. It is sometimes hard-won indeed, a factor that in itself serves to undermine the supposed 'commonality' among children that the process of statementing is, in theory, supposed to facilitate.

Notwithstanding the difficulties often encountered by parents and by children in achieving a satisfactory outcome, the introduction of SATs tests following the Education Act 1988 came hard up against the policies for special needs provision in school. This had a whole series of unforeseen, and rather uncomfortable, outcomes within the education system when they were put into practice in the context of the audit and inspection culture created by the Government as part of the process of reforming public sector services (Clarke *et al.* 2000). First, in the market-place of parental choice in schooling, created following the 1988 Education Act, the publication of league tables in newspapers of SATs results led to an increasing competitiveness between schools. There was, therefore, an increasing tendency for schools to want to 'statement' more children or, indeed, to remove them altogether from the school roll. This is a direct result of the fact that the test achievements of children who have special needs do not have to be included in the statistics of results for individual schools. It is tempting therefore for teachers, concerned about the public representation of their school by its results, to urge that those who they fear will not achieve the required grades be excluded from taking the tests. As a spokesperson for a teachers' association said:

> The trick here is to exclude children without admitting it. It's "jump before you're pushed"...Children whose faces don't fit, children who will never get the required number of A to C grades or whose

behaviour is disruptive: these children are removed off rolls. You cannot believe how easy it is.

(*The Guardian*, 7 March 2000)

A policy ostensibly designed to be inclusive – special needs provision – becomes in this way potentially exclusionary.

The integration of statemented SEN children into mainstream schools has had other unforeseen consequences too, particularly in relation to the mainstreaming of children with educational and behavioural difficulties. Following the policy of mainstreaming children, the number of permanent exclusions of children from school began inexorably to rise. Many teachers felt unable to cope with the extra demands made by such children in a context where there was little additional support given and school exclusions reached an all time high of 12,700 in 1997. In response, the Government announced policy measures in 1999 which would, they claimed, help to reduce the number of school exclusions and a target of a reduction by one third, by 2002, was set.

Thus, for example, the appeal panels that had been set up so that pupils who had been excluded could, if successful in their appeal, be readmitted into school, were instructed to exclude children *only as a last resort*. This strategy, to which teachers' unions objected strongly, was followed by an announcement that the Government intended to expand the provision of 'sin-bins' or, to give them their proper name, school-based learning-support units. These special units, where disruptive and violent pupils can be temporarily placed, had been already established in some schools under the previous administration and the Government announced its intention that these would be more than doubled in number by 2002. As the pupils who would be the occupants of the sin-bins would not be counted as having been excluded from schools – being simply rehoused within them – the Government's policy to cut the number of permanent school exclusions would remain intact, while the complaints made by teachers could also be addressed.

However, this neat political side-step led to further strong protests from head teachers and the teachers' unions, following the reinstatement of two boys who had been expelled the previous year from two schools in London for brandishing knives (*The Independent*, 2 August 2000). Teachers argued that such specialist units could not offer pupils sufficient supervised hours outside of mainstream classrooms and that, because sin-bins were on school sites, disruptive pupils would still be free to hang around the school gates. A warning was given that a flood of litigation would follow if the Government did not acknowledge the very real problems faced on a day-to-day basis by teachers, with a survey of teachers revealing that 71 per cent felt that they did not get enough help to handle violent, disruptive and abusive pupils. The Association of Teachers and Lecturers said that 'it was already preparing 13 negligence suits against local education authorities that allegedly failed to protect staff from the foreseeable dangers of returning troublemakers to the classroom' (*The Guardian*, 20 April 2000). This strong challenge forced the Government, therefore, to issue new guidelines on 1 August 2000. These stated that appeal panels should not normally reinstate pupils who had been excluded.

The twists and turns of these events are fascinating for the insight they provide into the cultural politics of childhood. They reveal the common-place of law in children's everyday lives (see Chapter 3) and underscore the role of children as active agents who contribute to its making, albeit here in a somewhat negative guise. The saga is also interesting in what it reveals about children's engagement with and participation in the social construction of 'childhood' and 'the child', and the ways in which the diversity of children's everyday experiences – what some children do when compared with others – is often at odds with the ideological commitment of the adult world to a particular version of children's lives that rests on the commonality of childhood (see Chapter 1). A political commitment to 'sameness', which ignores children's individuality, falls foul of the agency that children can and do exercise in the course of their everyday lives. As Hayden (1997) observes, this is particularly problematic with regard to primary school children:

> primary school children who are excluded from school are a tiny minority of all school children. We can decide through the way social policy is interpreted, adapted and reformulated whether we ignore this minority or plan and cater for it appropriately.
>
> (1997: 153–54)

Thus, for example, in commenting on the Government's exclusion policies in 2000, Jennifer Bangs, president of the Association of Teachers and Lecturers, argued that although the Government's social inclusion policy was laudable, teachers could not be expected to solve society's problems. She indicated that children with learning difficulties and emotional and behaviourial problems might find their interests better served, in fact, in special schools, a move which would also benefit the vast majority of other pupils (*The Guardian*, 20 April 2000). As she commented, this suggestion was made,

> not to marginalise them, not to exclude them, but to acknowledge candidly that in a civilised society caring for the many often means making specific provision for the few.
>
> (cited in *The Guardian*, 20 April 2000)

At the time of writing, there is little improvement in this situation, with figures showing that pupils with SENs are still four times as likely as their peers to be excluded from school. The teachers' union, the National Association of Schoolmasters and Union of Women Teachers (NASUWT) summed up the situation as follows, arguing that they were:

> in favour of educating children with SEN in mainstream education provided the appropriate resources and support are provided. We believe, however, that the policy of inclusivity cannot be unqualified. In some circumstances the principle of inclusivity must be subordinate to a consideration of the pressures on these particular pupils and the consequences of that for their teachers and other pupils...The blanket view on inclusion disadvantages the individual child. We take a more pragmatic view.
>
> (*The Guardian*, 9 June 2003)

Children's citizenship participation

The social engineering of 'childhood', measured by the criteria of quality standards and performance indicators in the many tests and league tables through which contemporary education policy is managed, has reached its apogee, perhaps, in the current drive of New Labour for the promotion of citizenship education. This policy, which like those in the spheres of crime, health and the family, is focused determinedly on the 'futurity' that 'the child' represents (Jenks 1996b and Chapters 6, 7 and 8), is designed to transform the child into not only an adult worker (as most schooling policies have always done) but also a future citizen and voter. This vision was made explicit in 1997 by the then Education Secretary, David Blunkett, when he identified the need for an education provision

> to ensure that *all* young people reach 16 with the highest standards of basic skills and a secure foundation for *lifelong learning, work and citizenship* . . . to encourage people to continue throughout their lives to develop their knowledge, skills and understanding to improve their employability in a changing labour market.
>
> (DfEE 1997 – cited in Jones and Bell 2000)

A year later, in 1998, in the context of growing political concern about the lack of participation in the democratic electoral process following a low turn-out in the general election, he commented again on the need 'to take seriously the development of young people, as learners, as earners but also as citizens of the future' (DfEE 1998 – cited in Green 1999).

But this future citizen is one who has been schooled or instructed into accepting a particular set of social values based on a particular vision of how the government thinks society should function – in this case, that of communitarianism. This is made quite clear in the endorsement of education for citizenship, given by the Minister for Education in 2000 and inscribed on the back cover of the book, *Active Citizenship:*

> the future of our democracy depends in large measure on the extent to which young people are encouraged to devote their energy, visions and enthusiasm to improving the quality of public and personal life. I warmly commend the work of CSV Education for Citizenship in furthering this cause.

However, as Ball notes 'the translation of the crude, abstract simplicities of policy texts into interactive and sustainable practices of some sort involves productive thought, invention and adaptation. Policies do not normally tell us what to do' (1994: 19). Thus, though the book that the Minister endorsed is sub-titled 'a teaching tool-kit', exactly what outcomes this would have for children themselves in terms of increased participation and the exercise of rights were not clear.

For example, although the proposals for citizenship education are rooted in an ideologically abstract discourse about citizenship, the means by which these are to be given practical expression are clearly articulated in both the 'teaching toolkit' produced by Francine Britton as part of this project (Britton 2000) and in the Final Report of the Advisory Group on Citizenship (hereafter referred to as the Report). Together, these spell out the eight key concepts that have been prescribed as among the 'essential elements to be reached by the end of compulsory schooling' (DfEE 1998: 44). However, as we have discussed elsewhere (James and James 2001b), the extent to which children's everyday life at school will permit them to engage intellectually with these concepts and to experience them in practice outside of the context of a lesson is far from clear.

Take, for example, the concepts of 'participative democracy' and 'co-operation', which are regarded as central to citizenship education. Although the idea of 'working as a group or team' and encouraging consensus is to be promoted, in spite of acknowledging the importance of children's own experience of the ethos and organisation of schools the Report decides against recommending that school councils, which might potentially provide the most powerful learning experience of all about co-operation and conflict, should be made compulsory (DfEE 1998: 27). The agency of children, it would seem, is perceived to be too risky to allow them to be citizens – even within their space of the school. Alderson's (1999) work on children's participation in school councils confirms this suspicion.

In this context, the main elements of the UN Convention on the Rights of the Child are listed by Britton (2000: 64) as values particularly relevant to citizenship. Included in these is 'the right to freely express an opinion in all matters affecting her/him *and to have that opinion taken into account*' (emphasis added). However, it is difficult to see how children might learn about fairness and justice when those who are responsible for educating them as prospective citizens do not think it necessary to make school councils compulsory in *all* schools for all children.

This is an especially peculiar state of affairs where research evidence suggests that if children *are* permitted full rights in a participative and democratic fashion, they wield them with integrity, fairness and justice – that is, fully in line with the other concepts seen as fundamental to citizenship education. A recent report, for example, suggested that in schools where pupil councils are taken seriously, they can work very effectively to change the ethos of a school and it was remarked that 'schools that took pupils' views seriously . . . were less likely to need to use exclusion as a sanction' (*The Guardian*, 24 October 2000). Noting that only around 50 per cent of secondary schools and 25 per cent of primary schools have councils, Peter Facey, Chief Executive at the British Youth Council, commented as follows:

> I've known schools that let the children debate litter control in the playground, and that's about it. But that sort of thing will only increase their cynicism – they've got to feel they are being listened to, and that their views are making a difference.
>
> (cited in *The Guardian*, 24 October 2000)

Derry Hannam, an advisor to the DfEE agreed:

> Children have a right to be heard, although that's never been a particularly prominent or acceptable position to take in this country . . . [but] children know a lot about what's working in school, as well as what's going on generally . . . Giving children a voice raises their self-esteem and self-image as learners, which in turn enhances their attainment . . . There are some things that can only be learned through participation, and that includes democracy . . . One of the main ideas behind the addition of citizenship to the curriculum is that children should develop participation skills and learn how to act as citizens, and you can only develop these by participating and taking action. There's a mountain of research to show you can't just lecture about democracy; it's simply in one ear and out the other.
>
> (cited in *The Guardian*, 24 October 2000)

However, in an increasingly authoritative educational environment, with emphasis being placed on issues of control, regulation and back-to-basics learning, and where a school such as Summerhill, with its emphasis on pupil choice and participation only just managed to escape closure through a spirited defence being made in a hearing held at the High Court, the notion that positive benefits may follow from children being allowed greater participative rights sits strangely. But this is only so, we suggest, because of the models of childhood through which children and children's education in the UK are contemporarily perceived. With undue emphasis placed on the commonality of 'childhood', on children's supposed similarity with one another, and therefore on a model of 'the child' which does not accommodate any notion of individual agency, the standardized child emerges as the measure against which all children's progress must be measured. In such a context, any difference risks reconstruction as deviance (see also Chapter 6).

However, there is ample evidence to suggest that acknowledging children's individual agency and using this as a base-line for policy-making need not lead to disaster, as is clear in the case studies reported by Arthur (2000). In addition, a report on an alternative school, which offers educational opportunities to children who have been excluded, or indeed have excluded themselves by persistent truanting, from mainstream schools, demonstrates the advantages to children, and hence to society, of trusting them to exercise their agency responsibly (*The Guardian*, 23 May 2000). At the Oaktree Educational Trust in Liverpool, children have a say in which teachers are appointed to the school and in what they learn; the school council is elected with candidates conducting their own election campaigns; the pupils make comments on their own school reports alongside the teachers' comments and children learn, alongside ordinary curricula, such topics as human rights and self-defence. The school day is divided into five sessions with time in between for breaks and circle meetings when staff and students meet to discuss any problems.

The benefits to children are clear as the report indicates. James, who for many years had been a school refuser, was gradually integrated into the school and now plans to go to university. Likewise, Sarah who truanted from school for 16 months because of persistent bullying, is now a keen pupil:

> I was really bored. The teachers used to say that the only place I was going to was the dole queue. Now I am looking at becoming an architect.
>
> (cited in *The Guardian*, 23 May 2000)

Similar illustrations can be found of other schemes that have drawn on children's agency to tackle such 'problems' as truanting, bullying and disruptive behaviour. For example, a highly successful initiative adopted by one school to tackle the problem of truancy and poor attendance was the use of a 'buddy system', which involved children helping each other to get to school on time. As the head-teacher explained:

> Where the kids take control of something themselves, it has a better chance of being successful... You can't rely on parents when they have problems themselves, such as drugs or long-term unemployment. The buddy system fosters friendships and a sense of belonging, which is an additional reason for going to school.
>
> (cited in *The Guardian*, 1 March 2001)

Examples can also be cited of other peer support systems being used to tackle discipline problems at school. A junior school in Plymouth which, prior to the introduction of the scheme, had frequent class-room punch ups, with class-room displays often being destroyed and children leaving because of the fear of intimidation, is now described as a 'place where the pupils respect property, their teachers and each other' (*The Guardian*, 28 November 2000). Commenting on how the school was transformed, the head teacher admitted that, at first, they got things wrong:

> we spent our time forever intervening and telling children what they should be doing. We were ignoring that they were the greatest asset we had in trying to improve things.
>
> (*The Guardian*, 28 November 2000)

Recognising this, the school developed a variety of techniques that placed children as the central decision-makers and arbiters of their own behaviour. For example, circle time was introduced for group discussions about what was, or was not acceptable behaviour; playground peacemakers were trained as mediators to sort out playground disputes; and a guardian angel scheme was set up, whereby a pupil who had difficulties nominated three others to whom they could turn for support. In addition, the children were involved in interviewing prospective teachers. One 10-year-old girl reflects on the scheme:

> Before I didn't want to go to school – if you had problems you had to be violent or keep them to yourself. Now it's different – things get sorted out... [two girls] were being horrible. I asked if they wanted me to do mediation. They did and afterwards became best friends. It was really good – it's like one of the best lessons at school.
>
> (cited in *The Guardian*, 28 November 2000)

However, as one head teacher observed, such a process involves taking on a rather different view of the child, childhood and children's education:

> It is contrary to the mechanistic, statistics-driven way in which education has been going. It has nothing to do with league tables and everything to do with individuals having the space and time in which to resolve their difficulties with one another.
>
> (cited in *The Guardian*, 28 November 2000)

Conclusion

From the three areas of education policy discussed, albeit briefly, in this chapter, it is clear that children in English schools are subject to a cultural politics of childhood which, despite the rhetoric of rights and responsibilities embedded in communitarian thinking and citizenship education, continues to reflect a high degree of prescription and selectiveness about what and how children should be taught. Given the evidence outlined above about children's experiences of the schooling process, it is no surprise then that, when asked to describe their ideal school in a recent national competition, children placed the need for 'respect' high up on their agenda:

> A respectful school where we are not treated as empty vessels to be filled with information, where teachers treat us as individuals, where children and adults can talk freely to each other and our opinion matters.
>
> (*The Guardian*, 8 June 2001)

For many children, this is precisely what is absent in their everyday experience of schooling where increasingly, as a consequence of current policies, children are being subject to greater and greater control by the state. Thus, ironically, through the use of home-school contracts, school exclusions and forms of assessment such as the SATs tests, the arenas within which children are able to express their greatest autonomy at school are being threatened with even greater restrictions at the very moment when the state is arguing the need for children's participation in and experience of the democratic process.

In 2003, the war with Iraq provided ample evidence of this contradiction when some of the children who had participated in the wave of school strikes as a protest against the war were themselves punished with suspension from school, whilst others who had wanted to participate were prevented from doing so by being locked in their schools. This is despite the fact that the 'the question of how a country can go to war without referring to public opinion' is precisely the kind of topic that could be addressed under citizenship education (*The Guardian*, 1 April 2003).

Here then is an illustration of the contradictory effects and outcomes of what Ball (1994) calls the mediation of ideologically abstract policy. Indeed, Wyness (1999) argues that in contrast to the child care context, where the Children Act 1989 at least appears to ensure a degree of participation by children (see Chapter 8), the drift in education policy over recent years has meant that, with a few exceptions, 'pupils have lost the few bargaining powers they once had' (1999: 358). Thus although schools' councils, peer mediation and advocacy systems provide instances of children's active participation in shaping the process of schooling, overall,

> the education system still seems to work on the basis that children are both ontologically absent and socially incompetent and therefore unfit to reflect on school choice and policy.
>
> (Wyness 1999: 366)

Thus, one of the ironies of the contemporary cultural politics of English childhood is that in the very social arena specifically set aside for childhood, children have little opportunity to influence the form it takes.

Notes

1 This discussion limits itself to education policy in relation to state schools in England, since in the UK there are effectively four different education systems in operation: England and Wales, Northern Ireland, Scotland and the independent sector.
2 The placement of children outside of society and public life is also found in J. S. Mills' writing on citizenship.
3 It is also the case that schools are becoming expert in manipulating statistics, such as absentee rates, and in training children to pass SATs tests in order that the combined results present a picture of a good school in the league tables. (*The Guardian*, 6 March 2000)

CHAPTER 6

Health

According to Fitzpatrick (2001), health promotion constitutes a new form of social control and state regulation, achieved through the representation of health scares and risk as matters of and for individual responsibility. At a time when, statistically, the life expectancy and health of people in Britain is far better than it has ever been, he argues that there appears to be a growing and widespread anxiety about the state of the nation's health and an increasing tendency toward the medicalisation of more and more aspects of everyday life. No longer simply focused on the eradication of illness and diseases, 'health' has come to take on additional moral qualities, such that the 'good life is not simply a longer life, but a longer life lived healthily, which is to say, virtuously' (Fitzpatrick 2001: 8).

And perhaps nowhere is the rhetoric of this message more powerful than when directed at children and young people, with scientific research over recent years head-lining the health risks hey face. It has been discovered that 20 per cent of children are overweight (*The Guardian*, 6 March 2000); that 25 per cent of under-18s are often stressed (*The Observer*, 29 October 2000); that 200,000 of British children are on psychiatric medication (*The Guardian*, 11 April 2000); that one in five 10-year-old boys drink at least one glass of alcohol a week (*The Independent on Sunday*, 15 October 2000); that children as young as six are suffering from anorexia nervosa with one in six young girls between 5 and 7 years old already dieting (*The Sunday Times*, 2 April 1995); that teenage pregnancies are at their highest for a decade, with around 56,000 babies being born each year to teenage mothers (*The Guardian*, 22 February 2001); that 20 per cent of teenagers smoke at least one cigarette a day (*The Guardian*, 21 February 2001); and, most recently, that children and young people are at risk of brain damage through their increasing use of mobile phones (*The Guardian*, 11 May 2000).

Such figures would seem to indicate that children in contemporary British society are hell-bent on a path of self-destruction and that therefore the very future of the nation – that which children represent – is itself under threat. The statistics present for the public gaze just how many of 'our' children are taking risks with 'their' health and deviating from the behavioural norms held to be appropriate for children and, being deemed so newsworthy, these figures urge that some counter-action be taken. And, indeed, following the publication of such reports, various initiatives at local and national levels are taken to implement policies and programmes to try to ameliorate matters. Thus the 'battle to cut teenage pregnancy rates' (*The Guardian*, 22 February 2001) was initiated by a report from the Government's social exclusion unit in June 1999 on teenage pregnancies. This advocated a four-pronged action plan focused on the combating of childhood neglect and deprivation, which was cited as the key cause. Similarly, primary school children's unhealthy eating habits are currently being tackled by the Government's pledge to provide free fruit at school to all children between 4 and 6 years old by 2003.

However, the perceived increase in the health risks faced by children, which are headlined in the press and government reports, ignores the fact that, as Fitzpatrick points out, 'infant mortality amongst the poorest families today is similar to that of the richest in the 1970s' and that a boy born in Britain today can expect to live until he is 75, a girl until over 80, figures that represent an increase of over 10 years life expectancy since the Second World War (2001: 5). Such reports also fail to underscore more positive interpretations about the statistical 'risk' to the future health of the nation: that, for example, 80 per cent of children are *not* overweight, that most primary school children do *not* drink alcohol and that 75 per cent of young people do *not* suffer from stress.

With these health paradoxes as its starting point, this chapter explores why 'child health' should be popularly represented in this way through taking, as extended examples, the issues for the cultural politics of childhood raised by current government policies in three specific areas of child health: nutrition, sex and drugs education, and children with special needs. In doing so, the chapter asks whether the alarmist discourse through which child health is represented constitutes yet another form of social regulation in the contemporary cultural politics of English childhood, through the construction and promulgation of a particular set of ideas about children's normalcy, risk and developmental needs (see Chapters 1 and 2).

Central to this discussion are, once more, the themes of commonality and diversity, structure and agency, the individual and the collectivity. As we argued in Part I, these are fundamental to a cultural politics of childhood and permeate our thinking. Here, they raise a number of specific questions. Is the perpetuation of standardised norms and indicators for child health helpful for our understanding of *individual* children's well-being or do they, instead, raise unnecessary anxieties? Does the use of a generalised concept of 'the child' mask the many inequalities in children's health status that are present nationally, with the result that those children who do need additional and special resources for health care become not only 'hard to reach' but are sometimes out of reach altogether? When, on the basis of such indicators of risk, health promotion initiatives are promulgated by government, to what extent are these experienced by children, and/or their parents, as enabling or is it the case, for example, that such measures come to work as insidious regulatory devices in the everyday lives of children by marginalising them from taking responsibility for their own health care? Such questions form the framework for this chapter in its consideration of the ways in which social policy and law work to produce particular understandings of child health as part of the cultural politics of childhood.

Childhood: a process of natural growth and development

Naturalistic and scientific approaches to health and the body hold that 'the capabilities and constraints of human bodies define individuals' and that the health differences and resultant inequalities, which are to be found in the social world, are simply manifestations of the 'determining power of the biological body' (Shilling 1993: 41). Thus, for example, sexual difference is a taken-for-granted feature of bodies and held to account for the 'natural' propensity of women for mothering and of men for dominance, bodily differences that in turn are often used to provide justifications for gendered social and political inequalities. In a similar way, as noted earlier in Chapter 1, childhood is naturalised through the child's body. Commonly envisaged as the literal embodiment of change over time – the phrase 'when you grow up' makes this quite explicit – concepts of childhood have long been seen through the lens of children's bodily development and change. Children's social identities as children are understood as a 'natural' outcome of their bodily difference from adults and their trajectory of physical development prized in terms of the 'futurity' of the nation (Jenks 1996b).

However, exactly, what is 'normal' and 'standard' in terms of children's development and the extent to which normalcy can indeed be generalised and measured in this way for all children, can be questioned both in terms of the hegemony of particular scientific paradigms and with regard to the social and political consequences for children themselves of employing such measures. Historians of childhood are, for example, beginning to document the ways in which ideas of standardisation, measurement and normalcy in relation to children's physical development emerged as devices with which to monitor and regulate children. Steedman, for example, argues that it was the 19th century that,

> fixed childhood, not just as a category of experience, but also as a time span ... [through] the development of mass schooling, and its grouping of children together by age cohort. In the same period the practices of child psychology, developmental linguistics and anthropometry provided clearer pictures of what children were like, and how they should be expected to look at certain ages.
>
> (Steedman 1995: 7)

During this period, the idea of a standardised path for child growth and development was used to underpin a whole variety of social, political and educational policies, policies designed to ensure a successful outcome for the whole child – that is, the achievement of adulthood:

> The building up of scientific evidence about physical growth in childhood described an actual progress in individual lives, which increased in symbolic importance during the nineteenth century, whereby that which is traversed is, in the end, left behind and abandoned, as the child grows up and goes away. In this way childhood as it has been culturally described is always about that which is temporary and impermanent, always describes a loss in adult life, a state that is recognised too late. Children are quite precisely a physiological chronology, a history, as they make their way through the stages of growth.
>
> (Steedman 1992: 37)

Thus, during the 19th century an understanding of the importance of child health was becoming central to the shoring up of the conceptual space of childhood for children, a space which was being carved out, simultaneously, in other areas through, for example, the institutionalisation of compulsory schooling (see Chapter 5)[1] and the Factory Acts that removed children, progressively, from the sphere of work. Thus, as Armstrong (1995) has shown, the wide-scale surveying of the child population gradually began to define certain limits of normality for children's bodies. This was exemplified in the height and weight growth chart, which was first introduced in the early 20th century and is still used routinely today to 'check' a child's development. Measurements are made of a child's height and weight at different points in time and these are then plotted against a three pre-inscribed growth lines, known as percentiles, which define the boundaries of normalcy for low, medium and high growth rates.

As Armstrong notes, the development of this chart meant that 'every child could be assigned a place on the chart and, with successive plots, given a personal trajectory' for the future, a process which, it was believed, would to reveal those children most at risk. Thus, as Steedman shows, the introduction of such devices enabled the plight of working-class children to be highlighted by the political activists and reformers of the period in their call for social change:

> [Child physiology] structured around the idea of growth and development... allowed for comparisons to be made between children, and, most important of all as a basis for a social policy on childhood, it... rooted mental life in the material body and the material conditions of life. In this way, working-class children could be seen as having been robbed of natural development, their potential for health and growth lying dormant in their half-starved bodies.
>
> (Steedman 1992: 25)

Such a view of children and childhood – the explicit linking of children's health to the future welfare of the nation – was a consistent feature of 19th century social and political thought. This in itself bears witness to the gradual ideological shoring up of childhood as a particular social space via social policy, through the notion that children have special and very particular physical and mental health care needs different from those of adults. Thus it was that paediatrics developed as a specialist branch of medicine in the early 20th century and, as the surveying and monitoring of the child population proceeded, other specialist children's clinics and services followed close behind. This was, Armstrong (1983) notes, accompanied by a shift from seeing 'pathology' as not just located within the body of the child but also in its environment – in poverty, poor education, bad parenting and dysfunctional families (see Chapter 8).

However, as Armstrong observes, although the height and weight chart claims to depict a child's unique and individual development, this uniqueness only exists in the context of a 'generalised' child, derived epidemiologically from the population as whole. Against this, the 'normality' or 'abnormality' of each individual child is measured and in this, 'age' – that is, time passing – is critical, for it provides the context within which 'successful' or 'pathological' height/weight trajectories are charted. Thus, the health of the child's body, he argues, is 'delineated not by the absolute categories of physiology and pathology, but by the characteristics of the normal population', shared and common characteristics that become standardised as 'normality' (1995: 397).

In this way, 'normality' for children has become firmly linked to the trajectory of a *collective* model of age-based change and development, inscribed upon and through the *individual* body (and mind) of 'the child'.[2] And one consequence of this charting of 'normalcy' is that any child is always potentially at risk of 'precocity' – doing things earlier than s/he *should* – or its opposite, developmental delay – doing things later than s/he *should*. Thus although, as Freeman (1992) notes, within any population individual deviations from the norms for the group are bound to be found, through the intense surveillance of children's growth and development the fear is that 'difference' becomes pathologised as 'deviance'.

Therefore, as Freeman also observes, what such statistically based surveillance techniques do is to open up 'an epistemological space in which the politics of social intervention . . . are played out' (1992: 36). Who gets what kind of intervention, why and when become, then, highly politicised issues of citizenship and of rights. The next section takes up this theme by critically examining three aspects of more recent health policy in the UK to explore the ways in which 'child health' is framed for children. It suggests that, through drawing on particular constructions of the 'child' and 'childhood', children remain marginalised from taking responsibility for their own health care, despite the Government's apparent recent commitment to promoting it (*Saving Lives: Our Healthier Nation*, 1999). This is just one of the many paradoxes of the cultural politics of childhood, a paradox paralleled by examples in our other case studies of education, crime and the family (see Chapters 5, 7 and 8).

Health policies for children?

Following the introduction of the free National Health Service for all in 1948, it can be argued that children's health improved significantly. Thus, for example, as Daniel and Ivatts reveal,

> whereas in 1948 1394 deaths were recorded from diphtheria, polio, measles and whooping cough, there were only sixteen such deaths in 1986; and deaths from the most virulent pre-war killer – tuberculosis – fell between 1938 and 1986 from 25623 to 376.
>
> (1998: 79)

However, despite the obvious benefits to children of the reduction in child mortality, many of the health policies that have emerged since the inception of the NHS cannot be regarded necessarily as child-centred, in the sense of prioritising services for children that meet their particular needs *as* children. On the contrary, it could be argued instead that they were – and are still – instituted primarily to underpin the State's need for a healthier adult workforce in the future.

It is significant, for example, that in terms of health policy children themselves were – and still are – not often positioned as 'consumers'. This means therefore that

> changes in health care designed to increase consumer choice may not be wholly sensitive to children's health needs and may by a verbal sleight of hand avoid the issue of children's rights to the best available care regardless of cost. Children certainly are among the least likely to have the relevant medical knowledge to make informed choices. It is others – parents, clinicians, health service managers, indeed politicians – who have to make judgements about the most appropriate forms of health care for children's health needs.
>
> (Daniel and Ivatts 1998: 86)

Thus, as Daniel and Ivatts indicate, reforms and legislation may well, ironically, reduce children's access to health care, in the name of greater economic efficiency. For example, although the Patients' Charter, introduced by the Conservative government in 1991, aimed to ensure patients' rights as 'consumers' of health care, it did little in the way of specifying children's particular rights. The Patients' Charter merely suggested that they have the same rights as other people, along with similarly marginal groups such as elderly or disabled people.

It did not, for instance, 'mention any right to availability in a child's local area of accident and emergency hospital care', which for many of the poorest children in Britain can be their main – if not only – source of health care and treatment (Daniel and Ivatts 1998: 86).

> The instant availability and access to hospitalised care in the case of serious injury make 'casualty' a highly valued part of the NHS ... It is also in casualty departments that children with unexplained injuries may first appear – like, for example, the children of Fred and Rosemary West, who attended the Gloucester Accident and Emergency Department on no fewer than thirty-one separate occasions.
>
>   (1998: 84)[3]

As Kurtz (1999) observes, even the guidelines on services for children under the Patient's Charter, which were later introduced in 1996, were 'addressed throughout to parents with respect to their children, and children's rights to health care [were] limited to the right to be registered with a general practitioner' (1999: 110).

It can also be argued that, although the White Paper *Health of the Nation* (1992) had the expressed intention of improving health for all by the year 2000, the everyday practical health needs of children were not prioritised sufficiently, despite the healthy future of the nation being the expressed intention of government policy. For example, although the White Paper identified accidents as the commonest cause of death in children over the age of 5 and made their reduction a priority target, by 1995 the then Health Minister was suggesting that, under the new NHS funding arrangements, hospital A and E departments might be closed. It was argued that their role could be taken on by primary health care teams. This was a rather worrying suggestion, given GPs' own reservations about their capacity to meet demand and, as noted above, the extensive use made of hospital departments by those families unable to register with a GP (Daniel and Ivatts 1998: 84–85).

A similar disregard for the specificity of children's needs and children as health care consumers in their own right was apparent elsewhere in the policy directions laid out in the 1992 White Paper. Thus, for example, although asthma had been one of the original sixteen targets set out by the Government for the year 2000, it was dropped when the targets were reduced to ten, even though it affects 10 per cent of children and cases are continuing to rise (Ranade 1997: 189). Similarly, although by 1991, when the NHS and Community Care Act was implemented, there had clearly been an overall improvement in the health of the general child population since the Second World War, the policy was, as Ranade argues, 'fundamentally flawed by the government's ideological inability to accept the centrality of poverty and social deprivation as causes of ill-health' (1997: 188). Thus the health of the future nation as embodied in its children was, in 1991, still at risk from the traditional and well-documented health inequalities that are wrought by social class and, to a lesser degree, by ethnicity, diversities that can be said to fracture 'childhood' as a shared conceptual space.

It remains the case, therefore, that there is an increased risk of mortality during childhood for all ages of children in lower social classes, with boys being at a higher risk than girls (Kurtz 1999). And, although class differences in morbidity amongst children are less pronounced, it is nonetheless apparent that parental unemployment, combined with low income, has a deleterious effect on children's mental health. Ethnicity too fractures the supposed commonality of child health, not only because of the susceptibility of certain ethnic groups to such diseases as sickle-cell anaemia, rickets and tuberculosis, but also because of the fact that many of the ethnic minority population experience low pay and poor housing conditions (Daniel and Ivatts 1998).

The net effect of this apparent unwillingness to recognise children as consumers of health care and to see them as active choice-makers is that, although good progress towards a healthier nation had been made in some areas by 1997 – for example, the decreases in the rates of adult coronary heart disease and breast cancer – amongst children, things had got worse:

> obesity, smoking by children and female alcohol consumption...are moving in the wrong direction. Smoking among 11–15 year olds is

particularly worrying, jumping from 8 per cent of the age group in 1988 to 12 per cent in 1994, twice the level it was targeted be.'

(Ranade 1997: 191)

More recent figures simply confirm this earlier trend with 20 per cent of UK teenagers admitting to smoking at least a cigarette a day at 13 years of age or younger (*The Guardian*, 21 February 2001) and one in five 10-year-old boys and one in seven 10-year-old girls drinking alcohol at least once a week (*The Independent on Sunday*, 15 October 2000). And to this list can be added the still relatively low rate of reductions in teenage pregnancies, giving the UK as a whole still the highest rate of teenage pregnancies in Western Europe (Bradshaw 2002).

It would seem therefore that government policy still struggles to address child health issues successfully. In part, we suggest, this is because it fails to recognise children as social agents who can – and do – take decisions about what the kinds of life-style behaviours they adopt. Thus, although the most recent White Paper, *Saving Our Lives: Our Healthier Nation* (1999), promises a new perspective on health care in which people are regarded as active partners and decision-makers – 'people can make individual decisions about their and their families' health' – the extent to which children and young people will also, in practice, be afforded such opportunities is as yet unknown. If, however, parallels are drawn with the citizenship-based approach currently being promoted through education and schooling (see Chapter 5) and in relation to crime reduction (see Chapter 7), this seems unlikely to happen on a wide scale.

For example, although for the most part in the White Paper children are still, as in the past, addressed only indirectly, as members of families who, it is assumed, will take proper responsibility for them, in the section entitled Health Foundation Skills (paras. 3.41–44), there *is* a more explicit focus on children and young people. However, despite the rhetoric, there is little evidence to suggest a radical change in policy. For example, children's health remains most important in terms of their futures – as the next generation of adults. Thus, a scheme to teach children about accident prevention is described as having the potential 'to produce a generation of children who will grow up with a different attitude to the risks and prevention of accidents' (para. 3.40), while the proposed Health Skills programme, to be developed as part of the citizenship component of the national curriculum in schools (see Chapter 5) will, it is argued,

> provide young people with new opportunities to learn and acquire skills which will help them to maintain their health as they move into adult life, including for example by resisting pressure from their peers to take risks with their health.
>
> (1999: para. 3.42)

But whether this new Health Skills programme will, as is claimed, meet 'young people's needs in a relevant, timely and effective way' depends, of course, on how those needs are being defined – and by whom (1999: para. 3.44). This is key within a cultural politics of childhood and, focusing on three different areas of child health, the chapter now turns to a consideration of this issue.

Children's diets

Despite the government's recognition of the importance of dietary factors in the prevention of adult coronary heart disease and strokes, contemporarily, children's diets remain high in fat, a known risk factor, and are also high in sugar with a large proportion of children failing to reach the recommended nutrient intake levels (Bradshaw 2002). This has led not only to a worsening of some children's health, signalled by rapid increases in childhood obesity and the recent emergence of early onset of diabetes in children, but has also laid down patterns of eating that children may take with them into adult life:

> If current medical thinking is correct, whereas with previous generations any physical symptoms caused by food deprivation and malnutrition were clearly apparent in childhood and adolescence, now the harm to children's health resulting from poor diets will not become apparent until later in adulthood. Meanwhile the true long-term health risks caused by poor eating habits among children and young people are obscured by physical appearances, and by the abundance of choice in food and the seeming affluence of many homes.
>
> (Daniel and Ivatts 1998: 102)

In sum, therefore, it could be argued that recent and current health policies aimed *at* children are not very effective health policies *for* children since they are only, rather belatedly, beginning to acknowledge children's agency and the effect on children's health of children's *own* behaviour and decision-making, something that has long been recognised by the manufacturers of sweets and 'junk food'!

Responses made by governments to the changing pattern of children's diet and the effect this potentially has on their health as adults, however, have been equivocal to say the least, and can be illustrated by examining the changing fortunes of the school meals service and the use of the school as site for nutritional education. Begun in 1930s, the school meals service was introduced at first for the children of the poor to ensure minimum nutritional standards for them, but under the provisions of the 1944 Education Act local educational authorities were expected to provide meals and milk for all children at a modest charge. The popularity of this service increased such that by 1970s around 70 per cent of children stayed at school for a midday meal, meals which had strict guidelines as to their nutritional value. However, under Conservative administrations the requirement for Local Education Authorities (LEAs) to provide meals for all was removed and under the 1980 Education Act the only obligation they had was to provide meals for those children entitled to free school dinners.

And alongside the abandonment of free dinners and free milk – summarily removed by 'Maggie Thatcher, Milk Snatcher', as the future Prime Minister became known – was the abandonment of minimal nutritional standards for their composition (Mayall 1996; Daniel and Ivatts 1998). By the 1990s, therefore, surveys were revealing that those school children who did take school meals were eating a high fat and sugar diet, dominated by chips, burgers, sausages, pizza, canned drinks and biscuits (Daniel and Ivatts 1998: 105). By eating school meals, therefore, those children entitled to 'free' school meals may simply have been compounding the potential health problems which, as noted above, poverty brings. These changes in the school meals service may, in addition to accounting for the rise in childhood obesity, also explain recent increases noticed in the incidence of childhood asthma, iron deficiency, anaemia and viral infections. As Daniel and Ivatts wryly note, 'once again, so it would appear, school meals are part of the problem of children's diets, and no longer, as they may once have been, for all too brief a period of our welfare history, a means of improvement' (1998: 106).

Recent government initiatives to tackle this problem seem somewhat tame by comparison with what it might be possible to achieve were the kind of school meals service that was available in the 1970s to be reintroduced. Despite a broad commitment in *Saving Lives: Our Healthier Nation* (1999) to setting up further Health Action Zones, in order to tackle the effects that poverty and social exclusion have on health, the bigger problem of *how* to change children's dietary habits receive little direct attention. Thus, while in some respects the strategy to provide free fruit to all children aged between 4 and 6 years old by 2003 represents a positive step, it begs the question as to whether children will actually eat the fruit, rather than the crisps or sugary snacks that might also be available to them! As social actors, children have – and do make – such choices.

This can be illustrated by another recent dietary trend amongst children and young people – the lowering of the age at which the slimming disease anorexia nervosa is being diagnosed. Until recently commonly believed to be a condition associated primarily with middle-class, teenage girls, anorexia nervosa is now appearing among children as young as six, and a recent report suggests that one in six children aged between 5 and 7 years old are already dieting (*The Sunday Times*, 2 April 1995). Six-year-old Lucy, who refuses food and makes herself sick and does press ups in her bedroom in order to stay thin explained her actions as follows:

> I can't eat because I've got a fat tummy. My sister's so fat she shouldn't wear jeans or skirts because her tummy rolls over it.
>
> (*The Sunday Times*, 22 April 1995)

To tackle such issues and find a viable solution involves, however, a rather radical shift in conceptions of childhood, one that sees children themselves, rather than their parents, as the targets for health policies and health education messages. It also means developing health education policies that address children and young people's needs and concerns as *they* see and understand them, rather than those which adults have identified for them.

Sex and drugs

As Kurtz notes, 'health in the traditional sense is not of great concern to young people' (1999: 103). Young people's concerns, even those living with chronic health conditions, are more often focused on friendships, careers and their increasing independence, than on health matters. A recent report confirms this in its finding that adolescents are the only group in the population whose death rates have not dropped in the last 50 years, leading David Hall, president of the Royal College of Paediatrics and Child Health, to comment that 'while it is readily accepted wisdom that we need to invest in tomorrow's adults, we seem peculiarly reluctant to do so' (*The Guardian*, 12 June 2003). This, as Kurtz argues, offers a

> challenge to the health system to find ways to encourage children and young people to make good use of services that can minimize any health problems they may have and not to neglect their health as a resource for living.
>
> (1999: 103)

However, this challenge is not, as yet, being systematically addressed.

Thus, for example, recreational drug use is becoming increasingly popular amongst young people with the British Crime Survey (1996) reporting that 'at least one in three will have tried an illicit substance by the age of 15' (Balding, cited in NACRO 1999). These figures suggest that this could be a key area for health education policies directed at young people and could enable them to use such drugs wisely without potentially causing lasting damage to their health (NACRO 1999). However, although the 1995 White Paper, 'Tackling Drugs Together', is ostensibly framed in such a way, it has been estimated that 'of resources devoted to dealing with drugs, two-thirds are spent on enforcement of legislation as against one-third on prevention, education and treatment services' (NACRO 1999: 19). Thus, despite an apparent invitation to young people to 'tackle drug use together' with adults, the 'criminalisation' of this activity persists as a major ideological frame surrounding young people's drug use.

Such a perspective may do little to address the ways in which many young people view their own use of illicit substances. As Ives and Clements (1996) note, although drug education has become a compulsory part of the national curriculum (DfE circular Drug Prevention and Schools, DfE 1995), whether it works to educate children about drugs is less than clear for 'there is little emphasis in drug education on asking young people what they want, or what they think would be effective forms of drug education, either for themselves or their peers' (Ives and Clements 1996: 19).

A comparable case would be the failure of government policy to reduce the conception rates of teenage girls. England continues to have the highest teenage pregnancy rate in Western Europe – 28.8 per thousand girls aged under 20 – with even higher figures for Scotland and Wales (Bradshaw 2002). However, if no account is taken of the choices which girls are actively making, and why they are making them, then policies to alter behaviour or life-style are doomed to failure. With respect to teenage girls' views on pregnancies, Simms makes the following observation:

> Affluent middle-class girls have higher education, careers and financial independence to look forward to. So becoming a teenage mother in error is not part of their plan. In this way they are no doubt supported by concerned parents who will help them to find their way to a legal abortion if that is what they desire. Girls from deprived backgrounds, with little education and doing under-paid repetitive jobs may find the notion of having a baby even at a very young age a more attractive proposition. Moreover, they know that they are not sacrificing much in terms of future prospects.
>
> (Simms 1993, cited in Dawson 1997: 254)

Simply explaining to teenagers how pregnancies occur via sex education lessons in schools will not, in itself, prevent them happening, if it is the case that for some young girls pregnancy is regarded as having a positive, rather than a negative, outcome for their adult futures. As Kurtz observes, what is 'difficult for many professionals is the capacity to listen to children and to learn from what they have to say about themselves' (1999:109). Thus, for example, while an advisory group recently set up by the government to report on teenage pregnancy has strongly advocated that teenagers should be able to get confidential advice on contraception at school, along with supplies of condoms and pills, Ministers would not commit themselves to act upon these recommendations (*The Guardian*, 1 December 2001). It was therefore left to the supermarket chain, Sainsbury's, to take up the initiative by starting a trial in August 2002 to sell the morning-after pill at its stores in areas known to be at high risk for teenage pregnancies.

This non-decision by the Government seems strangely at odds with the decision taken a year earlier, in October 2000, to launch a two million pounds advertising campaign directed at children and young people – *Sex. Are you Thinking About it Enough?* Although claiming not to lecture young people about keeping their virginity, the ideological thrust of the campaign as a whole, however, was more in that moral direction than the headline slogan would seem to indicate. The Health Minister, Yvette Cooper, advised that the campaign was launched to give children the facts about age and young people's sexual activity in the hope that it 'might encourage children to slow the headlong rush into sexual experience, as they discover that they are not as far behind the rest of the pack as they thought' (*The Daily Telegraph*, 10 October 2000).

Believing one of the main 'causes' of early sexual experimentation simply to be peer pressure, a belief as illustrated above reiterated in the latest White Paper, *Saving Lives*, returns us to a model of the passive child: to the child as a non-participant, a non-decision-maker and, in effect, a non-citizen. In addition, it conveniently ignores other factors through recourse to a traditional model of childhood innocence – that, for example, children are reaching sexual maturity at far earlier ages than ever before and that the changing social climate of a greater openness about sex, and about sex outside marriage, is something in which children and young people may themselves also wish to be involved.

Thus, in addition to the failure to appreciate that children and young people have their own perspectives and make decisions, current policy on sex education in schools, as set out in the Education Act 1993 (see Department of Education 1994, Circular 5/94), also fails to deliver a sex education that meets children's own needs as social agents. First, as Monk (1998) notes, that parents have the right to withdraw children from sex education classes means that schools may err on the side of caution in deciding what particular aspects of sex education to concentrate on in the curriculum. Moreover, the requirement in the Circular that 'sex education be taught within the context of moral considerations and the value of family life' has meant, for the most part, that it fails to address the realities of childhood sexuality by not constructing children as sexually active beings (Monk 1998: 299). As Monk suggests,

> the social and cultural ambivalence regarding young people's sexual activity results in a lack of clear consensus as to the purposes of sex

education and reinforces the conflict between preparing children for sexual adulthood and providing advice to sexual children.

(Monk 1998: 296)

Attempting to straddle both a moral as well as a sexual health programme, in which sexual activity is held to be most appropriately confined within marriage and the family, the Circular fails therefore to address the actual sexual practices of many young people, which may include non-reproductive sex such as masturbation, oral sex and homosexuality:

> the emphasis on marriage and criminal law reinforces the moral programme, excludes a positive approach towards alternatives to heterosexual married life and significantly fails to address the needs of sexually active pupils and, of particular significance in the context of HIV/AIDS prevention, the special needs of gay pupils.

(Monk 1998: 299)

As Monk goes on to point out, while the involvement of health education professionals such as sex education counsellors in schools is to be welcomed, which particular pupils receive those services in which schools is at the discretion of the school governors and head teachers and, in line with the Circular, may be only encouraged for those pupils whose sexual behaviour puts them 'at moral or physical risk or in breach of the law' (para. 40, cited in Monk 1998: 302). As Monk warns,

> this has the effect of marginalising those pupils and also problematises their sexuality to the extent that a sexual pupil is perceived as having a moral, health or legal problem, as opposed to an educational right to information.

(Monk 1998: 302)

In sum: health education policies that are built upon models of 'the child' that deny the agency of young people will not reach their target audience and yet, such models are core to the contemporary cultural politics of childhood.

Competent children

As suggested in the extended examples above, child health policy does not address children's own health needs primarily because

these 'needs' have been usually understood in relation to the pro-
spects they hold out for a healthy adult life in the future, rather
than in relation to children's present health concerns as children.
This has made children marginal as health care consumers in their
own right, confirming their status as non-citizens. Such a perspective is reinforced through recourse to views of 'the child' that place
incompetence, rather than competence, at their centre. Shored
up by developmental models (see Chapter 1), this construction
of 'the child' has meant that, in the past, children and young
people's rights to access particular kinds of health services and
to direct involvement in decision-making about their own health
care has been neglected.

However, despite the UNCRC and legislation such as the
Children Act 1989, which emphasise the importance of ascertaining
children's wishes and feelings, children are still not routinely
consulted in their everyday encounters with health care professionals and parents. Ironically, this continued failure to ensure
that children's rights to self-determination and involvement in
health care decisions are secured, can be seen as a direct consequence of the yardstick used to test children's competence that
emerged following the key legal decision made by the British
courts in 1986 (*Gillick v. Wisbech and West Norfolk Area Health
Authority*, [1986] AC 112). Summarised by Archard as follows, this
ruling held that,

> children under the age of 16 could consent to medical treatment,
> including contraceptive advice and treatment, if they have "sufficient
> understanding and intelligence" to comprehend what was proposed,
> as well as the emotional capacity to make a mature decision.
>
> (1993: 78)[4]

However, this apparent respect in law for children's rights is, as
Lewis (2001) has argued, not as strong as it might at first appear.
In many cases the courts 'have been reluctant to allow these
decision-makers complete autonomy, and have retained an absolute
power to override any decision involving the medical treatment of
a child on the grounds of the child's "best interests".'(2001: 151)
This latter notion, which is fundamental to the Children Act 1989
(see Chapter 4), can thus be drawn on by adults to overturn any

judgement a child might make about what his or her own interests are, *in spite* of the *Gillick* ruling.

Thus, for example, commenting on the *Gillick* ruling in the House of Lords, Lewis argues that in some instances, ironically, children may be required to demonstrate a *greater* competence than an adult would have in understanding the issues involved. A girl seeking contraceptive advice or treatment, according to the provisions set out by Lord Scarman,

> has to understand the "relevant moral and family questions", especially her relation with her parents; long term problems associated with the emotional impact of pregnancy and its termination; and ... the risks to health of sexual intercourse at her age, risks which contraception may diminish but cannot eliminate.
>
> (Lewis 2001: 153)

Many adults, let alone a 15-year-old girl, would not be able to pass such a test.

In other comparable medical cases, the setting of a higher standard of 'competence' for children has also worked against the exercising of their rights when set against the 'best interests', which *adults* have decided for them. In the case of a fifteen-and-a-half-year-old Jehovah's Witness with acute leukaemia, who was refusing blood transfusions and wished to be allowed to die (*Re E (a minor) (wardship: medical treatment)* [1993] 1 FLR 386), the judge held that the child was not '*Gillick* competent'. In this case, competence was defined in the following manner:

> I am quite satisfied that E. does not have any sufficient comprehension of the pain he has yet to suffer, of the fear that he will be undergoing, of the distress, not only occasioned by that fear but also – and importantly – the distress he will inevitably suffer as he, a loving son, helplessly watches his parents' and his family's distress. They are a close family, and they are a brave family, but I find that he has not realisation of the full implications that lie before him as to the process of dying. He may have some concept of the fact that he will die, but as to the manner of his death and to the extent of his and his family's suffering I find he has not the ability to turn his mind to it nor the will to do so. Who can blame him for that?
>
> (Ward J., cited in Lewis 2001: 154)

As Lewis wryly observes, this is an exceedingly high standard to impose on anyone, requiring them to come to terms with their own death prior to the event: 'the law of competence is thus distorted in order to provide a covert tool allowing the judge to avoid the consequences of the child's decision' (2001: 154).

But even when a child has been judged as '*Gillick* competent' and, for example, has taken the decision to refuse or indeed to consent to medical treatment, his or her decision can, nonetheless, still be overridden by anyone who has parental responsibility, by their claiming to act in the child's 'best interests'. Thus, if such claims are upheld (as has happened already), what we see occurring in the everyday exercise of law is, as Lewis notes, a failure 'to respect the proposition that a competent child should be taking responsibility for herself' and a 'distinct lack of respect for the child's right of self-determination and bodily integrity' (2001: 156). What we see, in effect, is the reinstatement of the view of 'the child' as both passive and incompetent, in the face of the more agency-based models of 'the child' that can be glimpsed in the provisions of the Children Act 1989 and the *Gillick* ruling. Instead, the competence that might be demonstrated by any individual child able to pass the *Gillick* test, and which might therefore highlight the diversity of experiences that children have, is threatened by legalistic recourse to the supposed commonality of the concept of 'the child'. This is achieved through the structuring of 'childhood' as an age-based, adult-determined context for children's lives, a key feature of the contemporary politics of childhood in England.

It is clear, then, that a universalistic model of childhood, while on the one hand offering children a recognised status, can, on the other, work against children's best interests. It can also deny them the opportunity to exercise their rights and to demonstrate their practical and everyday competence in matters of personal concern to them. This is clearly demonstrated by, for example, the case of *Re E* referred to above. On achieving his 18th birthday, this young man immediately exercised his right as an adult to refuse treatment, and died. As Freeman pointedly observes, 'no one can seriously believe that there is a real distinction ... between someone of 18 years and a day and someone of 17 years and 364 days' (Freeman 1992: 35). His death at 18 years not only acted as a salutary reminder of his long-term commitment to his faith but also that this was a commitment that he had made as a *child*. Similarly, Bluebond-Langner's (1978) now classic study of young children with cancer in the USA revealed very clearly that children who are chronically ill and dying are, as far as it can be possible to ascertain, fully aware of the distress that their death will bring to their family.

Such evidence calls into question the concerns raised by Ward J. about children's competence and suggests that children can exercise competence in dealing with their own health care and treatment. This confirms the suspicion that their oft assumed 'inability' is, in large part, a function of adult expectations (and legal judgements) about what children in general *should* be able to do – rather than what children, on an individual basis *are* able to do. In this sense, then, although the *Gillick* case offers an example of the way in which ideas of childhood can be changed through the actions of children – in this instance, just one child – continued adult resistance to that change tempers the impact it has, in practice, for children.

Alderson's (1993) UK research into children's consent to surgery illustrates well this interrelationship between children's agency and adult constructions of their competence, as she reveals the complex and varied social contexts within which children of different ages are facilitated or hindered in giving their consent to surgical procedures. In her study this occurred through different interpretations being made by adults – parents and medical staff – of the legal requirement that children be of 'sufficient understanding to make an informed decision' (Children Act 1989, Part V, s. 43 (8)). In some instances, parents and medical staff were willing to listen to what children had to say about their feelings with respect to prospective leg-lengthening surgery and respected these in the process of decision-making. In other cases, however, children's views were given but little credence, the assumption being that young children are not able to make informed and competent choices. Citing the remarks made by one surgeon, Alderson depicts the pitfalls of assuming a singular age-based model of children's competence that ignores social experience:

> One surgeon thought, "The variation is absolutely enormous. I know lots of adults who can't make decisions". He had "come across a couple of children who are able to make decisions remarkably well" at 8 years, and thought some 13-year-olds were "much more sensible than their parents." He repeated the terms "manage" and "deal with", referring to the child's emotional maturity to cope with hard concepts: "If they

ask an appropriate question leading on from the information, I think
you can assume that you are able to communicate something they've
taken in, and understood and can deal with."

(1993: 154)

As Alderson concludes

competence is more influenced by the social context and the child's
experience than by innate ability and to respect children means we
must not think in sharp dichotomies of wise adult/immature child,
infallible doctor/ignorant patient, but to see wisdom and uncertainty
shared among people of varying ages and experience.

(1993: 158)

Health and the special needs of children

If, as argued above, the particular health needs of children are
not being fully met by current health policies, what might a more
child-centred health policy in England look like? First, as indicated
above, it would be able to engage with the issues that children
identify for themselves as being important, as well as those that
adults identify for them; and second, it would involve children
directly in decision-making. Although such a perspective pervades,
as noted, current government thinking concerning children and
citizenship, the extent to which this will be realisable in the field
of health, given its rocky path so far in the educational sphere,
remains in doubt. In this final section, then, we consider this issue
in more detail through looking at a relatively neglected area of
child health – children with mental health or behavioural problems
of different kinds – and the ways in which policy might be made
sensitive to the needs children have, as expressed and articulated
by children themselves.

For example, in recent years there has been considerable
controversy over the treatment of the condition Attention Deficit/
Hyperactivity Disorder (AD/HD), which manifests itself in 'problems' that are

characterized by an apparent inability to conform to social and pro-
cedural rules, in the home and the school; extreme difficulty in maintaining effort and interest in school and leisure activities, particularly
those involving sustained attention and problems of over-activity

and impulse control that make the individual appear self centred and antisocial.

(Cooper 2001: 392)

Notwithstanding the importance of the cultural context in the contemporary framing of such behaviour as especially 'problematic' – the condition itself has a clinical history which can be traced back at least 200 years – children diagnosed with AD/HD are often treated with the controversial drug, Ritalin. This works to reduce their hyperactivity, thereby 'normalising' their behaviour to fit into the demands of contemporary life at school and at home. It is worth noting, therefore, that the use of Ritalin is increasing at an astonishing rate, with prescriptions escalating by an estimated 270 per cent between 1996 and 1997 to over 90,000 (NACRO 1999: 17).

Other estimates that nearly 200,000 children are on psychiatric medication have fuelled heated debate over whether such treatment is 'necessary' or whether 'naughty children' are simply being rendered quiet and passive, through the use of medication (*The Guardian*, 11 April 2000). But what do children themselves make of it? Whilst there is little research into children's own experiences of such treatment, what little there is suggests that,

> where [children] had a more contextualised view, which related the condition to the demands of schooling, and their own motivations, there was much more of a sense of the students being 'in charge' of the condition and seeking medication, for example, as a tool for helping them achieve their goals.'

(Cooper 2001: 393)

As Cooper argues, involving children themselves more closely in dialogue about AD/HD, rather than excluding them from it, repositions children as active agents and as 'consumers' of health care who can assist in determining, with adults, the nature of their own treatment and its outcomes.

Other psychological problems that children have may, however, go unrecognised by adults or may not be seen as warranting attention or immediate concern, for one important consequence of the dominant model of 'the child', which positions children as innocent, care-free and safe inside the garden of childhood, is that the existence of mental health and psychological problems amongst children seems counterintuitive. If childhood is supposed to be

happy, safe and protected (Ennew 1986), it is difficult to acknowledge the fact that many children are not only unhappy but also
experiencing a range of mental health problems, from mild anxiety
through to psychoses. A recent report by the *Young Minds* organisation reveals 'a huge increase in recent years in the number of
children, as young as four, seeking treatment for severe mental
health problems' (*The Observer*, 29 October 2000). Given that suicide
counts for one-fifth of all deaths of young people (Bradshaw 2002),
listening to what children say about their worries and concerns,
rather than assuming that because they are children they do not
have them or that their problems are only be minor, might produce
better policies – and better health.

A good example of the impact of such an approach is the
changes in *adult* attitudes towards bullying that have taken place
over recent years. It is now recognised that, for children, bullying
can have severe psychological consequences. In the past, however,
adults simply repeated to children the aphorism 'sticks and stones
can break your bones but names can never hurt you', leaving
bullying unremarked by adults as a 'problem' faced by children.
That this old adage has now finally been laid to rest is, we suggest,
a direct consequence of children's own voices and views on bullying finally receiving attention from the adult world. Bullying at
school has become recognised as the problem for children that it
is – for example, Bullying on-line, an internet site launched in
April 1991 that offers advice to children and their parents,
received around 3700 e-mails during its first year. Recognition
of this children's problem as a problem means that schools in
England are now required, by law, to have anti-bullying policies
and in October 2000, a 17-year-old school boy successfully sued
his LEA for their failure to protect him from bullying (*The Guardian*,
31 October 2000).

Other issues such as problems in forming friendships and
social relationships, family breakdown, bereavement, and exam
and testing overload are all seen as sources of stress and anxiety by
children themselves and are thus likely to create mental health
problems (Armstrong *et al.* 2000). However, attempts to ameliorate
these stressors have to be carried out in ways in which young
people have confidence:

> young people wanted adults to provide information about issues that
> worried them, such as sex, drugs and careers. However, the quality of

information, and hence the expertise of the adult providing it, was seen as crucial if young people were to take any notice of what they were told.

(Armstrong *et al.* 2000: 67)

This may also explain the success of the charity *Childline*, which provides confidential telephone advice and support service for children about matters which concern them. Originally set up to provide a help line for children suffering from sexual and physical abuse, *Childline* now deals with a wide range of other issues that children themselves are identifying as problems.

In contrast to developments such as these, which have arisen in response to children identifying their own health care needs, for those children with 'special needs' the tendency has been, however, to develop policies that are driven more by adult agendas concerning what those needs might be. These have often been underpinned by research that, as Priestly (1998) has argued, is characterised by an over-preoccupation with the nature of the impairment, with the special vulnerability of these children and with the kinds of services and institutional arrangements that are available for their care and support. In his view, such an approach works to generalise children with special needs within a pathological model of childhood that compounds their double marginalisation, as 'disabled children'.

When, however, disabled children themselves are asked about their needs, research suggests that these needs do not seem very different from those of other children:

'disabled children's aspirations about future employment and family life seem to reflect those of non-disabled children' and are more a reflection of their gender and socio-economic backgrounds than their status as children with disabilities.

(Priestley 1998: 217)

As Petrie and Poland argue, in their evaluation of play services for disabled children, what these services offer, despite many shortcomings in the level and adequacy of provision, is the chance for disabled children to experience levels of 'self-realisation not easily available in other settings' (1998: 293).

However, the policies that underpin provision of such play services are still often couched in adult-centred terms, seen as offering parents 'child care' or 'respite' from the hard work of looking after disabled children. As Petrie and Poland show, however, although this is one aspect of the service which parents do appreciate, what parents also gain from play services are the 'advantages for their children which are the child's of right: the right to play, recreation, art and cultural activities' as set out in the UNCRC, Articles 18 and 31 (1998: 294). What such research shows, therefore, is that the 'special needs' of a disabled child are not necessarily special or different from those of other children. Facilitating this understanding in practice would make health policies for children with special needs properly child-centred. As Petrie and Poland conclude, play services for disabled children,

> are services which have the potential, in the words of the Children Act, to 'put children first'. Yet this potential will not be fully realised until public policy ensures that all services provide the standards of care which disabled children require.
>
> (1998: 294)

Conclusion

This chapter has explored the ways in which particular health policies have contributed to the cultural politics of contemporary English childhood and therefore also to the ways in which children's health experiences and encounters take place. As described, despite current government rhetoric and a more communitarian approach that encourages people to take responsibilities and decisions for themselves, all too often the failure to deliver truly child-centred health policies has been because of a failure to recognise and give weight to a child's standpoint. Identified by Alanen, this means recognising 'the generational structures within which childhood as a social position is daily produced and lived' (Alanen 2001:131) and also taking note of the agency that children can – or cannot – exercise from that position.

In the area of health policies, therefore, it would seem that the government is more concerned about child health with respect to the structural position of children as the next adult generation, rather than what this might mean for the current health status of children as actors and agents in their own right. Thus, for example, while strong emphasis is currently being placed on combating childhood obesity as a health problem, since childhood patterns of eating are said to be highly predictive of later adult behaviour, relatively little attention is given to the health matters that children themselves identify as being of most concern to them – for example, mental or sexual health. However, given the prevailing cultural politics of childhood, such issues are likely to be ignored since dominant discourses of happy and innocent childhood tend to obscure children's potential to experience such problems.

Even if a 'child' stand point *were* to be adopted, however, health policies may, nonetheless, still fail to address health issues in ways that are appropriate for children and young people – witness, for example, the increase, rather than decrease, in drinking, smoking and drug taking amongst young people and the failure to reduce teenage pregnancy rates, despite all of these being targeted through health education campaigns. All of these are health-related behaviours over which children themselves have most control in terms of the exercise of their agency. It is ironic, therefore, that it is precisely through children's exercise of their agency in these more 'adult' areas of social action that their subsequent health status as adults may also be adversely affected. Such are some of the paradoxes of a cultural politics of childhood.

Notes

1 The emergence of a 'standardized' child in the sphere of health was matched, as Hendrick (1997a) notes, by the appearance of the 'schooled' child as part of the creation of a 'national childhood', a political act that disguised the inequalities and differences in social experiences that existed between children.

2 Such conceptual slippages between 'children' and 'the child' are, as Chapter 1 suggested, a critical aspect of the cultural politics of childhood, one way in which children are separated out as a group apart.

3 However, it could also be argued that were children's accidents always treated by a General Practitioner (GP), known to the family, then better watch could be kept on repeated non-accidental injuries to children, and children's rights might be better protected. Adequate funding is the issue here.

4 If a child is sixteen or seventeen competence is presumed, until proved otherwise, in the same way as it is for adults.

CHAPTER 7

Crime

Having considered in Chapters 5 and 6 the way in which the cultural politics of childhood is reflected in the production and reproduction of childhood in the key spheres of education and health, we now wish to consider recent developments in what appears to be, in the UK at least, the almost axiomatic relationship between children, childhood and crime. This issue is not, at first sight, as pervasive in its reach as either education or health, which are by definition issues for *all* children. It is, however, the case that the law as it relates to the criminal activities of *some* children applies potentially to *all* children and young people. Moreover it is also the case that there is a widespread view, amongst both policy-makers and adults more generally, that there *is* a clear relationship between the developmental/social space of childhood and crime such that it requires special measures that is, different from those deemed to be necessary for adults to deal with it.

As we argued in Chapter 3, following the work of Pearson (1983), the criminal behaviour of children, especially the younger they are, has generated particular concerns throughout recent centuries. This is partly because the rebelliousness and non-conformity of the young has long been seen as representing a threat to the hegemony of the adult order and values, a threat which requires special measures in order to deal with it. In addition, however, the offending behaviour of the young challenges not only the power and authority of the adult generation to control children but also valued and often idealised notions of childhood. It is interesting to pause, in passing, and consider that if we talk not of criminals but of child or young *offenders*, it raises the question of what else it might be they offend against other than the criminal law. Our answer would be that their offence is also against hegemonic adult perceptions of what childhood and children are. Part of these is how they should behave and in this sense, their offending behaviour is also offensive to adults. Thus, as well as the identification of the particular needs of children as a corollary to the emergence of childhood as a separate social status, we have also seen the increasing identification of crime as being a particular problem associated with childhood.

As Pearson observes,

> The fact that young people are over-represented in the criminal statistics is repeatedly rediscovered in each successive wave of concern as a particularly 'new' and shocking feature of the problem.
>
> (Pearson 1983: 209)

In short, the way in which adults respond to the crimes of the young is yet another component of the cultural politics of childhood that helps us to understand how childhood is produced and reproduced. Indeed, as Pearson argues, it is a phenomenon that belongs 'within the idiom of continuity' rather than that of change (Pearson 1983: 212). However, Pearson also poses an important question about the predominance of young people in the criminal statistics and, it has to be said, in discourses of law and (dis)order: he asks – 'is it because young people are more uncontrollable? Or is it that the lives of young people are subject to more public regulation', which biases the crime statistics towards the young?

We shall argue in this chapter that the more significant consideration in understanding this phenomenon, whether in the UK or elsewhere, is what the rebellious child represents – viz. a symbolic challenge to the adult status quo and to the *ideology* of childhood, made possible by children's looser attachment to the values and social institutions of adulthood, rather than a serious threat to law and order or to social democracy, for it is this that results in the more extensive regulation of childhood rather than their offending behaviour *per se*.

Such regulation is therefore not, in the final analysis, aimed at buttressing cultural and social systems threatened by incipient breakdown and anarchy. Rather its universal role in the cultural politics of childhood, regardless of social and cultural context and local diversity, is to reassure adults of the rectitude and continuity of their world views and to buttress their ideologies of childhood. This may vary in its components, both historically and culturally, and may include, *inter alia*, idealised images of childhood as a time of innocence, naïvety, youthful high spirits, learning, or apprenticeship for adulthood. Ultimately, however, it hinges upon the denial or suppression of the agency of children, the denial of the importance of their ideas, and the reinforcement of their dependence on adults. Such processes and perspectives are fundamental to the developmental paradigm that Woodhead describes as 'a regulative device that diminishes the status of children's learning and thinking' (1999: 12), reinforcing the 'asymmetrical power relationships between adults and children, teachers and learners' (10).

As we have argued elsewhere (James and James 2001a), in recent years children in the UK have become increasingly the subjects of other regulatory devices, both overt and covert, reflecting the perceived crisis in childhood (Scraton 1997; Wyness 2000). This 'crisis', reflected across a variety of social, legal and political arenas, is one in which children are depicted as spiralling out of control, although as Scraton and Wyness both observe, it is debatable whether or not such a 'crisis' *is* actually taking place. None the less, however, a consequence of this perceived crisis has been to increase adults' concerns and to increase the monitoring and regulation of children's lives. As a result, the opportunities children and young people have to be relatively free from adult control have been greatly reduced (Valentine 1996) and contemporary moral discourses that construe society as being 'at risk' from children or, conversely, children as 'at risk' from society (Scott *et al.* 1998) are continuing to tighten the net of social control on children's lives.

Crime, youth justice and the community

As a result of growing concern about the apparently increasing lawlessness of children, and following the remarks of the judge in the Bulger trial, James and Jenks argued that 'the government's response to the growing moral panic about the nation's children has been to establish a set of controls upon children's activities' (1996: 327). The lead set by the Conservatives in this regard during the 80s and early 90s seems to have been eagerly taken up by New Labour as part of its pursuit of a 'third way' in politics for, as Crawford observes,

> crime, as a compelling symbol of lost community, has a particularly salient place in communitarianism. The perceived decline of a 'sense of community' and the fracturing of actual communal institutions in

the late twentieth century, are associated in the minds of communitarians with a crisis of social regulation.

(1999: 194)

Since youth crime in particular had become an increasingly prominent political issue in the latter part of the 20th century, the manifesto commitments made by New Labour in relation to crime were both clear and predictable: a fast-track punishment for persistent young offenders; a crackdown on petty crimes and neighbourhood disorder (mostly attributable to children and young people); crime prevention (targeted often at the kinds of crimes committed by children and young people in the more deprived areas); and more police officers on the beat (deployed in these same areas as part of the efficient use of resources in the pursuit of crime prevention strategies and targets). Both implicitly and explicitly, therefore, children and young people were the primary targets of New Labour's crime reductions policies aimed at being tough on crime – indeed, they were seen as being one of the principal causes of the crime problem.

The first expression of these policies in legislation was the 1998 Crime and Disorder Act. By virtue of its broader focus on community safety, however, this effectively broadened the law and order debate by recognising:

> that 'social harm' and victimisation can come about as a result of non-criminal as well as criminal activities ... Labour's effective endorsement of the principle of *social crime prevention* ... places emphasis on early intervention and support for young persons at risk of future or further offending (hence the focus on youth offender teams and the plethora of measures on youth justice) and the importance of families and communities as networks of social control.
>
> (Charman and Savage 1999: 202 – emphasis in original)

As a consequence of such an approach, however, the range of behaviours that need to be controlled is extended to include potentially a much wider range of behaviours that many children and young people engage in that are defined by adults as 'anti-social', particular in areas of poor housing where there is multiple deprivation. What such an approach also reveals, however, is that the concern about victims is primarily a concern about *adult* victims and yet, ironically, children and young people are more likely to be victims of high volume crimes such as theft from the person, assault ... [and] 95% of crimes committed against children and young people are not reported.

(Hall 2001: 8)

The victimisation of children, however, receives little or no attention in crime reduction strategies.

The Crime and Disorder Act 1998 also made explicit the perceived links between crime, education, and parenting, for as the Home Office guidance on the Act makes clear, 'tackling youth crime is likely to require action to deal with some of the underlying causes of youth offending, such as truancy and school exclusions' (Home Office 1998: para. 2.13). The provisions of the Crime and Disorder Act 1998 – for example, the anti-social behaviour order (s. 1), parenting programmes made available through parenting orders (s. 8) (or voluntary attendance on such programmes as part of a less formal mechanism for dealing with offending behaviour) – provide clear evidence of an extension of explicit control over children and childhood.

They also represent, however, the drive to reassert adult and parental responsibility for and authority over children in the face of the challenge of youth crime. Parents who fail to exercise control over their children in effect allow them degrees of freedom and agency that are not normally permitted. Thus, in order to reestablish the 'proper' – that is, asymmetrical – power relationships between adults and children, parents who fail in this respect are defined, through mechanisms such as parenting orders and parenting programmes, as dysfunctional or inadequate and in need of training – in effect, they are seen as needing resocialisation. Warburton (2001) argues that recent evidence (Policy Research Bureau 2001) strongly suggests that many parents welcome assistance with the far from easy task of parenting and that many parents living in poor environments found that they experienced parenting as difficult and had a number of significant anxieties about their role. In particular, he argues that:

they are not sure what constitutes 'normal' behaviour for children and young people, they worry about the right approach to discipline and have particular concerns about coping with teenagers.

(Warburton 2001: 11)

Whilst such findings may provide some welcome reassurance in relation to any libertarian concerns raised by such interventions, it highlights yet again the thrall that developmental theory holds over children and the normative straitjacket that dominates discourses about childhood. Whilst this influence is restrictive enough in terms of their biological and psychological development, its possible extension to children's behaviour must be cause for serious concern. In particular, we should ask who will be the arbiter of children's normalcy and whose criteria will be used?

As we have argued elsewhere (James and James 2001a), other more subtle changes have occurred recently that signify an important shift of emphasis in the construction of the cultural politics of childhood in the UK. For many years, the Department of State with responsibility for children's issues (other than education and social security) was the Department of Health, a structural/political location that clearly linked children and childhood with health and welfare discourses that implicitly acknowledged the special developmental needs of children. Apart from the significant changes it made to the measures available for the legal and social control of youth crime, the Crime and Disorder Act 1998 marked a shift of emphasis in terms of Ministerial responsibility in relation to such issues – away from the Department of Health and towards the Home Office.

The links that had been established in the political psyche between youth crime and the family were also reflected in the fact that the Ministerial Group on the Family – which produced the recent Green Paper, *Supporting Families* (Ministerial Group on the Family 1999), in which considerable prominence was given to the provisions of the Crime and Disorder Act 1998 – was chaired by the Home Secretary. In addition, in 1999 it was the Home Office that allocated over £1 million out of its Family Support Grant, established in 1998, to target services and projects that help parents cope with their teenagers.

The Home Office was also instrumental in the recent establishment of the National Family and Parenting Institute that, with its intention of establishing what it calls the 'millennial family', speaks volumes about the government's vision for a 'third way'. With its implied overtones of future prosperity, happiness and good governance, it is through better parenting and the reconstruction of 'the family' that the future of children, and by implication 'proper' childhood, can be ensured. As Jenks notes:

the modern family enabled the modern State to invest in 'futures'. The ideology of care both lubricated and legitimised the investment of economic and cultural capital in the 'promise' of childhood. Childhood is transformed into a form of human capital which through modernity has been dedicated to futures.

(1996b: 15)

The Institute will be working closely with, amongst others, the Trust for the Study of Adolescents. This trust, which currently has an active research programme within secondary schools, is also providing advice and support for those responsible for developing parenting programmes in response to the requirements of the Crime and Disorder Act 1998. The development of the latter is being supported to the tune of over £3.9 million of grants from the Development Fund of the Youth Justice Board to 'encourage the development of programmes for parents of children at risk of offending and parents of young offenders, so that parents will be involved in helping their children towards a crime-free life' (Home Office Press Release 323/99, 15 October 1999). Any consideration of children's own views, responses and contribution to the parenting relationship is noticeably absent from these initiatives (James 1999).

A more obvious social control mechanism is the introduction of child safety orders and local child curfew schemes (Crime and Disorder Act 1998, s.14), both of which can be aimed at children younger than 10 who are not under the supervision of a 'responsible adult' between 9 p.m. and 6 a.m. Such schemes have a distinctively communitarian flavour. When first introduced, they were to be employed only after discussion with the police and the local community, this support being regarded as essential to the success of such schemes. Although few Local Authorities have yet introduced a local child curfew and very few anti-social behaviour orders have so far been made, it is their availability which is significant: first, it registers an increase in the breadth and depth of the surveillance of childhood or, more correctly, particular types of childhood; second, it signifies the extension of a pseudo-parental responsibility to the community as a whole, outwith the family; and third, it works to deny children's autonomy and their right to be responsible and govern their own behaviour.

However, a recent study of a pilot curfew scheme in Scotland concluded that rather than help to create the communitarian vision of a safer, revitalised community, the initiative had in fact elevated the "risk consciousness" of local people; reduced the level of contact between different sections of the community; and helped entrench divisions that already existed ... further, by increasing the authority of the police – and their level of activities within this community – there is a danger that rather than creating a "responsible" community, local people will hand over their ownership and responsibility for the behaviour of local young people, to the police.

(Waiton 2001: 145)

The price paid for this initiative was high: a significant increase in the restrictions placed on primary school children and their opportunities to develop their independence; more authoritarian policing based on actions before any offence has been committed; the problematising of peer relationships between young people themselves (by increasing the suspicion of young people towards peers who are not known); and a decline in the contact between generations.

In spite of such evidence, the Criminal Justice and Police Act 2001 (s. 48 and 49) recently increased the upper age limit for child curfews from 10 to 15 and increased the powers of the police to apply for such orders. In a transparent attempt to disguise this extension of social control as a measure aimed at protecting and enhancing the welfare of children, the responsible Home Office Minister, Beverley Hughes, argued that:

Extending the age range will ... provide better protection for communities as well as young people themselves [and that] by extending child curfew orders to include children up to the age of 15, police and local authorities are also better able to protect them from the risks of being unaccompanied on the streets at night; from adults such as drug dealers or pimps, or older peers encouraging them into criminal activities.

(Home Office News Release 01/08/2001)

In the same year, electronically monitored curfew orders were made available to the Youth Courts for use with specified juvenile offenders, whilst it was also reported (*The Times*, 8 October 2000) that the Government has announced plans to grant the police the power to impose *blanket* curfews on areas according to postcode. The especial significance of these proposals is that *innocent* children will also be confined to their homes during specified hours merely because they live in a particular area. If a child breaches such an order, parents will face fines of up to £1000 with the ultimate penalty of imprisonment and the placing of their children in care. It is hard to conceive of a more graphic illustration of policies designed to extend and reinforce the control of adults over children and to deny their citizenship.

The 1998 Crime and Disorder Act also represented a sea-change in terms of the links that have been created between the police and local authorities in relation to community safety. As Innes has argued in a recent review of the development of zero tolerance policing in Britain and America,

> the fundamental flaw with making policing overly accountable to community demands, is that it can all too easily become a tool for the expression of the 'tyranny of the majority', where policing strategies are used to target stigmatised, unpopular minority groups.
>
> (Innes 1999: 407)

Through such devices then, it might be suggested that a wedge is also being driven between those children inhabiting 'correct' as opposed to 'incorrect' childhoods (cf. Ennew 1986: 22).

Other schemes, such as the use of volunteer mentors (predominantly white females), drawn from the community, to change problem behaviour in primary school children (Roberts and Singh 1999) also cross the school/community divide. Recommended by the Audit Commission (para. 37, 1996), such schemes aim to target selected children in order to have the maximum impact on reducing the likelihood of subsequent criminal behaviour. It is worth noting in passing that the Connexions Strategy envisages a major expansion of the use of the National Mentoring Network (DfEE 2000: para. 2.7) since mentors will have an important role within the new service.

The Youth Justice and Criminal Evidence Act 1999 continues the process of reforming the youth justice system that was started by the Crime and Disorder Act, 1998, by introducing the power to refer offenders to a youth panel. Unless the court thinks an absolute discharge or custody are appropriate, young offenders aged between 10 and 17 appearing before the court for the first time and who plead guilty will be referred to a youth panel made up of people recruited from the local community who have an interest or expertise in dealing with young people and including a member from the local Youth Offending Team.

The task of the panel will be to agree to a contract with the young person and their family aimed at tackling their offending behaviour and its causes, setting out clear requirements that they will have to fulfil. These might include, *inter alia*, making an apology or reparation to their victim, complying with arrangements that have been made for their education, carrying out community work, refraining from doing certain things or going to certain places, and/or taking part in family counselling or drug rehabilitation, all with the aim of achieving their reintegration into the law-abiding community. It is perhaps worth reiterating the fact that such measures can be applied to children as young as 10 for a first offence.

The funding role of the Home Office in such developments is also not without significance. As the Audit Commission, in its review of youth justice, recommended, 'all public services should co-operate with institutions that socialise young people – such as families, schools, religious institutions and community organisations – to ensure that children *have the opportunity to become* responsible and capable citizens' (para. 45, 1996 – emphasis added). It also identified local government as providing the necessary structure in which such a co-ordinated policy could be delivered. Significantly, statements such as this also provide a clear indication of the denial of the citizenship of children, a point we shall return to later in this chapter.

As part of these recent developments, we should also not lose sight of the significance of the creation of multi-disciplinary Youth Offending Teams and the Youth Justice Board for England and Wales, which are ultimately responsible to the Home Office and the Home Secretary. As Goldson observes, these originally saw the light of day as Youth Justice Teams but

> the substitution of the term justice by offending signals a conceptual shift within which children in trouble are increasingly regarded, and thus treated, as "offenders" first and "children" second.

> (Goldson 2001: 5)

For much of the 20th century, responsibility for providing support and services for juvenile offenders was located largely within the framework of local authority social service provision, providing clear practical and symbolic links between services for juvenile offenders and mainstream child-welfare services. The creation of Youth Offending Teams, managed under the umbrella of multi-agency steering groups as part of local 'crime and disorder reduction' and 'community safety' strategies has fundamentally changed such linkages, however. As a consequence, issues to do with children and young people in trouble have been effectively separated from concerns about child welfare and children's rights, which have traditionally been a part of child care policies and practices. The main point of reference for the youth justice system now therefore is the criminal justice system rather than the child welfare system, finally breaching the connections forged so carefully in the 1960s between not only welfare services for *all* children but also between the values and ethos of child welfare provisions and those for juvenile offenders. It is arguable that this development is but another facet of one of the main tenets of New Labour's social policies – that welfare dependency is both a cause and a consequence of crime.

The increasing emphasis on multi-agency initiatives such as these, together with the drive for increased consultation, also reflects the government's agenda for reforming local democracy and its desire that all sections of the community should be involved in such consultations including, *inter alia*, '[r]elevant hard-to-reach groups [such as] young men [and] children' (Home Office 1998: para. 3.52). Indeed, the Home Office argued that 'it will be essential to involve young people as part of the solution to local crime and disorder issues, not just part of the problem' (Home Office 1998: Executive Summary). Such consultation is part of a wider process 'whose ultimate aim is to maximise community control and to involve the community in the delivery of community safety' (NACRO, 1999a: 8 – emphasis added).

Recent research suggests that a significant proportion of young people in some areas may well be interested in such consultation and involvement but that there is a degree of cynicism on the part of some who believed that even where consultation does take place, it will make little difference. More importantly, there was some evidence that it is the most cynical who are the least likely to seek involvement in such consultation processes, compounding the problem of achieving the effective involvement of hard to reach groups (Liddle *et al.* 2001). Other evidence suggests that there remains much to be done in this area and that with one or two exceptions, such as the Hastings Young Person's Council (NACRO 1999a: 5) and a small number of school-based schemes

(Home Office 1998), '[e]fforts to engage young people as part of the community rather than as a problem to be dealt with by the community were less in evidence' (NACRO 1999b: 6).

Central to these ideas, however, is the intention that all such initiatives should be targeted on deprived communities with high crime rates. As Crawford argues, 'the need to restore a "sense of community" around issues of crime and its control, therefore, implies an assumption that high crime areas lack sufficient "community"' (1999: 199). It is important to note in addition that, to the extent that the focus is on the prevention of offending and not just *re*offending, the focus for this communitarian initiative is upon children and young people as an *entire* social category, and not just young offenders. Such a policy defines young people as a threat that must be controlled and yet tries to encourage them to accept their responsibilities to the community while not necessarily acknowledging their rights (Scraton 1997). As James and Jenks observe, 'such public accountability for children represents a revival of the concepts of "the child" as public property taking us back to the pragmatic origins of mass education, the economic policy of "human capital" and the educational ideology of vocationalism' (1996: 327–28).

Such reactions and concepts are not easy to reconcile with a political philosophy that espouses the need to link responsibilities with rights, authority with democracy unless, of course, it is the case that children and young people are not seen as being members of the community and therefore as having only responsibilities and no rights, and only the need to conform and to obey authority, rather than to participate democratically (Roche 1996b).

Children in court and in custody

The ambiguous attitude of adults towards children in the UK is perhaps nowhere better reflected than in how we respond to children who offend, since they elicit an entirely different and often highly punitive response that for many involves temporary removal from the community. Such punitive responses are, as we have suggested above, because children who break the law also offend against hegemonic adult perceptions of what childhood is and how children should behave. In this sense, children and women are in a similar position in terms of the criminal law since it is widely accepted that female offenders are also seen to be

guilty of offending against similarly idealised images of woman-
hood. As Hudson observes,

> by and large the criminal law is imposed by whites on blacks; by the
> advantaged classes on the disadvantaged; by the elderly on the young,
> and by men on women.

(Hudson 1987: 95)

When the idealised images of childhood are shattered by the
actions of children themselves, the protective mantle of adult care
that normally provides protection and nurture, as a response to
the special needs of children, is suddenly set aside. It took the
judgements of the European Court of Human Rights in T *v.* UK
and V *v.* UK 'the cases brought by John Thompson and Robert
Venables, the killers of James Bulger' to determine that the trial of
these two young boys in an adult Crown Court had been inappro-
priate and for the Lord Chief Justice to issue, in February 2000,
a Practice Direction (*Trial of children and young persons in the Crown
Court*). In this, he makes clear that the purpose of a trial is not
to expose the young defendant to avoidable intimidation, humili-
ation or distress; that regard must be had for the welfare of the
young defendant; and that all possible steps should be taken
to ensure that a young defendant is able to understand and participate in the proceedings.

In spite of this, however, the Practice Direction allows judges
considerable discretion in relation to how far trial proceedings
should be modified to take account of such considerations when a
juvenile is tried jointly with an adult, and it does not apply to com-
mittal proceedings or appeals. The evidence thus far is that while
some courts have embraced the spirit and the letter of the practice
direction, 'others have merely paid lip service to it or even shown
a flagrant disregard for it. In general, the older the defendant, the
less willing the courts seem to be to modify the trial process'
(Butcher 2000: 16).

Of more fundamental significance and importance, however, is
the fact that in spite of the recommendation of the UN Committee
commenting on the first UK response to the UN Convention on
the Rights of the Child that 'serious consideration' should be given to
raising the age of criminal responsibility throughout the areas of
the United Kingdom (DOH 1999: Appendix A, para. 36), the Crime
and Disorder Act 1998 went in the opposite direction. Perversely,

it abolished the limited protection that the long-established presumption of *doli incapax* (which required the prosecution to prove that a child being prosecuted for an alleged offence knew what s/he was doing was wrong) gave to children between the ages of 10 and 14. This change in effect reduced the age of criminal responsibility to the age of 10, treating children of this age as if they were the same as adults in terms of their competence and maturity in the eyes of the criminal law. It also undermines Article 40(3) of the UNCRC which requires signatories to promote the establishment of laws, procedures, authorities and institutions specifically applicable to children.

As a result, at 10 in England and Wales and 8 in Scotland, the UK has one of the lowest ages of criminal responsibility in Europe. In France, a child under 13 is presumed to be incapable of crime and cannot be prosecuted; in Germany the equivalent age is 14, as it is in Italy; in Norway, Sweden and Denmark, the age is 15 whilst in Spain and Belgium, the age is 16 (Johnston 1995).

This retrograde step offers a clear reflection of the changing political context in which criminal justice policy in relation to child and young offenders is currently being formulated and the changing attitudes that underpin this. It also highlights starkly the ambiguity of adult attitudes toward children for, as Piper (2000) has pointed out, whilst children as young as 10 are now deemed to be as capable of forming criminal intent as adults, in proceedings under the Children Act 1989, children under the age of 16 are viewed legally as subjects with a 'disability', whose wishes and feelings may be marginalised, ignored or over-ruled as a consequence.

In the name of crime reduction and curbing the offending behaviour of children and young people, the UK imprisons more children and young people than almost any other country in Western Europe. In 1998, for example, 3.6 per cent of the prison population in England and Wales were under 18 years of age, making them 7th out of the 40 countries in relation to which the Council of Europe produces figures, and only behind countries such as Andorra, Albania, Romania and Estonia (Council of Europe, Penological Information Bulletin No., 22, 2000 – Table 2: 62).

In the UK, the punitive attitude towards young offenders and in particular those of minority ethnicity, is also evident not only in the number of children who are given custodial sentences but also in how they are often treated once in custody (Goldson and Peters

2000). Once in prison, their particular needs are also often over-looked in the context of a penal system that continues to struggle to provide even a basic level of care to some of its youngest prison-ers because it is primarily designed to cater for the needs of an adult population. Consequently, child prisoners are often exposed to intolerable conditions. Indeed, in August 2000 the Governor of Feltham Young Offenders Institution, the conditions of which had been described 2 years earlier by the Chief Inspector of Prisons as 'unacceptable in a civilised society', felt he had no option but to resign in protest at the conditions in which he was forced to keep the children and young people in his custody. With over 100 boys locked in graffiti covered cells for up to 22 hours a day, he described the conditions in Feltham as 'more suitable to a Dickens novel than the 21st century' (Day 2000: 15).

Even in institutions where there is less overcrowding and more training facilities are available, prisons in the UK do not provide an education friendly environment. Thus, although young people in prison have a right to education, they are entitled only to 15 hours education a week, compared to the OFSTED recom-mendation that secondary school children should receive 24 hours education a week; internet access is denied to most young people in prison; and many juvenile units in prisons do not offer all of the National Curriculum subjects, including science and modern languages (Atkinson 2000).

This bleak picture was confirmed in a recent study by Atkinson (2001), which found that more than 300 out of over 2000 children in UK prisons at the turn of the century were below school leaving age. Interviews, conducted with over a third of all 15-year-old boys in prison revealed that

> Many boys, not only the most able . . . wanted to learn, to gain qualifi-cations and new skills. But many were unhappy with the education in prison. Some felt the teachers had low expectations of them. Others were unhappy about not being given choices . . . Boys were rarely con-sulted for their views.

> (Atkinson 2001: 8)

In addition, it is sadly the case that many of these children resort to self-harm or even suicide. Between 1989 and 1999, over 30 young people committed suicide in Young Offender Institutions (Goldson and Peters 2000).

As Muncie (2001) has argued, throughout Europe in the 1990s, there was an opening up of juvenile justice with a widespread decline in the use of custodial sanctions. In England and Wales, however, there has been a reversion to custody that is in direct contradiction of the UNCRC, Article 37 of which states that imprisonment for children should only be used as a last resort and then only for the shortest appropriate period of time, while Article 40 requires alternatives to institutional care to be sought to ensure that children are dealt with in accordance with their well-being.

Notwithstanding these provisions, and a recommendation from the UN Committee that 'law reform be pursued in order to ensure that the system of the administration of juvenile justice is child-oriented' (DOH 1999, Appendix A, para. 35), the Government proceeded with the introduction of the Detention and Training Order in early 2000 (which the Crime and Disorder Act 1998 allows to be extended to children as young as 10), as a consequence of which the number of children sent to prison, often for relatively minor and even first-times offences, increased by 10 per cent, presumably because the sentencers were attracted by the supposed training element (Day 2000: 15). As Muncie argues, in terms of how we deal with child and young offenders, 'the human rights of British children are not being upheld' (Muncie 2001: 7).

In spite of this evident enthusiasm for the development of a more punitive approach to dealing with child and young offenders, reconviction rates for those discharged from custody remain high. This therefore begs the question of why such harsh treatment is meted out if it has such little demonstrable impact on youth crime. Faced with such evidence, the rhetoric of evidence-based practice, which also underpins many aspects of New Labour policy, looks highly vulnerable to the demands of political expediency.

Currrent and future developments

The way we have come in the UK in relation to dealing with children who offend is clear and well documented (see, for example, Newburn 2002). The way ahead is, of course, more speculative but recent policy statements have made it fairly clear that the general direction taken by the Labour Government since 1997 will continue. A recent document outlining the Government's vision of the future of the criminal justice system (Home Office 2001a) reasserts the view that confronting crime 'requires concerted action across Government, in local communities, in schools and homes' (para. 3).

There are four key elements of this strategy as it relates to young offenders. The first is the investment of £45 million over 3 years from April 2000 in a new Intensive Supervision and Surveillance Programme to deal with 2500 of the most difficult offenders. Some 50 Youth Offending Teams are to be given grants to work with 50–60 hardcore repeat young offenders. The programme for each offender will last at least 6 months and will combine:

> close surveillance by the police and other agencies with a highly struc-
> tured daily programme tackling the causes of offending. The where-
> abouts of each young offender on the programme will be checked at
> least twice daily with 24 hours a day, seven days a week surveillance
> where this is necessary. Techniques may include electronic tagging,
> voice verification (where a young offender must call in at appointed
> times to confirm their whereabouts), tracking (staff accompanying
> young offenders in person) and intelligence led policing.
>
> (Home Office 2001a: 32)

The second element includes the provision of 400 additional secure training centre places providing intensive supervision and high quality programmes for young people in custody. The third is to provide 30 hours a week of education, training or similar development work for young offenders in custody. And the fourth is to establish a new Referral Order, under which young offenders appearing in court for the first time will be referred to Youth Offender Panels, chaired by a member of the community, with victim involvement where the victim consents.

These elements are based on the view that 'any strategy to tackle persistent offenders must get to grips with persistent young offenders and, just as importantly, *those at risk of graduating into that group*' (Home Office 2001a: para. 2.6 – emphasis added). A new dimension is thereby added to the *protection* of children and the nature of the risks to which they are exposed – the need to protect them against the risk of becoming offenders. This is used to justify the extension of the net of social control to include parents of at-risk children, high crime areas with children out on the streets, and children excluded from or truanting from school, by no means all of whom will necessarily go on to become the persistent young offenders at whom such policies are purportedly aimed.

Such proposals reinforce the relationship that is already evident in recent policy developments between control, the community and custody. Whether this particular heady mixture of intensive, high-tech surveillance, community involvement and a more positive approach to custody will be effective in reducing offending by young people is not the issue for a book such as this. It should be noted in passing, however, that such measures do nothing to address the many structural disadvantages faced by so many young offenders. It is also the case that the history of the provision of training in custody does not hold out much promise either, not least because the introduction of such improvements may well serve to make the use of custody for young offenders more attractive, thereby increasing the number of those given such sentences. This may well in turn, as the recent experience with the introduction of the Detention and Training Order suggests, lead to overcrowding that makes the provision of such enhanced regimes impossible to deliver.

More important for our purposes, however, is what such proposals represent – a continuation of policies aimed at increasing the authority of parents (an authority that does not, as with some other areas of policy such as health, appear to diminish with the increasing age of the child) and at expanding the measures for the control and punishment of young offenders. Policies such as these also serve to reinforce the emerging cultural politics of childhood in the UK in which young people as social category need ever stricter, more intrusive methods of supervision and socialisation before they can be granted the adult status of citizen.

This cultural politics of childhood is, however, very much a product of the same social and political forces that have shaped criminal justice policies in the late-modern UK more generally. As Garland has recently forcefully argued,

> Today's world of crime control and criminal justice . . . was created by a series of adaptive responses to the cultural and criminological conditions of late modernity . . . During the late 1980s and 1990s, the political culture that articulated these social relations . . . was more exclusionary than solidaristic, more committed to social control than to social provision, and more attuned to the private freedoms of the market than the public freedoms of universal citizenship. The institutions of crime control . . . have adjusted their policies, practices

and representations in order to pursue the social objectives and invoke the cultural themes that now dominate the political domain.

(Garland 2001: 193–94)

Nor are such developments unique to the UK. Garland draws exactly the same conclusions in relation to recent developments in the US where, as Melton has argued, there has been

> a steady erosion of the juvenile court in most states through reduction of the court's jurisdiction, increased *transfer* of juveniles to criminal courts, and deemphasis of its historic rehabilitative purpose.

(Melton *et al.* 1997: 417)

Consequently, as Grisso and Schwartz (2000) demonstrate, since the 1980s, most states in the USA have increased the range of charges for which juveniles could be tried as adults in criminal courts, lowered the age at which this could be done and changed their laws to prioritise punishment and punitive training, such as boots camps. Such developments have led to cases such as those reported in *The Independent* (28 July 2001), which covered the case of a Florida boy who killed his teacher when he was aged 13, who was sentenced to 28 years in prison, drawing attention to the way that states such as Florida insist on trying juvenile defendants as adults. The case occurred only months after another young boy was sentenced to life imprisonment without parole for killing a 6-year-old girl when he was aged 12 by carrying out a professional wrestling move on her.

In such a political and social context, criminal justice policy as it relates to children and young people has become increasingly instrumental in two particular senses – one is in terms of the increasing importance attached to managing crime (see Feeley and Simon 1992) and the fear of crime (as opposed simply to punishing offenders) which, as we have argued above and elsewhere (James and James 2001) has extended the boundaries of law enforcement and criminal justice policy well beyond the traditional boundaries of detection and enforcement into the community more generally. The other is that it has become an integral part of the panoply of social policy initiatives and measures that are increasingly being deployed to address late-modern concerns about the decline of civic society more generally and the role of the family as one of the key institutions in bringing about its reassertion.

Similar trends are also evident in Canada, where popular conceptions about increases in youth crime have generated much public attention. In response to criticisms of the criminal justice system and consistent with populist politics centring on law and order issues, successive federal governments have sought to devise appropriate legislative responses 'in response to popular representations of media-fed "moral panics" concerning youth crime' (Campbell *et al*. 2001: 272). As they argue:

> the field of criminal policy encompasses a much broader space of social relations than that which is normally defined as strictly penal. Globalisation and neo-liberal forces, coupled with the difficulty of political systems in containing conflict arising from economic and socio-cultural anxieties, has prompted an increasingly instrumental use of criminal justice systems, both quantitatively and qualitatively, in attempts to alleviate social problems. Examples of this include the criminalisation of mental illness, the criminalisation of deviance in schools and, in particular, increases in the number of youth processed through criminal justice systems [reflecting] recurrent calls from advocacy groups and politicians for harsher penalties for youth, an increased concern for societal protection, [and] an erosion of the notion of special needs of young offenders.
>
> (Campbell *et al*. 2001: 275–76)

Such an analysis undoubtedly sheds important light on similar developments through the Western World. They are, at least in part, a response to the massive impact of 'youth culture' in the latter part of the 20th century as this cohort, expanded by the baby boom of the 1960s, 'occupied a newly extended period between childhood and full-time work and family commitments' (Garland 2001: 80), which has come to be seen as one of the 'threats' to the established social order, to be 'managed' in part by renewing and reiterating the responsibility of parents for raising law-abiding children and their authority to do this.

However, as Garland argues,

> Crime control today does more than simply manage problems of crime and insecurity. It also institutionalizes a set of responses to these problems that are themselves consequential in their social impact. In Britain and America today, 'late modernity' is lived – not just by offenders but by all of us – in a mode that is more than ever defined by institutions of policing, penalty and prevention ... we now find the

imposition of more intensive regimes of regulation, inspection and control and, in the process, our civic culture becomes increasingly less tolerant and inclusive, increasingly less capable of trust.

(194–95)

Such developments seem to us to be particularly evident in the targeting of crime control at children and young people outlined above, a process which, as Garland suggests, both reflects the attitudes and beliefs of adults about children whilst also reducing our trust in them and extending the desire to respond to the percieved threat they are seen to represent.

The emergence of such policies of control are part of a backlash against the 'wave of anxiety about the breakdown of the family, the relaxation of institutional disciplines, and the collapse of informal norms of constraint' (Garland 2001: 195) during the latter part of the 20th century. As a consequence,

a reactionary politics has used this underlying disquiet to create a powerful narrative of moral decline in which *crime* has come to feature – together with teenage pregnancies, single parent families, welfare dependency and drug abuse – as the chief symptom of the social malaise.

(p. 195 – emphasis in original)

It is interesting to note that most, if not all, of the indicators of moral decline listed by Garland are associated primarily, and in some cases exclusively, with young people. Indeed, it might be argued that because of this, the seat of this moral decline is often seen to lie in the youth culture created during the same period. This, as Pearson has argued in relation to earlier historical periods, helps to explain the particular focus of crime control and criminal justice policy on young offenders and the consequent problematisation of childhood and youth as social categories since it is these that are, indeed, the main challenge to the adult status quo.

Conclusion

Crime is a complex problem that is, in one important (sociological) sense, 'normal'. It is a problem, however, that few if any societies feel able to ignore, although how they respond varies according to a range of political, cultural and economic factors. It is therefore reassuring that this complexity is increasingly being recognised, since it offers some prospect that the social responses to the offending of children will not be simplistic. The links between children, education and crime have already been made (NACRO 1998) and are clearly reflected in many of the initiatives discussed in this chapter. Further evidence of this understanding is to be found in the relationship between children, crime and health, since research suggests that there is a complex relationship between crime and the health of children and young people who get into trouble with the law, many of whom have a variety of difficulties associated with poor health (NACRO 1999c). This element is also addressed in part by these same initiatives insofar as they deal with substance misuse as a factor associated with the offending behaviour of a number of children and young people.

That there is a hard core of persistent young offenders who commit the majority of those crimes that are commited by young people, and that this same hard core will in many cases go on to become the hard core of adult offenders is beyond doubt. What is of concern, however, is that in the process of developing multi-faceted, multi-agency approaches to dealing with the complex phenomenon of youth crime, the social space of childhood, the space in which children can experiment, can test out their ideas against those of adults and can 'be' children, unencumbered by adult intervention and surveillance, is being increasingly eroded by policies that demonstrate more than a little intolerance of children, not only in terms of their behaviour but also their difference. As Melton has argued,

> Respect for personhood demands that we err on the side of promotion of autonomy. Therefore the presumption should be in favour of self-determination and those special entitlements that assist youth in developing the capacity for full exercise of autonomy.
>
> (Melton 1989: 157)

The relentless pursuit through social policy and law of universality, normality and conformity in children, rather than the nurturing of their particularity, diversity and difference seems a high price to pay for the criminal careers of a few children and young people that, in the large majority of cases, are short lived and do not continue long beyond the years of childhood into adulthood.

CHAPTER 8

The Family

The family has long occupied an ambiguous status in the eyes of Western governments. It is valued on the one hand as providing the very foundation of social stability, a bulwark against change, and the primary means of social reproduction and, for the last two decades in the UK, increasingly as an area of private life in which intervention by the state should be minimised. It is feared on the other hand precisely because of the inability of the State to control it. It therefore has potential to subvert the State and to undermine social policies and their implementation. As Mount has argued,

> The family...is the ultimate and only consistently subversive organisation. Only the family has continued throughout history and still continues to undermine the State. The family is the enduring enemy of all hierarchies, churches and ideologies.
>
> (1982: 1)

The family is also regarded as subversive in that, as an institution that fosters selfishness and privatism, it 'stands in opposition to the common good and the civic virtues' (Berger and Berger 1983: 185) and thus undermines democracy. As we shall argue, the 'third way' as espoused by Giddens and developed by New Labour is clearly intended to address this concern. Increasingly therefore, as we have demonstrated in the previous chapters in Part II, it is being targeted for its role in the production of not only children's non-conformity in relation to, for example, education, employment, crime and anti-social behaviour, but even in relation to the institution of marriage itself.

Simultaneously, however, the family is also inherently deeply conservative, not only in terms of its universality and its continued existence throughout history but also in terms of its structuring of adult/child relationships as part of the cultural politics of childhood.

Regardless of cultural context, it is within the family that children learn to be adults and that adults use what they learned as children to help their own children to become adults. The family thus has a paradoxical relationship with the State through the mechanisms of law. On the one hand, it resists State intervention and clings tenaciously to its privacy; on the other, it relies on the law as a superordinate mechanism to reinforce the power relationship between adults and children. Thus, for example, the continued use of corporal punishment within families in the UK as part of the exercise of parental authority over children depends on the defence in domestic law of parents' right to use 'reasonable chastisement' in controlling and disciplining their children *and* the Government's willingness to defend this right against pressure from the UN Committee on the Rights of the Child to abolish it.

As we have argued throughout our analysis, therefore, a major challenge in analysing such issues is to understand the influence of law on social policy and social practices, and the relationship between these in the everyday cultural politics of childhood. In this chapter, therefore, we wish to consider, by way of illustration, the extent to which the rhetoric of the UN Convention and the Children Act, 1989 about children's autonomy and agency is being – or, indeed, can be – put into practice in family law and family life in the context of the communitarian-based policies of New Labour.

Such issues will be considered in the context of the emergence for the first time in the UK of a nascent family policy as outlined in the *Supporting Families* Green Paper (Ministerial Group on the Family 1998). Unlike many other countries, although the UK has had policies that affect families, this is the first occasion on which any government has attempted to delineate a comprehensive family policy. Such a development has potentially far-reaching implications for children and childhood and what these signify in terms of the contemporary cultural politics of childhood. They should also be considered in the context of the appointment in 2003 of the first ever Minister for Children and the forthcoming Green Paper, *Children at Risk* which, it is widely anticipated will, when published, outline a reform agenda for the development of a range of services for children for which she will be responsible.

The scope of the *Supporting Families* consultation document is wide, but here we shall explore in detail the issues this raises with reference to the debate surrounding divorce. This acts as a powerful lens, which magnifies political and cultural understandings of the family and the nature of childhood. Through this we intend to shed further light on the relationship between adults and children, and the central role of the law in defining and regulating this.

Emerging family policy in the UK

Supporting Families marks a watershed in terms of the political landscape of the UK, not only in terms of what it symbolises but also what it attempts to provide – a coherent framework for the development of social policies relating to the family. This being the case, as Maclean observes, it is perhaps at first sight

> surprising that the impetus for change has come, with the energetic support of the Prime Minister, from the Home Office, with its responsibility for public order, the police and prison services.
>
> (2002: 65)

rather than from other Departments of State such as the Department of Health, which have had a long-established brief for many aspects of family life and, in particular, the welfare of children in families.

If the Green Paper is understood less as a policy statement in its own right, however, and more as an exercise in 'joined up thinking' by a government that has become increasingly interventionist in family life – at least in relation to the perceived failure of some families to raise their children properly (see Chapter 7) – then the apparently strange provenance of the Green Paper is more readily comprehensible. As Maclean argues,

> It is ... fascinating to see the developing convergence of policy through the different sources of government activity, including penal policy, economic policy and family law reform.
>
> (2002: 66)

The Government's interest in the family therefore springs less from its concern to support the family *per se* and more from its concern to control childhood and children and, in particular, 'from its interest in juvenile delinquency and thus in approaching the family as an ally in the battle for social control' (Maclean 2002: 65). In this sense, however, when it 'fails', the family can also be seen as the enemy, a view that is reflected in Tony Blair's proposals 'to cut child benefit for the parents of unruly youngsters' (*The Independent*, 26 April 2002).

As the Home Secretary states in his Foreword, the Green Paper 'is about the practical support the Government can provide to help parents do the best they can for their children'. (1998: 3) Thus, although it states clearly that 'the interests of children must be paramount' (1998: 4), the emphasis throughout is actually on parents (and ideally *married* parents), especially as a source of stability and in terms of their role in controlling children – 'Parents raise children, and that is how things should remain' (1998: 4). As it goes on to argue,

> Families ... educate us, and teach us right from wrong. Our future depends on their success in bringing up children. That is why we are committed to strengthening family life.
>
> (1998: 4)

Such a perspective makes no acknowledgment of children's agency in the context of family life or even to their greater participation in the emergent democratic family as envisaged by Giddens (1998). Although the document tells us that 'Children must come first' (1998: 52), as Maclean (2002) observes, it is actually parenting that lies at the heart of the policy and that 'an element of social control is also present' (2002: 66). Parents are clearly seen as being a source of stability – in other words, control – as well as of nurture.

The sweep of the Green Paper is therefore broad. It explores the question of how to provide better services and support for parents through the establishment of a national helpline and a National Family and Parenting Institute. It proposes an enhanced role for health visitors who are seen as being well placed to provide advice and support to parents who are 'uncertain about what to expect at each stage of their child's development' (1998: 11, para. 1.29), a proposal that further reinforces the process through which a standard 'national childhood' is created (see Chapters 5 and 6). Additional support services for families with young children are also to be provided through outreach workers employed under the *Sure Start* programme in order to target areas of greatest need since, it is argued, 'The early years of a child's life are critical to their future success and happiness' (1998: 13, para. 1.37). Thus children are firmly embedded in the family where they are to be controlled by parents, with those who are seen as being least well-equipped to provide such control being 'supported' by a variety of services.

The Green Paper also considers how best to provide financial support for families, exploring a range of provisions for working families, lone parents and parents in receipt of child support following the breakdown of a relationship. It also discusses the problems faced by many families of balancing the demands between work and home in order 'to provide quality care within the family...and provide role models for adult employment' (1998: 27, para. 3.19). The development of 'family-friendly employment practice' is also seen as providing wider social benefits – more stable families, fewer broken relationships between parents, better support for children during the years of their education, and reduced levels of delinquency – that will strengthen both families and the communities in which they live.

Childhood is therefore, as noted in earlier chapters, identified as the site of key social problems and children are, once again, defined in terms of their futurity rather than being recognised in their own right. At the same time, their futurity is also, by implication, regarded as potentially problematic and needing to be shaped by government, through social policy and the law, in order to produce the next generation of compliant citizens (for which, perhaps, we should read voters) and workers. Such perspectives are foundational to the particular form that the cultural politics of English childhood takes.

Thus Chapter 4 of the Green Paper argues for the strengthening of marriage, parenting and the family, in order 'to provide the best basis for raising children and for building strong and supportive communities' (1998: 30). Of particular significance, however, is Chapter 5 – 'Better Support for Serious Family Problems'. On reading it, however, one might be left wondering whether the real concern of the Government is with serious problem families! The chapter includes, for example, sections on 'Problems with children's learning' (including truancy and exclusions, agreements between home and school to reduce these, and discipline in the home); 'Youth Offending' (including parenting orders, child safety orders to control children under the age of 10, local child curfews to help parents control children by making them stay at home); 'Tackling teenage parenthood' and 'Domestic Violence'. It is only the very last of these that does not, under the guise of supporting families, problematise children and key aspects of childhood.

The Green Paper is thus a powerful signifier of the current cultural politics of childhood in England. In Chapter 5 of the Green Paper, as Barlow and Duncan argue, *social* problems are redefined as family problems (2000: 29), although these are for the most part, in terms of the Green Paper, the problems caused by children. It is interesting to note therefore that many of the solutions proposed involve intervention in *individual* behaviour rather than tackling any of the structural factors that might contribute to such problems, and that the focus is on the behaviour of *parents* rather than their children. Such an approach is a central element of New Labour's version of communitarianism. As Barlow and Duncan go on to point out,

> The New Labour government believes that law facilitates and, additionally, legitimates particular kinds of behaviour and will thus use it, coercively if needs be, to achieve its "moral reform crusade"
>
> (Barlow and Duncan 2000: 142)

in relation to the family and parenting behaviour. It is, however, this very focus on parenting and the willingness to resort to coercion in order to improve parenting that demonstrates clearly the sub-text of *Supporting Families* – that it is the *control* of children that is paramount, rather than the promotion of their interests or the encouragement of their agency or participation. This sub-text thus further reinforces the perception and presentation of children as non-citizens. It also illustrates clearly, once more, the relationship between the rule of law and the social response, and the role of Law as mediator between social order and custom and practice that we outlined in Chapter 3, elements at the core of the cultural politics of childhood.

Communitarianism, children and childhood

Such developments in the UK need to be understood in the context of the shifts in the political and ideological context that occurred with the emergence of New Labour. Of particular significance is the influence of communitarianism that was central to the reconstruction of traditional Labour politics and policies through the reinvention of social democracy by means of defining a 'third way' in politics. Giddens, one of the major architects and proponents of this new approach, argues strongly that the causes of so many political and social ills are located in the civic decline that is evidenced in 'the weakening sense of solidarity in some local communities and urban neighbourhoods, high levels of crime, and *the break-up of marriages and families*' (Giddens 1998: 78 – emphasis added).

The family was thus moved to the very centre of social policy, with Giddens arguing for its democratisation as a social institution, through the promotion of 'quality, mutual respect, autonomy, decision-making through communication and freedom from violence' (op.cit.: 93). Such a 'manifesto' does, however, raise crucially important questions about the place of children in the family, as we have argued elsewhere (James and James 2001). Thus, as Roche observes,

> As adults we take it for granted that we will participate in key decisions in our lives; we might not "get our way" but we will be players most of the time. With children it is different; there is no automatic expectation of participation. Of course some "good parents" might encourage participation within the family, but in civil society children do not count.
>
> (Roche 1999a: 67)

This argument is of central importance in terms of any vision for the development of the democratic family for, since the family is the primary site in which the boundaries and tensions between age and generation are managed and negotiated, the notion that children 'do not count' in civil society, that they have no right to participate, and that their behaviour must be controlled – if necessary by physical coercion – represents a denial of their agency. This is thus a major obstacle in terms of any movement towards the family becoming more democratic. Here we have a classic struggle between structure and agency, the existence of which is implicitly recognised in Etzioni's exposition of communitarian ideology. He notes that 'there is a fundamental contradiction between the society's needs for order and the individual's quests for autonomy', a contradiction which can place obstacles in the path of realising a communitarian agenda (1996: 3).

In the particular case of children and families, this difficulty is compounded since families (as well as communities) also have a moral as well as a developmental responsibility to provide socializing structures that will foster both children's autonomy *and* their ability to conform. Part of the 'problem' of children is precisely that they are still in the process of acquiring values, norms, meanings and identities on their journey towards the achievement of citizenship status, and this is a process over which parents in families and adults in communities feel bound to retain control and are, indeed, expected to do so by the State. Children have therefore to be encouraged to explore their agency, their difference, and their individuality, but only within a broader, common societal framework (James 1993) defined and constructed by adults. In this context the family becomes the key mechanism for the social control of children, as well as their socialisation.

However, although the rights of children, as articulated in the UNCRC and the Children Act 1989, would seem to suggest that children's status as citizens is unequivocal, the reality of much social policy and many social practices is that they are, in fact, seen and treated as non-citizens. Thus, for example, in terms of UK social policy in relation to education and crime, we have identified (James and James 2001) policies that produce active and proactive forms of social control aimed at children through, largely, the reassertion of 'family' values. Whilst such forms of social control are clearly visible there are, in addition, other less obvious but equally important mechanisms at play. As we shall show through our discussion of divorce, these also hinder the development of a culture in which children's agency and, by implication, their citizenship, is acknowledged.

Children and divorce

We have argued above that the family is the quintessential social institution of age and generation, a key institution in which children are socialised and develop the values, norms, meanings and identities that will eventually enable their transition into adulthood and citizenship. If, however, as Giddens suggests, the family is also under pressure to be 'democratised', it is instructive to consider more closely how the family functions in terms of the extent of English children's participation in the decisions surrounding divorce and family break-up. Once again, as in previous chapters, this allows us to consider the influence of law and social policy over the way in which childhood is constructed in this particular context and what this might tell us about the impact of this on children themselves, in terms of their lived everyday experiences as children – in sum, it allows us to explore the cultural politics of childhood.

It is, of course, the case that in England and Wales the Children Act 1989 *did* place much greater emphasis than hitherto on the importance of taking account of the wishes and feelings of children in family proceedings. Children's involvement in child protection proceedings, for example, was considerably enhanced as a consequence of the Act. Similarly, in other areas of childcare policy, such as the Quality Protects initiative for children in local authority care (Robbins 2001), greater emphasis is now being given to consulting and responding to the views of children. However, recent research (James *et al*. 2002) has shed some additional light on these issues. It suggests that the provisions of the Children Act to give children an effective voice in family proceedings are, notwithstanding the provisions of the UNCRC, considerably less effective than has been supposed.

In considering the way in which welfare professionals work with children in situations of family breakdown, in the context of the Children Act 1989, and in exploring how they construct their understanding of childhood in this particular context, this research identified two dominant images of childhood that are embedded in the way in which these professionals talked about childhood. Thus they talked positively of childhood as a time to be carefree but, more negatively, they also talked of childhood as a time of powerlessness. In addition, however, the data also revealed that children are seen to occupy two rather different status categories: first, 'the child' as an age-based social status and second, 'the child' as kinship/generational status, both of which are firmly rooted in the developmental paradigm (see Chapter 2).

While of course not mutually exclusive – any one child is always a member of both status categories – in practice, and at any one time, these were used as discrete and distinct attributions in the accounts of practitioners. It can be argued, therefore, that practitioners discriminate between 'the child' as a social (kinship) and a legal (age-based) construct. This comprises what we have called the 'double status' of children. Yet within such conceptualisations 'the child' is described primarily as an *object*, rather than a subject – as the object of legal rulings or the outcome of parenting practices. In both cases, the individual agency of children is obscured through the use of these categorical terms. Although it is possible to see the child as some kind of *subject*, using these same categories – for example, by referring to the child as *a minor* or the child as *a family member* – neither of these new descriptions tell us much more about the child as an individual or as a person in their own right.

Such an approach to understanding 'childhood' confirms the view, therefore, that it only derives its meaning from adulthood and, in particular, from parenthood. So even if we do conceptualise the child as *minor* or as *family member*, the meaning attributed to the concept of 'the child' is in terms of a status that is derived from the experience of being parented: the child as the *object* of parental love, care and protection. There is no space here for the person-hood of children as competent actors in the social world and their agency is therefore once more conceptually denied. Thus, as an age-based legal status, the process of protecting 'children' from responsibilities can be experienced by them as a denial of rights. As a kinship status, however, 'the child' who is care-free is also made so as a result of being protected and cared for by parents and/or other family members – a dependence that is once again experienced as a form of powerlessness by children.

Such theoretical and conceptual mapping is not, however, simply an exercise in logic. It has, we suggest, a number of potentially quite significant implications in the context of the Children Act 1989, in terms of the ways in which a child's welfare is to be deter-mined. If, as this analysis would suggest, 'the child' is nearly always conceived of as a product of *parenting*, and 'childhood' is generally assumed to be about the experience of *being parented*, there is little room in such conceptualisations for 'the child' to be seen as having an identity in his/her own right – that is, there is little room for the agency of children.

This contention is clearly illustrated by two recent cases. As Roche (2002) notes, in the case of *Re H (Residence Order: Child's Application for Leave)* [2000] FLR 780, a 12-year-old boy who wanted to apply for a residence order in the context of his parents divorce, in order to ensure that he ended up living with his father, was refused leave to apply. This was on the ground that since the father agreed with his son, there was no argument that he might put to the court himself that would not be advanced, on his behalf, by his father! The paradoxical message this conveys is, Roche contends, very clear: 'the child who is the very reason for the court sitting need not necessarily be seen or heard directly... [and] [i]n their own interests children should not be witness to the resolution of the conflict in which they are central' (Roche 2002: 68). This, he suggests, reveals the continued judicial disquiet with the idea of the visible, participating child.

In the second case, that of *Re W (Contact: Joining Child as Party)* [2001] EWCA Civ 1830, a father appealed against an order, made by a district judge, that there should be no contact between him and his son. This order was made on the basis of the son's view and an independent social worker's report, following a deterioration in the existing arrangements for the son to have staying contact with his father. On appeal, the most senior family court judge in England and Wales (Dame Elizabeth Butler-Sloss P) allowed the appeal. She argued that 'the child had a right to a relationship with his father, *even if he did not want it*, and his welfare demanded that efforts be expended to make contact possible' (Bridge 2003: 225 – emphasis added). This uniquely judicial construction of the concept of the child's right, which does not embrace the right of the child *not* to have contact with his father, demonstrates not only the centrality of the law and the impact of legal constructions of 'the child' in the cultural politics of childhood, but also the power of the language of welfare to over-ride a child's wishes and feelings and to deny their agency.

As these cases illustrate, family law routinely allows no separate identity for or agency of 'the child', other than that which it has in the context of being parented. Unless children *are* conceptualised as having active agency, however, it may be hard for adults to give real credence to the importance of children's thoughts, wishes and feelings when making decisions on their behalf, because it is precisely these things that express each child's individuality and agency. Such practices (which are social as well as legal, since they are embedded in and reflect the views of adults more generally about the proper ordering of relationships between adults and children) make the realisation of children's right to be heard in such proceedings under Article 12 of the UNCRC almost impossible. It also follows that the pervasive and much-used concept of 'the best interests of the child' is at risk of being devalued and of becoming simply a generalised socio-legal concept (rather than an individualised human concept). It threatens to become a rhetorical device that is given meaning by reference to the generalities of 'children' and 'childhood', from which is then derived what is, in effect, no more than an inferential understanding of the particular 'child' (see also Chapter 1).

And the role of law in all of this is critical. Law defines both 'childhood' and 'the child' in ways that clearly reflect widely held adult assumptions. It does so by defining and regulating the boundaries between adulthood and childhood, both through statute and case law, in various social spheres – for example, employment, health, education and the family. In performing this function, the law leans heavily on the objectivity of judgements based on chronological age, which provides the accepted basis for the determination of 'age' for the purposes of law, rather than more subjective, experiential definitions of competence. Thus, 'childhood' is defined as an age-bounded part of the life course during which, until the appropriate legally defined chronological threshold is passed, children are regarded, especially in family law, as legal subjects requiring protection. Viewed in this way, children cannot be seen as competent actors, as persons capable of independent thought and of exercising judgement. As we argued in Chapter 7, however, there is an important and paradoxical exception to this in terms of the criminal law: the recent *de facto* change to the age of criminal responsibility in England and Wales means that now, children as young as 10 are viewed as being as competent as adults in exercising independent thought and judgement in relation to the commission of crimes.

By defining 'childhood' in this way, therefore, the law (and therefore those adults who construct and interpret the law) mediates between, and simultaneously helps to *construct* 'the child' – as a minor, vis à vis the range of political and social rights associated with obtaining one's majority; and as a family member, vis à vis its parents upon whom children are deemed dependent. By the same token, and using exactly the same mechanisms, the law also therefore acts to regulate and reinforce the boundaries between adulthood and childhood.

In practical terms therefore domestic statutes, case law, and international conventions all define different aspects of childhood and children. In particular, it is worthy noting that family law in England and Wales (in the context of the Family Court Rules) defines a child as 'a person with a disability', and therefore denies all but the most limited scope for children as *actors* to exercise their agency. By the same token, welfare professionals working within the framework of and with the constructs provided by the law in general, and the Children Act 1989 in particular, also circumscribe children's ability to participate fully and effectively. By making assessments and offering 'expert' advice that draw on constructions of 'childhood' and 'the child' that are derived from the process of parenting and children's experiences of being parented, these welfare professionals are unable, as a consequence, to acknowledge sufficiently what being a child means in terms of that child's experience, agency and personhood. They therefore cannot enable fully the voice of the child to be heard in family proceedings. Rather, what is offered is an adult construction of what is in 'the best interests of the child' that attempts to resolve the ambiguity inherent in the task of allowing 'the child's wishes and feelings' to be heard in a system that struggles to acknowledge children as actors.

Children and family mediation

Such processes are also evident in other aspects of the family justice system in the UK. A significant development in recent years has been the growing interest in the development and application of mediation for the resolution of a range of community-based disputes, be these between employers and employees, victims and offenders, neighbours, or parents. This provides a mechanism whereby the community, rather than the State (through the courts) resolves conflict, an approach that chimes well with the main tenets of communitarianism to foster an active civic society. Of particular interest in this context is the recent emphasis on the use of mediation as a means of resolving disputes between parents over children when marriages and other parenting partnerships break down. The Children Act 1989 provided the legal context in which family mediation developed in the UK and, although its development reflected a range of social and political pressures (see James 1990) as well as the increasing pressure of rising divorce rates on the legal system – not to mention the public purse! – mediation was presented in such a way as to reflect the principles underpinning the legislation.

In this context, family mediation also reflects the new orthodoxy of child welfare in divorce. This hinges on the importance currently ascribed to continuing post-divorce contact between children and both parents, albeit with an apparent emphasis upon the responsibilities of parents in this respect, rather than their rights. The provision of mediation was central to the provisions of the Family Law Act 1996, the child welfare rhetoric of which was equally powerful. Its aim was to ensure the paramountcy of the child's welfare by arguing that it is in 'the best interests of the child' that post-divorce parenting should be as conflict-free as possible and that parents should agree on the arrangements for this, rather than seeking resolution of any disagreements about residence and contact through the courts and the legal process.

The centrality of mediation to the Family Law Act 1996 and the emergence of the 'new' divorce professional in the form of the mediator also brought with it the expectation that mediation would bring children to the centre of the divorce process and would recognise

> the need to admit the voice of the child into a parent-centred process... by means of consultation either directly within mediation or indirectly by mediators helping parents with ways to listen to their children.
>
> (Piper 1999: 91)

However, it has become clear that not all mediators wish to use direct consultation since they

> work within the same discursive constraints as the "old" divorce professionals: parental responsibility and particular notions about the risks of talking to children "inappropriately" again provide barriers to asking children what they think.
>
> (Piper 1999: 92)

This is partly because, as Piper argues, children's role in divorce in the UK has been located firmly within the welfare discourse and is linked only to a 'caretaking' version of children's rights. As National Family Mediation argued in its document outlining policies and standards in relation to consultation with children in mediation (NFM 1998), mediators

> have a special concern for the welfare of the children of the family and must encourage participants to focus upon the needs of their children... [and] to consider their children's wishes and feelings.
>
> (1998: 1)

The document goes on to define family mediation as 'a process of decision making by adults', arguing *à propos* the involvement of children that

> Indirect Consultation is the preferred form of consultation of children during mediation . . . [it] enables children's views to come into mediation via the parents . . . There must be a positive reason for seeing the children . . . Mediators will need to challenge parents as much as possible to ensure there is a positive reason for direct consultation and that this is agreed.
>
> (NFM 1998: 2–3)

This perspective is reflected in the UK College of Family Mediators' (2000) policy on children's involvement in mediation. Although this indicates that the Family Law Act 1996 extended the philosophy of the Children Act 1989 by emphasising the central importance of hearing the voice of the child in the making of decisions in mediation, it goes on to argue that the statutory requirements of publicly funded mediation in England and Wales only require mediators to have arrangements designed 'to ensure that the parties are encouraged to consider the welfare, wishes and feelings of each child, and also, *whether and to what extent* each child should be given the opportunity to express his or her wishes and feelings in mediation' (UK College 2000 – emphasis added). As the policy document notes, this highlights the priority that is attached to *parents* themselves consulting their children, rather than any professional.

Thus, as we argued above in relation to the divorce process more generally, children's voices are *not* heard in mediation – it is the voice of parents, at best repeating but also quite possibly interpreting (or misinterpreting) their children's views and what they think, or would like to believe, that their children have said. Such responses are firmly rooted in parents' perceptions of their children's competence, viewed in the light of the developmental assumptions on which these are based (see also Chapter 6). Indeed, as Leach notes,

> Mediation culture currently presumes that children will *not* be active participants in the process. Mediation practice is based on the principles that the mediator is the impartial manager of the process, that parents "know what is best for their children".
>
> (Leach 2000 – emphasis added)

Leach, a mediation development advisor with National Children's Homes, a UK NGO, argues that this is because parents are either resistant to the notion – or dangerously keen – that children should provide the solution. She observes that '[t]he majority of mediators seem paralysed by the notion that an encounter with a child will be damaging to the child' (Leach 2000). Her view seems to be confirmed by recent research (Murch *et al.* 1998), which revealed that the direct involvement of children in mediation is comparatively rare and that '[m]ediators have generally considered this is not the preferable way of working' (para. 5.5). (see also Chapter 6).

The study by Murch and his colleagues (1998), which admittedly was based on a sample that included a number of mediators with relatively little experience, found that only a very small minority (less than 10 per cent) of mediators always or often discussed with parents the appropriateness of the direct involvement of their children and over three quarters of mediators reported the direct involvement of children in fewer than 5 cases in 1997, with 28 per cent reporting no cases in which children were directly involved at all. Perhaps more important however, was the finding that out of a sample of over 450 mediators, less than 60 per cent *always* encouraged parents to consider children's views in mediation.

The policy of the UK College of Family Mediators also makes it clear that the decision about whether or not to consult a child directly in mediation is also to be made by agreement between mediators and parents, rather than in response to any expression by children of a desire to be consulted. This, we would suggest, is a very weak interpretation of the child's supposed right under Article 12 of the UNCRC ('to express those views freely in all matters affecting the child' and 'be provided the opportunity to be heard in any ... proceedings affecting the child'). Indeed, it is an interpretation that serves only to highlight the powerlessness of children, their lack of substantive rights, and their total dependence upon adults in such circumstances – and yet they, just as much as their parents, are going to have to live with the consequences of the decisions that are made in relation to them, sometimes for many years.

There is by now a considerable body of evidence that reveals the importance to children of being given the opportunity to be involved and being given information when their parents are separating or divorcing (see, for example, Smart *et al.* 2001).

Children should get a say in things, they shouldn't be left out. I mean it's their life as well, they shouldn't be stuck with someone they didn't want to be with.

(Mark aged 15 – quoted in Neal and Wade 2000: 36)

I think there should be some kind of agreement between the children and the parents as to what should happen.

(Jake aged 11 – quoted in Neal and Wade 2000: 32)

The children should get a say, and the parent should be able to sort things out for everyone – they should be able to act like adults about it really.

(Ursula aged 19 – quoted in Neal and Wade 2000: 33)

Such views expressed by children make it abundantly clear, to those who wish to hear what they are saying, that what they want is not necessarily to make the decisions but to be informed about issues that affect them, to be given the opportunity to express their views, and to have these valued (see also O'Quigley 2000).

There is nothing intrinsic to the process of divorce, or mediation as part of that process, that makes it necessary for children to be marginalised or 'protected'. Thus, for example, the Scottish Law Commission stated clearly, in the course of its deliberations about the place to be given to children's wishes and feelings in divorce, that

the child's own views . . . we believe, ought to be taken into account *in their own right* and not just as an aspect of welfare.

(cited in Piper 1999: 79 – emphasis added)

Similarly, recent developments elsewhere have indicated the benefits of children's involvement in mediation. A major Australian study (Commonwealth of Australia 1998) revealed not only the benefits to parents of their children's involvement in mediation but showed

a strong consensus amongst the children . . . that when parents are in conflict, children benefit from having a chance to talk about how it is for them . . . regardless of their parents' capacity to respond differently, the children interviewed felt that the chance to talk *in their own right* was beneficial.

(1998: 4 – emphasis added)

The report concluded that '[t]he Child Inclusive Mediation Project, which combined parent education with direct child consultation, produced strong positive short term outcomes for both parents and children' (1998: 53). Importantly, however, the children interviewed also pointed out that direct consultation with children was not a *universal* panacea and that 'a case by case rather than a "recipe" approach remains essential' (1998: 68). In other words, as a cultural politics of childhood recognises, there are many different childhoods, the diversity of which must be acknowledged; and it is the child as an *individual* actor whose needs must be considered in the context of their own childhood, not the needs of *all* of those who share the status of being 'children'. Nonetheless, the report *has* been an important element in the development of a strategy for the development of child inclusive practice in Australia in the wake of the 1996 amendments to their Family Law Act 1975, which gave legal force to the aspiration of securing 'the best interests of the child'.

Such developments do, of course, pose significant challenges for practitioners and, as a related report comments,

> [p]ractitioners bring with them aspects of themselves from their past, and counsellors are inevitably "adult-centric", so practitioners working with children need to grow smaller, to see the world through the child's eyes.
>
> (Mackay 2001: 19)

It is also interesting, in terms of the policy context of such developments, to note an issue raised by this study that underlines the adult focus of mediation, even in the context of developing child inclusive mediation – the report poses the question 'is it legitimate to offer a service from which children may gain more than their parents . . . ?' (Commonwealth of Australia 1998: 63)

Part of the difficulty in securing the effective involvement of children in England and Wales lies, we would suggest, in the role of law and lawyers, in that mediation has fallen increasingly under the thrall of law as a result of recent policy developments in relation to the public funding of mediation by the Legal Services Commission. It is interesting to note, in the context of the Children Act 1989 and the Family Law Act 1996, there is no duty on solicitors in divorce cases to take into account children's wishes and feelings and, in the main, solicitor mediators also do not consider it appropriate for children to be involved in the process, other than through their parents (Leach 2000). This reflects an increasing trend in the UK – 'mediation continues to be subsumed into legal practice and is in danger of becoming constrained by the ideology of legal practitioners' (Leach 2000; see also James 2003). This trend is all the more significant because, undoubtedly, additional costs would accrue if children were to be more extensively involved in mediation!

As Roche argues in his analysis of the law relating to divorce, although children's welfare is central to the decision-making of courts and welfare professionals, 'an "adult" consensus has emerged around the need to keep children out – albeit for their own good' (1999a: 55). He continues by asking:

> Today, when the child does get to speak what does the law hear? The words of the child are filtered through the lens of the concerns of mediators and other welfare professionals operating the current family justice system ... children are either ... victimised or demonised. The law is implicated in this. The words of the child are inherently suspect.
>
> (Roche 1999a: 70–71)

Family mediation is therefore presented as being synonymous with securing the welfare of children in divorce by virtue of its focus on reducing the conflict between parents that can be so detrimental to children's welfare (James 1995). Since, however, there is no requirement to involve children directly in mediation, a practice that is widely resisted by mediators,

> a major consequence of this arguably ... is that even the currently limited child welfare safeguards of the formal legal process may be being further weakened and a particular model of the passive, dependent child increasingly endorsed.
>
> (James and James 1999: 199)

Such a blatant denial of agency sits uneasily with the rhetoric of children's right to be heard and represents a powerful denial of their personhood and citizenship. It is therefore also a passive but symbolically important mechanism for their regulation, which effectively acknowledges that it is only through the passage of time, combined with and through the operation of the law, that children achieve adulthood, and thus citizenship and personhood. Thus, we would contend, in order to be able to control and regulate the status differential between children and adults, and the access that the achievement of adult status allows individuals to the rights, responsibilities and competencies of adulthood, the law in practice both actively and passively *dis*ables children. Consequently, the way in which 'the child's right to be heard' is expressed in practice represents, in effect, a means of avoiding the fundamental tension between adult control and children's agency. By giving children a right to be included in the decision-making process but then interpreting it in this particular way, adults avoid

> choosing between the child's self determination ... and paternalism ... Thus the languages of welfare and rights meet.
>
> (Roche 1999a: 59)

Indeed it is arguable that this *must* be so – without the category of non-personhood and non-citizenship called 'child', the achievement of the status of adult would have no or many fewer meanings and the language of welfare would be irreconcilable with the rhetoric of children's rights.

These issues also have profound implications for the supposed democratisation of the family as propounded by Giddens. As Roche argues, such practices in the context of divorce make it clear that 'the private world of the family is no place for the languages of democracy' (1999a: 64) and that in England and Wales, the language of citizenship appears to cease to have any purchase at the front door of the family home. In marked contrast, however,

> In Sweden the language of citizenship is increasingly applied to children – whereas in many other countries the "private enslavement" of children by their parents "is scarcely noticed".
>
> (Roche 1999a: 68 – quoting Beck 1997)

Similarly in Norway, as Kjørholt notes, '[b]elonging to a community ... and the right to participate in society are core issues in the construction of a good Norwegian childhood (2002: 71).

As this analysis suggests, in the context of UK family law and the welfare model that is embedded therein, the child is constructed, as object (and subject), apart from the adult world and that for the child to be recognised as an actor, it must become part of and party to the adult world. For Roche too, '[t]he core problem with welfare is its objectification of the child' (Roche 1999a: 56). The law seldom treats the child as an actor, however (and even then, only with major qualifications on the extent to which the child can participate and subject ultimately to adult endorsement), and if a child is never defined and addressed as an actor, none of the rhetoric or the devices used can ever ensure the effective participation of children in family proceedings. As we have argued elsewhere,

> Under the present law, in spite of a child-orientated rhetoric, it is adults – judges, magistrates, parents and welfare professionals – rather than children who remain in control when it comes to divorce and separation and thus, in relation to divorce, the Act can be said to be fostering a particular model of 'the child' in which ideas of agency are underplayed and those of structure fore-grounded.

> (James and James 1999: 198)

Conclusion: culture, politics and childhood

Running through our analysis in Part II of recent political initiatives with regard to children and the regulation of childhood is a key analytical strand concerning the relationship between the State, social policy and law and the way in which these not only reflect the changing cultural and political landscape but comprise the cultural politics of childhood that we are concerned to map out – communitarianism.

Throughout much of the Western World, the communitarian political perspective that has been adopted by New Labour and labelled as the 'third way' has been prominent in shaping political thinking and public policy. The redefinition of the relationship between the community and the State that is central to this has, however, seen the transfer of significant social control functions, together with the creation of new control mechanisms, to the community. As we have argued, however, such policies, although they abound with the rhetoric of participation, citizenship and empowerment, are essentially about the selective empowerment of adults and a more widespread increase in the control over children as a group, and delinquent children in particular.

Thus, for example, while the *Supporting Families* Green Paper offers many tempting morsels to those who would wish to see the development of some form of family policy, closer examination of the paper, including its provenance (i.e. an inter-departmental committee chaired by the Home Secretary) suggests that it has a strong social control agenda embedded within the rhetoric – for example, the early years initiative, greater use of grandparents, the role of health visitors in terms of policing families for child abuse, etc. The production of the 'millennial' family and, presumably, 'millennial children' is its thrust. It is arguable therefore that the communitarian philosophies of New Labour are having the effect, at least in part, of incorporating the family and the community into the social control mechanisms of the state. Thus as Jenks argues, following Donzelot:

> the child has become the meeting place of the political contract and the psychological complex...[thus] developing a wider argument about the functioning of control in modern life. The contemporary political state no longer addresses the polity as a whole but rather treats the family as its basic unit of control.
>
> (Jenks 1996a: 80)

In this context, we have argued that rather than the democratisation of the family, the family agenda of New Labour will result in the continuation of adult control over children. To the extent that this is largely covert and concealed beneath the rhetoric of children's welfare and the *extension* of their rights, it might even be argued that such an approach in fact represents the consolidation and reinforcement of control over children. As Pryor and Rodgers argue,

> listening to what children say...is a surprisingly contentious issue. There is a deep ambivalence about children's roles and rights of participation in determining their well-being. Why might this be? One answer is that to take children seriously poses a fundamental challenge to power issues within the family and within the wider community...Beliefs about childhood in general influence our views about children's roles in families and their participation in decision-making.
>
> (Pryor and Rodgers 2001: 112)

As Archard (1993) observes, this struggle revolves around two interrelated issues – the completely arbitrary and culturally specific distinction between childhood and adulthood, and the similarly culturally determined presumption that children are incompetent. This is, as we have argued, a presumption that is firmly embedded in UK law and one that is also buttressed by the 'caretaking' thesis which, as Roche (1999a) points out, ultimately belongs within a welfare discourse. This argues that 'children should not be free to make autonomous decisions' (Archard 1993: 52), a denial of the right to self-determination justified on the basis that 'children lack the requisite rationality to be able to make intelligent decisions and because they are emotionally immature' (Roche 1999a: 56). Such is the pervasive influence and power of the developmental paradigm in determining the cultural politics of childhood in Britain.

In the context of the family, family policy and family change, children's views are located firmly in the context of a welfare discourse, which is, in turn, firmly embedded within the legal framework within which such issues are dealt. There is an alternative legal framework, however, which is that of 'rights'. Thus law is not a homogeneous or unitary phenomenon. As a giver of rights, it *does* have the potential to acknowledge the child as a social actor, a person with agency, although as a provider of protection, it can also deny that agency. As Roche argues,

> In our arguments about childhood, children's rights and citizenship, we are arguing about ourselves and our place in the world: it is an argument about politics and how we want to be and live our lives.
>
> (1999b: 484)

As Roche also argues, however, the evidence of a range of disappointing jurisprudential and social policy developments since the Children Act 1989 was implemented demonstrates that the children's rights project is fragile and, as Freeman (2002) observes in reviewing progress in the implementation of the UNCRC, any complacency about children's rights in England is totally misplaced. This is because it is also 'a cultural project', straddling the private and public spheres, which requires adults to rethink their attitudes towards children and childhood (Roche 2002).

Thus the power struggle, which is therefore both cultural and political, is a struggle between the minority of adults who seek to use law as a means of giving rights to liberate children, and the majority who seek to use it as a mechanism for giving care and protection to children, a mechanism that simultaneously also keeps them dependent upon adults and thereby also defines the cultural politics of childhood.

Concluding Thoughts – Continuity and Change

In the course of the preceding chapters, we have sought to develop and articulate a theoretical model that addresses the complexities of childhood, both as a social phenomenon and as an experience. Our purpose has been not only to increase the explanatory power of models that are currently available but, by drawing on a range of disciplinary perspectives, to provide a heuristic model that might take the social study of childhood a little further.

Central to our analysis is the fact that childhood as a social space is structurally determined by a range of social institutions and mechanisms, including Law, social policy and the family, which combine to provide inter-generational continuity of the nature and dimensions of that social space. Equally important, however, is the recognition that this does not imply any kind of immutability since those structural determinants change over time, reflecting cultural shifts. Some of these are the direct consequence of the behaviours of children, both as individuals and as a collectivity, and some are the product of a wide range of external influences that are part of the process of globalisation. Such shifts not only allow for but also sometimes facilitate changes in childhood, as well as continuity.

It follows from this that within that social space, children as objects and subjects are also structurally and culturally determined, since in any given society, it is that unique combination of political, economic, social and cultural forces that constitute the cultural politics of childhood. What we have also demonstrated in the case studies we have offered, however, is that within the social space of childhood, children are not just social actors, playing a multitude of roles in relation to the increasing range of adults with whom their lives mesh as they move through their own childhoods towards adulthood. They are also social agents in that they shape those roles, both as individuals and as a collectivity, and they can create new ones that alter the social space of childhood to be inherited by the next generation.

Thus, although childhood and the category of children are both structurally determined, within the lived experience of their own childhoods children experience varying degrees of autonomy as actors, in which they can and do play a variety of roles. And yet, although many of those roles might also be culturally determined, they are often differently situated within and between cultures so that each child brings to those roles their own interpretation.

Thus, although it is the roles and role sets associated with childhood, many of which are constructed in relation to adults, and to kinship groups in particular, which provide one of the main mechanisms for the inter-generational continuity of childhood itself, each child, within its own occupancy of the life-space of childhood, has the ability to act – that is, to effect change and to create new roles or new interpretations of existing roles. These may change that child's experience of childhood, but may also affect childhood itself more generally by transforming adult perceptions. In turn, this change in adult perceptions may result in policy and legal responses that will change childhood, since it is adults who are the principal arbiters of its boundaries.

It is clear that this process is neither uniform nor unilinear, either within or between societies. It will vary according to the particular configuration of the cultural politics of childhood in each country. It is also clear, however, that as globalisation increases, so does the potential for external pressures to influence national constructions of childhood. This will sometimes trigger change and transformation, sometimes resistance and retrenchment. In either case, however, there are shifts in the status quo, thereby perpetuating the dialectical process of cultural change.

The model we have articulated suggests that it is Law that provides a key institutional and social mechanism in the construction and reconstruction of childhood, not only in the maintaining of social order but also in the change process. Although there may be other mechanisms that we have not yet identified, Law, and the institutions and mechanisms of the law – be these religious or secular – incorporates and enforces the boundaries between childhood and adulthood, and those between children and adults. It is the laws made by adults that determine, for example, the age of majority, the age at which children can marry, have sexual relations legally, be educated, give or withhold consent to medical treatment, fight, smoke, work, vote and so on. That these various age boundaries can and often do differ within societies may reflect some confusion about the nature of childhood, but what they also reflect are the changes in perceptions that have occurred over time. Whatever the degree of internal consistency, it is through law that adult views about children and childhood are expressed.

It is also the case, as we have argued and demonstrated, that law does not necessarily operate uniformly at any given time, or over time, in terms of enforcement procedures. These vary depending upon cultural shifts and historical/temporal exigencies. Thus in addition to the body of the law, be this common, statute or religious, we must also consider the nature and extent of enforcement, since this will not only reveal something about the relationship between law and social practices, but will also tell us something about those areas in which processes of change may be under way. Thus, for example, the extent to which laws relating to the age at which children may lawfully engage in sexual intercourse are enforced may not only give important clues about changing sexual mores in a given society but also about changing adult perceptions of the sexual maturity and responsibility of children, and thus of the nature of childhood itself.

What we have also argued, however, is that in addition to national laws and jurisdictions, which define and construct childhood within any given society, we must increasingly take note of the influence of the development of international law. With the globalisation of law in general, and in particular of child law, we are also witnessing the tentative emergence, through instruments such as the UNCRC, of a global childhood. Whilst it is clear from the evidence we have reviewed that there are varying degrees of resistance to such developments, it is also clear that they are potentially of huge importance as a catalyst to cultural change and thus the gradual modification of national laws and the childhoods these construct.

For example, implicit in and central to law is the concept of rights and it is thus to the rights of children that international law is addressed. Rights are also, however, closely associated with citizenship and it is therefore inevitable that, as a result of such developments, the spotlight is being turned increasingly on the rights of children, as well as on their relationship with adult society. By so doing, the emerging international discourse about childhood is also highlighting the extent to which children are regarded as citizens in different societies and, simultaneously, the extent to which childhood, as a major social space, is occupied by those with few or without any rights at all.

Such debates are important in their own terms since they identify potential means by which to achieve sought after ends. Perhaps more important, however, is that they provide us with important insights into the relationship between childhood and adulthood, and the worlds of adults and children, providing in the process some important potential clues to understanding a range of social processes and problems. In the absence of any rights, for example, children remain social objects. As such, they may have little incentive to develop a commitment to conformity and without a commitment to conformity, rooted in the experience of being a social subject and a bearer of rights, the adult who emerges from childhood may have only tenuous links and commitments to society and citizenship.

This possibility focuses attention on another important issue to emerge from our attempts to achieve a greater understanding of the social construction of childhood. Since adults were once children themselves, we should consider what they might take from their experiences as children and then bring to the understandings and interpretations of childhood. How do they deploy these as adults in their task of arbitrating the boundaries of childhood – be this as parents, teachers, politicians, social workers or judges? For some adults, this may comprise a wish/determination that their children (or those to whom they relate as adults) will experience the same kind of childhood that they had – the preservation and passing on of what was good, ensuring that childhood experiences provide a rigorous schooling for the freedoms and challenges of adult life. For others, this may produce a wish to change the nature of childhood experiences for the better a wish that may find expression through the organised activities of professionals such as lawyers or pressure groups such as children's NGOs.

This combination of perspectives within each and every generation and the resultant tensions between the desire for both change and continuity (which are reflected in cultural and political radicalism, liberalism and conservatism) create a cultural dialectic that produces change over time, the pace of that change depending upon the pressures produced by these tensions and the countervailing pressures exerted by existing forms of social order. Thus both continuity and change necessarily imply the existence of social order. Without order there could be no continuity and without continuity, there would be nothing to change.

At the level of the individual 'child', the dual processes of continuity and change are reflected in the experience of developmental continuity. This carries with it the experience of biological and social change as the child moves towards adulthood – the individual order. At the level of 'children', there is a collective experience of progress as part of a peer group, cohort or generational group through a socially defined space occupied by children but controlled substantially by adults – the collective order. At the level of 'childhood', there is continuity, since the social and developmental space occupied by children continues between generations as different generations of children move through it. However, the children who move through that social space also constitute and reconstitute it. Thus, the nature of the social space they occupy changes over time, with changes in culture, law, politics and economics – the institutional order. Continuity and change are therefore central to the individual child's experience of childhood, as well as to the perspectives that adults take into adulthood from their own experiences as children.

A considerable proportion of those experiences are gained in the context of the family and it is also the case that families are not only inherently diverse – in that some families offer much greater scope for children to exercise their agency compared to others – but they are also becoming ever more diverse in terms of their definition and structure. Thus families, however defined, offer children a huge range of childhood experiences. But regardless of cultural context, in that the family is a key social institution, it plays its part in the inter-generational transmission of culture, transecting in varying degrees all of those key areas of social policy and practice that constitute the cultural politics of childhood.

Thus in terms of the UK, for example, the family and the child within the family are at the centre of a complex of overlapping policies and regulatory frameworks. Each family, in the context of its own community, is affected, to varying degrees by health policy, education policy, family policy and criminal justice policy. Increasingly in the UK, the Government, in its pursuit of its ambition of joined-up thinking and policies, is seeking to close the gaps between the family and these different policy areas, a process that is becoming progressively evident as its family policy unfolds: the family is being ever more closely involved with the school and the educational process; the family is becoming ever more central to the delivery of health care in the community; and the family is increasingly the target of intervention in terms of both the prevention and the treatment of crime.

It is therefore, increasingly, only in the gaps between such adult structures and the reach of these policy areas that children have the opportunity to exercise and experiment with their agency for, in spite of the rhetoric of participation, there is a long way to go before they will experience participation in policy-making as meaningful rather than tokenistic. Currently, however, such gaps are progressively being closed as the State seeks to exercise ever more control. For example, the Internet, one of the few remaining areas where children are not yet regulated and controlled, is fast becoming an arena within which children are being deemed 'at risk' and therefore in need of protection.

All such experiences are taken forward into adulthood by today's children as they relinquish the space of childhood for the next generation, experiences that will help inform their ideas as adults of what children are or should be. In turn, each successive generation of children will, like their parents, continue to find new ways of exercising their agency and constructing their own childhoods and those of other children. And it is, therefore, through the complex shifts and negotiations in and around these different status and experiences that the cultural politics of childhood can be seen taking place.

References

Alanen, L. (2001) 'Childhood as a generational condition: children's daily lives in a central Finland town'. In L. Alanen and B. Mayall (eds) *Conceptualising Child–Adult Relations*. London: Falmer.

Alderson, P. (1993) *Children's Consent to Surgery*. Buckingham: Open University Press.

—— (1999) 'Civil rights in schools', *Children 5–16 Research Briefing 1*. London: ESRC.

—— (2000) 'School students' views on school councils and daily life at school', *Children and Society*, 14(2): 121–35.

Archard, D. (1993) *Children: Rights and Childhood*. London: Routledge.

—— (2001) 'Philosophical perpectives on childhood'. In J. Fionda (ed.) *Legal Concepts of Childhood*. Oxford: Hart.

Aries, P. (1962) *Centuries of Childhood*. London: Jonathan Cape.

Armstrong, D. (1983) *The Political Anatomy of the Body: Medical Knowledge in Britain in the Twentieth Century*. Cambridge: Cambridge University Press.

—— (1995) 'The rise of surveillance medicine', *Sociology of Health and Illness*, 17(3). 393–404.

Armstrong, C., Hill, M. and Secker, J. (2000) 'Young people's perceptions of mental health', *Children and Society*, 14(1): 60–72.

Arthur, J. with Bailey, R. (2000) 'Schools and community: the communitarian agenda in education'. London: Falmer Press.

Asquith, J. (1996) 'Children, crime and society'. In M. Hill and J. Aldgate (eds), *Child Welfare Services: Developments in Law, Policy, Practice and Research*. London: Jessica Kingsley.

Atkinson, L. (2000) 'A right to education', *The Howard League Magazine*, 18(4): 15.

—— (2001) 'Missing the grade', *The Howard League Magazine*, 19(3): 11.

Audit Commission (1996) *Misspent Youth: Young People and Crime: Summary*. Audit Commission: London.

Ball, S. J. (1994) *Education Reform: A Critical and Post-structural Approach*. Milton Keynes: Open University Press.

Barlow, A. and Duncan, S. (2000) 'Supporting families? New labour's communitarianism and the "rationality mistake" – Parts I and II', *Journal of Social Welfare and Family Law*, 22(1 and 2): 23–42 and 129–43.

Beck, U. (1997) 'Democratisation of the family', *Childhood*, 4(2): 151–68.

Berger, B. and Berger, P. (1983) *The War Over the Family: Capturing the Middle Ground*. Penguin: Harmondsworth.

Bernstein, B. (1971) 'On the classification and framing of educational knowledge'. In M.F.D. Young (ed.) *Knowledge and Control*. London: Coliler and Macmillan.

Beveridge, F., Nott, S. and Stephen, K. (2000) 'Addressing gender in national and community law and policy-making'. In J. Shaw (ed.) *Social Law and Policy in an Evolving European Union*. Oxford: Hart.

Blatchford, P. (1998) *Social Life in School*. London: Falmer Press.

Bluebond-Langer, M. (1978) *The Private Worlds of Dying Children*. Princeton: Princeton University Press.

Bourdieu, P. (1971) 'Systems of education and systems of thought'. In M.F.D. Young (ed.) *Knowledge and Control*. London: Coliler and Macmillan.

Boyden, J. (1997) 'Childhood and the policy makers: a comparative perspective on the globalisation of childhood'. In A. James and A. Prout (eds) *Constructing and Reconstructing Childhood*. London: Falmer (Second edition).

Boyden, J. and Myers, W. (1994) *Exploring Alternatives to Combating Child Labour: Case Studies from Developing Countires*, Child Rights Series no. 8, Florence: Innocenti Occasional Papers.

Boyden, J., Ling, B. and Myers, W. (1998) *What Works for Working Children?* Sweden: Save the Children/UNICEF.

Bradshaw, J. (2002) *The Well-being of Children in the UK*. London: Save the Children.

Bridge, C. (2003) 'Contact' (Case Report), *Family Law*, 33, April.

Britton, F. (2000) *Active Citizenship: A Teaching Tool Kit*. London: Hodder and Staughton.

Buckingham, D. (2000) *After the Death of Childhood*. Cambridge: Polity Press.

Burman, E. (1994) *Deconstructing Developmental Psychology*. London: Routledge.

Burney, E. (1999) *Crime and Banishment: Nuisance and Exclusion in Social Housing*. Winchester: Waterside Press.

Butcher, H. (2000) 'Juveniles in the Crown Court', *The Howard League Magazine*, 18(4): 16.

Campbell, K., Dufresne, M. and Maclure, R. (2001) 'Amending youth justice policy in Canada: discourse, mediation and ambiguity', *The Howard Journal of Criminal Justice*, 40(3): 272–84.

Charman, S. and Savage, S. (1999) 'The new politics of law and order: labour, crime and justice'. In M. Powell (ed.) *New Labour, New Welfare State?: The 'Third Way' in British Social Policy*. Bristol: The Policy Press.

Child Rights Information Network (2002) *Time for Action: The United Nations Special Session on Children*. London: CRIN.

Children and Young People's Unit (2001) *Learning to Listen: Core Principles for the Involvement of Children and Young People*. Department for Education and Skills: London.

Children's Legal Centre (2002) 'UNGASS: the views of young people', *ChildRight*, 187, June.

Children's Rights Alliance (2002) *Report to the Pre-Sessional Working Group of the Committee on the Rights of the Child, Preparing for the Examination of the UK's Second Report Under the CRC*. Children's Rights Alliance for England: London.

Children's Rights Development Unit (1994) *UK Agenda for Children*. London: CRDU.

Children's Rights Information Network (2000) CRIN Newsletter, No. 13, November. CRIN: London.

—(2001) CRIN Newsletter, No. 14, June. CRIN: London.

—(2002) CRIN Newsletter, No. 15, March. CRIN: London.

— (2002a) Special Session Update No. 1, Tuesday 7 May 2002 – NGOs working together for the UN General Assembly Special Session on Children, crin_specialsession@ domeus.co.uk

— (2002b) Special Session Update No. 3, Thursday 9 May 2002 – NGOs working together for the UN General Assembly Special Session on Children, crin_specialsession@ domeus.co.uk

— (2002c) Special Session Update No. 4, Friday 10 May 2002 – NGOs working together for the UN General Assembly Special Session on Children, crin_specialsession@ domeus.co.uk

ChildRight News (2002) 'Children give evidence before Human Rights Committee', *ChildRight*, 187, June.

Christensen, P. (1999) *Towards an Anthropology of Childhood Sickness: An Ethnographic Study of Danish School Children*. Unpublished PhD Thesis, University of Hull.

Christensen, P. and James, A. (2001) 'What are schools for? The temporal experience of children's learning in Northern England'. In L. Alanen and B. Mayall (eds) *Conceptualizing Child–Adult Relations*. London: Falmer.

Christensen, P., James, A. and Jenks, C. (2001) ' "All we needed to do was blow the whistle": children's embodiment of time'. In S. Cunningham-Burley and K. Backett-Milburn (eds) *Exploring the Body*. London: Palgrave.

Clarke, J., Gewirtz, S., Hughes, G. and Humphrey, J. (2000) 'Guarding the public interest? Auditing public services'. In J. Clarke, S. Gewirtz and E. Mclaughlin (eds) *New Managerialism, New Welfare?* London: Sage.

Cockburn, T. (1998) 'Children and citizenship in Britain', *Childhood*, 5(1): 99–117.

Coleman, J. (2000) 'Young people in Britain at the beginning of a new century', *Children and Society*, 14(4): 230–42.

Coles, R. (1986) *The Political Life of Children*. Boston: Atlantic Monthly.

Combe, V. (2002) *Up for it: Getting Young People Involved in Local Government*. JRF/National Youth Agency: Leicester.

Commonwealth of Australia Department of Family and Community Services (1998) *Child Inclusive Practice in Family and Child Counselling and Family and Child Mediation*. Commonwealth Attorney General's Department: Canberra.

Cooper, P. (2001) 'Understanding AD/HD: A brief critical review of literature', *Children and Society*, 15(5): 387–95.

Corsaro, W. (1979) ' "We're friends, right?": Children's use of acces rituals in a nursery school', *Language in Society*, 8, 315–36.

Corsaro, W. (1997) *The Sociology of Childhood*. Thousand Oaks, California: Pine Forge Press.

Council of Europe (2000) *Penological Information Bulletin*, No. 22.

Crawford, A. (1999) *The Local Governance of Crime*. Oxford: Oxford University Press.

Cunningham, S. and Lavalette, M. (2002) 'Children, politics and collective action: school strikes in Britain'. In B. Goldson, M. Lavalette and J. McKechnie (eds), *Children Welfare and the State*. London: Sage.

Daniel, P. and Ivatts. J. (1998) *Children and Social Policy*. London: Macmillan.

Dawson, N. (1997) 'The provision of education and opportunities for future employment for pregnant school girls and schoolgirl mothers in the UK', *Children and Society*, 11(4): 252–63.

Day, C. (2000) 'Hard Times', *The Howard League Magazine*, 18(4): 15.

Department of Education (1994) *Education Act 1993: Sex Education in Schools*. Circular 5/94, HMSO.

Department for Education and Employment (DfEE)(1998) *Education for Citizenship and the Teaching of Democracy in Schools*. London: TSO.

Department for Education and Employment (DfEE)(2000) *The Connexions Strategy Document*. http://www.gov.uk/strategy.htm

Department of Health (1999) United Nations Convention on the Rights of the Child: Second Report to the U.N. Committee on the Rights of the Child by the United Kingdom, 1999. London: TSO.

Department of Health (1999) *Saving Lives: Out Healthier Nation*. London: TSO.

DfES (2003) Excellence and Enjoyment: a strategy for primary schools. HMSO

Donnan, H. and McFarlane, G. (1997) 'Anthropology and policy research: the view from Northern Ireland'. In C. Shore and S. Wright (eds) *Anthropology of Policy*. London: Routledge.

Donzelot, J. (1979) *The Policing of Families*. London: Hutchinson.

Douglas, M. (1973) *Natural Symbols*. London: Penguin.

Driver, S. and Martell, L. (1997) 'New labour's communitarianisms', *Critical Social Policy*, 17(3): 27–44.

Ennew, J. (1986) *The Sexual Exploitation of Children*. Cambridge: Polity Press.

Etzioni, A. (1996) 'The responsive community: a communitarian perspective', *American Sociological Review*, (61): 1–11.

Ewick, P. and Silbey, S. (1998) *The Common Place of Law*. University of Chicago Press: London.

Feeley, M. and Simon, J. (1992) 'The new penology: notes on the emerging strategy of corrections and its implications', *Criminology*, 30(4), 449–74.

Field, N. (1995) 'The child as labourer and consumer: the disappearance of childhoold in contemporary Japan'. In S. Stephen (ed.) *Children and the Political Culture*. Princeton, NJ: Princeton University Press.

Fionda, J. (2001) 'Legal concepts of childhood: an introduction'. In J. Fionda (ed.) *Legal Concepts of Childhood*. Oxford: Hart.

Fitzpatrick, M. (2001) *The Tyranny of Health*. London: Routledge.

Flekkøy, M. G. (1991) *A Voice for Children*. London: Jessica Kingsley.

Flekkøy, M. G. and Kaufman, N. H. (1997) *The Participation Rights of the Child: Rights and Responsibilities in Family and Society*. London: Jessica Kingsley.

Fortin, J. (1998) *Children's Rights and the Developing Law*. London: Butterworths.

—— (2002) 'Children's rights and the impact of two international conventions: the UNCRC and the ECHR'. In M. Thorpe and C. Cowton (eds) *Delight and Dole: The Children Act 10 years on*. Bristol: Jordans/Family Law.

Freeman, M. (1992) 'The limits of children's rights'. In M. Freeman and P. Veerman (eds) *The Ideologies of Children's Rights*. Martinus Nijhoff Publishers.

—— (1995) 'Children's rights in a land of rites'. In B. Franklin (ed.) *The Handbook of Children's Rights: Comparative Policy and Practice*. London: Routledge.

—— (1998) 'The next children's act?', *Family Law*, 28: 341–48.

—— (2002) 'Children's rights ten years after ratification'. In B. Franklin (ed.) *The New Handbook of Children's Rights: Comparative Policy and Practice*. London: Routledge.

Freeman, R. (1992) 'The idea of prevention: a critical review'. In S. Scott, G. Williams, S. Platt and H. Thomas (eds) *Private Risks and Public Dangers* Aldershot: Avebury.

Garland, D. (2001) *The Culture of Control: Crime and Social Order in Contemporary Society*. Oxford: Oxford University Press.

Giddens, A. (1976) *The New Rules of Sociological Method*. London: Hutchinson.

—— (1979) *Central Problems in Social Theory*. London: Macmillan.

—— (1998) *The Third Way: The Renewal of Social Democracy*. Cambridge: Polity.

Gillis, J. R. (1996) *A World of their Own Making*. Oxford: Oxford University Press.

Goldson, B. (ed.) (1999) *Youth Justice: Contemporary Policy and Practice*. Aldershot: Ashgate.

—— (2001) 'Reconfigured "justice": reconstructed childhood', *The Howard League Magazine*, 19(4): 5.

Goldson, B. and Peters, E. (2000) *Tough Justice – Responding to Children in Trouble*. The Children's Society: London.

Green, D. R. (1999) 'Political participation of youth in the United Kingdom'. In B. Riepl and H. Wintersberger (eds) *Political Participation of Youth Below Voting Age*. Vienna: European Centre for Social Welfare Policy and Research.

Griffith, R. (1996) 'New powers for old: transforming power relationships'. In M. John (ed.) *Children in Our Charge: The Child's Right to Resources*. London: Jessica Kingsley.

Griffiths, A. and Kandel, R. F. (2000) 'Legislating for the child's voice: perspectives from comparative ethnography of proceedings involving children'. In M. Maclean (ed.) *Making Law for Families*. Oxford: Hart.

Grisso, T. and Schwartz, R. (eds) (2000) *Youth on Trial: A Developmental perspective on Juvenile Justice*. Chicago: University of Chicago Press.

Habermas, J. (1996) *Between Facts and Norms: Contributions to a Discourse Theory of Law and Democracy*. Cambridge: Polity.

Hall, J. (2001) 'Children and crime reduction – victims not villains', *The Howard League Magazine*, 19(4): 8.

Halliday, T. and Karpik, L. (1997) 'Postscript: lawyers, political liberalism and globalization'. In T. Halliday and L. Karpik (eds) (1997) *Lawyers and the Rise of Western Political Liberalism: Europe and North America from the Eighteenth to Twentieth Centuries*. Oxford: Clarendon Press.

Hart, R. (1992) *Children's Participation: From Tokenism to Citizenship; Innocenti Essays No. 4*. Florence: UNICEF International Child Development Centre.

Harvey, R. (2002a) 'A missed opportunity: reviewing the UN Special Session on Children', *ChildRight*, 186, May.

—— (2002b) 'The UK before the UN Committee on the Rights of the Child, *ChildRight*, 190, October.

Hayden, C. (1997) *Children Excluded from Primary School*. Buckingham: Open University Press.

Hendrick, H. (1997a) *Children, Childhood and English Society 1880–1990*. Cambridge: Cambridge University Press.

—— (1997b) 'Constructions and reconstructions of British childhood: an interpretive survey, 1800 to the present'. In A. James and A. Prout (eds) *Constructing and Reconstructing Childhood* (Second edition). London: Falmer Press.

Heywood, C. (2001) *A History of Childhood*. Cambridge: Polity Press.

Hockey, J. and James, A. (1993) *Growing Up and Growing Old*. London: Sage.

—— (2003) *Social Identities Across the Life Course*. London: Palgrave.

Holly, D. (1973) *Beyond Curriculum*. St Albans: Paladin.

Home Office (1998) Guidance on Statutory Crime and Disorder Partnerships: Crime and Disorder Act 1998. Home Office Communication Directorate: London.

—— (2001a) *Criminal Justice: The Way Ahead*, Cm 5074. London: TSO.

—— (2001b) *Antisocial Behaviour and Disorder: Findings from the 2000 British Crime Survey*. London: Research, Development and Statistics Directorate, Home Office.

House of Lords/House of Commons Joint Committee on Human Rights (2003) *The UN Convention on the Rights of the Child*: Tenth Report of Session 2002–03, HL Paper 117/HC81. London: TSO.

Houston, S. (2001) 'Beyond social constructionism: critical realism and social work', *British Journal of Social Work*, 31: 845–61.

Hudson, B. (1987) *Justice Through Punishment*. London: Macmillan.

Innes, M. (1999) ' "An iron fist in an iron glove?" The zero tolerance policing debate', *The Howard Journal*, 38(4): 397–410.

Ives, R. and Clements, I. (1996) 'Drug education in schools: a review', *Children and Society*, 10(1): 14–27.

James, A. (1993) *Childhood Identities*. Edinburgh: Edinburgh University Press.

James, A. (1999) 'Parents: a children's perspective'. In A. Bainham, S. Day Sclater and M. Richards (eds) *What is a Parent?* Oxford: Hart Publishing.

James, A. and James, A. L. (2001) 'Children and childhoods: towards a theory of continuity and change', *Annals of the American Institute of Political and Social Sciences*.

James, A. and Jenks, C. (1996) 'Public perceptions of childhood criminality', *British Journal of Sociology*, 47(2): 315–31.

James, A. and Prout, A. (1990) 'Re-presenting childhood: time and transition in the study of childhood'. In A. James and A. Prout (eds) *Constructing and Reconstructing Childhood*. Basingstoke: Falmer Press.

James, A. and Prout, A. (1990) (eds) *Constructing and Reconstructing Childhood* London: Falmer

James, A., Jenks, C. and Prout, A. (1998) *Theorising Childhood*. Cambridge: Polity Press.

James, A. L. (1990) 'Conciliation and social change'. In T. Fisher (ed.) *Family Conciliation within the UK: Policy and Practice*. Bristol: Family Law/Jordans.

—— (1992) 'An open or shut case? Law as an autopoetic system', *Journal of Law and Society*, 19(2), 271–83.

—— (1995) 'Social work and divorce: welfare, mediation and justice', *International Journal of Law and the Family*, 9, 256–74.

—— (2003) 'Squaring the circle – the social, legal and welfare organisation of contact'. In A. Bainham, B. Lindley, M. Richards and L. Trinder (eds) *Parent–Child Relationships and Contact*. Oxford: Hart Publishing.

James, A. L. and James, A. (1999) 'Pump up the volume: listening to children in separation and divorce', *Childhood*, 6(2): 189–206.

—— (2001a) 'Tightening the net: children, community and control', *British Journal of Sociology*, 52(2): 211–28.

—— (2001b) 'Teaching children to be children: how law and education policies construct the child', *Children in their Place*, Conference, Brunel University.

James, A. L., James, A. and McNamee, S. (2002) 'The legal and social construction of childhood' paper presented to the Socio-Legal Studies Association Annual Conference, Aberystwyth, 3–5 April.

Jenkins, R. (1992) *Pierre Bourdieu*. London: Routledge.

—— (1996) *Social Identity*. London: Routledge.

—— (2002) *Foundations of Sociology*. London: Palgrave.

Jenks, C. (1996a) *Childhood*. London: Routledge.

—— (1996b) 'The Postmodern child'. In J. Brannen and M. O'Brien (eds) *Children in Families*. London: Falmer.

John, M. (1996) 'In whose best interest?'. In M. John (ed.) *Children in Our Charge: The Child's Right to Resources*. London: Jessica Kingsley.

Johnson, N. (1999) 'The personal social services and community care', in M. Powell (ed.) *New Labour, New Welfare State? The 'Third Way' in British Social Policy*. Bristol: The Policy Press.

Johnson, V., Hill, J. and Ivan-Smith, E. (1995) *Listening to Smaller Voices: Children in an Environment of Change*, London: Action Aid.

Johnston, H. (1995) 'Age in Criminal Proceedings in Europe', in *Child Offenders: UK and International Practice – A Report by the Howard League*. The Howard League for Penal Reform: London.

Jones, G. and Bell, R. (2000) *Balancing Acts: Youth, Parenting and Public Policy*. New York: YPS/Joseph Rowntree Foundation.

King, M. and Piper, C. (1990) *How the Law Thinks About Children*. Gower: Aldershot.

Kjørholt, A. T. (2002) 'Small is Powerful: Discourses on "children and participation" in Norway', *Childhood*, 9(1): 63–82.

Kurtz, Z. (1999) 'The health care system and children'. In J. Tunstall (ed.) *Children and the State: Whose Problem?* London: Cassell.

Lansdown, G. (1996) 'Implementation of the UN convention on the rights of the child in the UK'. In M. John (ed.) *Children in Our Charge: The Child's Right to Resources*. London: Jessica Kingsley.

—— (1998) 'Children's rights and the law', *Representing Children*, 10(4): 213–24.

Leach, P. (1994) *Children First*. Harmondsworth: Penguin.

Leach, V. (2000) 'Children Unseen and Unheard – A Challenge to the Practice of Family Mediation', International Society of Family Law 10th World Conference, Brisbane.

Lee, N. (2001) *Childhood and Society*. Buckingham: Open University Press.

Lewis, P. (2001) 'The medical treatment of children'. In J. Fionda (ed.) *Legal Concepts of Childhood*. Oxford: Hart Publishing.

Liddle, M., Reid, S., Solanki, A.-R., Feloy, M. and Fraser, P. (2001) *The Southwark Youth Involvement Study: Key Findings and Lessons*. London: NACRO.

Lyon, C. (1995) 'Representing children – towards 2000 and beyond', *Representing Children*, 8(2): 8–18.

Mackay, M. (2001) *Through a Child's Eyes: Child Inclusive Practice in Family Relationship Services*. Department of Family and Community Services and the Attorney General's Department: Canberra.

Maclean, M. (2002) 'The Green Paper *Supporting Families*, 1998'. In A. Carling, S. Duncan and R. Edwards (eds) *Analysing Families: Morality and Rationality in Policy and Practice*. London: Routledge.

Marshall, T. H. (1950) *Citizenship and Social Change*. London: Pluto.

Mayall, B. (1996) *Children. Health and the Social Order*. Buckingham: Open University Press.

—— (2002) *Towards a Sociology for Childhood*. Buckingham: Open University Press.

McGlynn, C. (2000) 'A family law for the European Union?' In J. Shaw (ed.) *Social Law and Policy in an Evolving European Union*. Oxford: Hart.

Melton, G. (1989) 'Taking *Gault* seriously: toward a new juvenile court', *Nebraska Law Review*, 68: 146–81.

Melton, G., Petrila, J., Poythress, N. and Slobogin, C. (1997) *Psychological Evaluations for the Courts: A Handbook for Mental Health Professionals and Lawyers*. (Second edition) Guilford Press: New York.

Ministerial Group on the Family (1998) *Supporting Families: A Consultation Document*. London: TSO.

Monk, D. (1998) 'Sex education and HIV/AIDS: political conflict and legal resolution', *Children and Society*, 12(4): 295–305.

Montandon, C. and Osiek, F. (1998) 'Children's perspectives on their education', *Childhood*, 5(3): 247–63.

Mount, F. (1982) *The Subversive Family: An Alternative History of Love and Marriage*. Unwin: London.

Muncie, J. (1999) *Youth and Crime: A Critical Introduction*. London: Sage.

—— (2001) 'Lessons from Europe', *The Howard League Magazine*, 19(4), 6–7.

Murch, M., Douglas, G., Scanlan, L., Perry, A., Lisles, C., Bader, K. and Borkowski, M. (1998) *Safeguarding Children's Welfare in Uncontentious Divorce: A Study of s. 41 of the Matrimonial Causes Act 1973: Report to the Lord Chancellor's Department*. Cardiff Law School: Cardiff.

NACRO (1998) *Children Schools and Crime: A Report by NACRO's Committee on Children and Crime*. London: NACRO.

—— (1999) *Children, Health and Crime*. London: NACRO.

—— (1999a) *NACRO Briefing – Putting the Community into Community Safety: Community Consultation*. London: NACRO Crime and Policy Section: London.

—— (1999b) *Community Safety, Community Solutions: Tackling Crime in Inner City Neighbourhoods 'Summary*. London: NACRO.

—— (1999c) *Children, Health and Crime: A Report by NACRO's Committee on Children and Crime*. London: NACRO.

National Family Mediation (1998) *Policies and Standards: Consultation with Children*. London: NFM.

Neale, B. and Wade, A. (2000) *Parent Problems! Children's Views on Life when Parents Split Up*. East Molesey: Young Voice.

Newburn, T. (2002) 'Young people, crime and youth justice'. In M. Maguire, R. Morgan and R. Reiner (eds) (2002) *The Oxford Handbook of Criminology*. (Third edition) Oxford: Oxford University Press.

O'Neill, J. (1994) *The Missing Child in Liberal Theory*. Toronto: University of Toronto Press.

O'Quigley, A. (2000) *Listening to Children's Views: The Findings and Recommendations of Recent Research*. New York: Joseph Rowntree Foundation.

Ondrácková, J. (1996) 'The rights of children in a post-totalitarian country'. In M. John (ed.) *Children in Our Charge: The Child's Right to Resources*. London: Jessica Kingsley.

Parsons, T. (1962) 'The law and social control'. In Willian M. Evan (ed.) *The Law and Sociology: Exploratory Essays*. New York: Free Press.

—— (1978)' Law as an intellectual stepchild'. In Harry M. Johnson (ed.) *Social Systems and Legal Process*. San Francisco: Jossey Bass.

Pearson, G. (1983) *Hooligan: A History of Respectable Fears*. London: Macmillan.

Petit, J. M. (1996) 'World changes and social policies in Uruguay'. In M. John (ed.) *Children in Our Charge: The Child's Right to Resources*. London: Jessica Kingsley.

Petrie, P. and Poland, G. (1998) 'Play services for disabled children: mothers' satisfaction', *Children and Society*, 12(4): 283–94.

Piper, C. (1999) 'The wishes and feelings of the child'. In S. Day Sclater and C. Piper (eds) *Undercurrents of Divorce*. Dartmouth: Aldershot.

Piper, C. (2000) 'Assumptions about children's best interests', *Journal of Social Welfare and Family Law*, 22(3): 261–76.

Policy Research Bureau (2001) *Parenting in Poor Environments: A Study of Parents and Stress*. London: Policy Research Bureau.

Pollard, A., Broadfoot, P., Croll, P., Osbornm, M. and Abbot, D. (1994) *Changing English Primary Schools? The impact of the Education Reform Act at Key Stage One*. London: Cassell.

Pollock, L. A. (1983) *Forgotten Children: Parent–Child Relations from 1500 to 1900*. Cambridge: Cambridge University Press.

Postman, N. (1983) *The Disappearance of Childhood*. London: W. H. Allen.

Priestley, M. (1998) 'Childhood disability and disabled childhoods: agendas for research', *Childhood*, 5(2): 207–24.

Prout, A. and James, A. (1990) 'A new paradigm for the sociology of childhood? Provenance, promise and problems'. In A. James and A. Prout (eds) *Constructing and Reconstructing Childhood*. Basingstoke: Falmer.

Pryor, J. and Rodgers, B. (2001) *Children in Changing Families: Life After Parental Separation*. Oxford: Blackwell.

Pupavac, V. (2001) *Children's Rights and the New Culture of Paternalism*. Sheffield: Sheffield Hallam University Press.

Qvortrup, J. (1990) 'A voice for children in statistical and social accounting'. In A. James and A. Prout (eds). *Constructing and Reconstructing Childhood*. Basingstoke: Falmer.

—— (1994) 'Childhood matters: an introduction'. In J. Qvortrup (ed.) *Childhood Matters*. Aldershot: Avebury.

Ranade, W. (1997) *A Future for the NHS? Health Care for the Millenium*. Second edition. London: Longman.

Roach Anleu, S. (2000) *Law and Social Change*. London: Sage.

Robbins, D. (2001) *Transforming Children's Services: An Evaluation of Local Responses to the Quality Protects Programme*. The Stationery Office: London.

Roberts, I. and Singh, C. (1999) *Using Mentors to Change Problem Behaviour in Primary School Children*. Research Findings No. 95, Home Office Research and Statistics Directorate: London.

Roche, J. (1996a) 'Children's rights: a lawyer's view'. In M. John (ed.) *Children in Our Charge: The Child's Right to Resources*. London: Jessica Kingsley.

—— (1996b) 'The politics of children's rights'. In J. Brannen and M. O'Brien (eds) *Children in Families*. London: Falmer.

—— (1999a) 'Children and divorce: a private affair?' In S. Day Sclater and C. Piper (eds) *Undercurrents of Divorce*. Dartmouth: Aldershot.

—— (1999b) 'Children: rights participation and citizenship', *Childhood*, 6(4): 475–93.

—— (2002) 'The Children Act 1989 and children's rights: a critical reassessment'. In B. Franklin (ed.) *The New Handbook of Children's Rights: Comparative policy and practice*. London: Routledge.

Rose, N. (1990) *Governing the Soul*. London: Routledge.

Save the Children Fund (1995) *Towards a Children's Agenda*. London: Save the Children Fund.

Scheper-Hughes, N. and Sargent, C. (eds) (1998) *Small Wars: The Cultural Politics of Childhood*. Berkley: University of California Press.

Scott, S., Jackson, S. and Backett-Milburn, K. (1998) 'Swings and round-abouts: risk anxiety and the everyday worlds of children', *Sociology*, 32(4): 665–89.

Scraton, P. (1997) (ed.) *Childhood in Crisis*. London: UCL Press.

Shilling, C. (1993) *The Body and Social Theory*, London: Sage.

Shore, C. and Wright, S. (eds) (1997) *Anthropology of Policy*. London: Routledge.

Smart, C., Neale, B. and Wade, A. (2001) *The Changing Experience of Childhood*. Cambridge: Polity.

Stainton-Rogers, R. and Stainton-Rogers, W. (1992) *Stories of Childhood: Shifting Agendas of Child Concern*. London: Harvester Wheatsheaf.

Steedman, C. (1992) 'Bodies, figures and physiology: Margaret McMillan and the late nineteenth-century remaking of working-class childhood'. In R. Cooter (ed.) *In the Name of the Child: Health and Welfare, 1880–1940*. London: Routledge.

Steedman, C. (1995) *Strange Dislocations: Childhood and the Idea of Human Interiority 1780–1930*, London: Virago.

Stephens, S. (ed.) (1995) *Children and the Politics of Culture*. Princeton: Princeton University Press.

Teubner, G. (1989) 'How the law thinks: towards a constructivist epistemology of law', *Law and Society Review*, (23): 727–57.

Thorne, B. (1993) *Gender Play: Girls and Boys in School*. New Brunswick, NJ: Rutgers University Press.

Todorova, V. (2000) 'The Builgarian Children Act: a battlefield for adult policies or a genuine commitment to children?' In M. Maclean (ed.) *Making Law for Families*. Oxford: Hart.

Tucker, K.H., Jr (1998) *Anthony Giddens and Modern Social Theory*. London: Sage.

UK College of Family Mediators (2000) *Children, Young People and Family Mediation: Policy and Preliminary Practice Guidelines*. London: UK College.

Valentine, G. (1996) 'Children should be seen and not heard? the role of children in public space', *Urban Geography*, 17(3): 205–20.

Van Bueren, G. (ed.) (1993) *International Documents on Children*. London: Save the Children/Martinus Nijhoff Publishers.

Wade, H., Lawton, A. and Stevenson, M. (2001) *Hear by Right: Setting Standards for the Active Involvement of Young People in Local Democracy*. Local Government Association/National Youth Agency: London and Leicester.

Waiton, S. (2001) *Scared of the Kids? Curfews, Crime and the Regulation of Young People*. Sheffield Hallam University Press: Sheffield.

Warburton, F. (2001) 'Crime prevention and parenting: What works with families?' *Safer Society: The Journal of Crime Reduction and Community Safety*, No. 9, Summer: 11–12.

Willow, C. (2002) 'The state of children's rights in 2002', *ChildRight*, 187, June.

Woodhead, M. (1996) 'In search of the rainbow: pathways to quality in large-scale programmes for young disadvantaged children', *Early Childhood Development: Practice and Reflections*, 10, The Hague: Bernard van Leer Foundation.

—— (1999) 'Learning relationships with children: conceptual, methodological and ethical issues', paper presented at the 'Sites of Learning' Conference, University of Hull, 14–16 September 1999.

Woodhouse, B. B. (2000) 'The status of children: a story of emerging rights'. In S. Katz, J. Eekelaar, and M. Maclean (eds) *Cross Currents: Family Law and Policy in the US and England*. Oxford: Oxford University Press.

Wright, S. and Shore, C. (1997) *Anthropology of Policy*. London: Routledge.

Wringe, C. (1996) 'Children's welfare rights: a philosopher's view'. In M. John (ed.) *Children in Our Charge: The Child's Right to Resources*. London: Jessica Kingsley.

Wyness, M. (1999) 'Childhood, agency and education reform', *Childhood*, 6(3): 353–69.

—— (2000) *Contesting Childhood*. London: Falmer Press.

—— (2001) 'Children, citizenship and political participation: English case studies of young people's councils', paper presented at 'Children in Their Places' conference, Brunel University, 21 June 2001.

Zelitzer, V. A. (1985) *Pricing the Priceless Child: The Changing Social Value of Children*. New York: Basic Books.

Index